THE SKEPTICAL JUROR

AND

THE TRIAL OF

CAMERON TODD WILLINGHAM

THE SKEPTICAL JUROR

THE SKEPTICAL JUROR SERIES

The Trial of Byron Case
The Trial of Cory Maye
The Trial of Cameron Todd Willingham

SKEPTICAL JUROR MONOGRAPHS

Regarding The Trial of Susan B. Anthony (forthcoming)
Regarding The Rate of Wrongful Convictions (forthcoming)

THE SKEPTICAL JUROR

AND

THE TRIAL OF
CAMERON TODD WILLINGHAM

First Edition, October 2010

ISBN 978-0-9842716-2-7
Published by Allen & Allen Semiotics, Inc., www.semiotics.com

Cover design by Ed Lewis, www.edlewisdesign.com
Cover design © 2010 Ed Lewis

Printed on acid-free paper in the United States of America

TABLE OF CONTENTS

PRELUDE

Tuesday, 17 February 2004
Huntsville Unit, Huntsville, Texas

He refused to walk. It was one of the few freedoms he had left to him on Death Row. He wouldn't struggle, but he wouldn't walk to his own execution.

Twelve years earlier, the fire investigator assured the jury it was arson.

"The fire tells a story. I'm just the interpreter. I'm looking at the fire, and I'm interpreting the fire."

So now they would have to carry him. It shouldn't be too much trouble. They were many and the death chamber was nearby.

"That's what I know. That's what I do best."

The guards strapped him to the gurney.

"The intent was to kill the little girls."

The medical team inserted the needles.

"Have I ever been wrong? Not to my knowledge."

He had prepared a final statement. "The only statement I want to make is that I am an innocent man convicted of a crime I did not commit. I have been persecuted for twelve years for something I did not do. From God's dust I came and to dust I will return, so the Earth shall become my throne."

"If I have, sir, I don't know. It's never been pointed out."

He went beyond the script and thanked the forty-seven year old French teacher who had tried for so long to exonerate him. "I gotta go, road dog. I love you Gabby."

"And the fire does not lie."

Then he shouted invectives at his ex-wife who had only recently turned against him. "I hope you wrote in hell, bitch."

"It tells me the truth."

INTRODUCTION

The story you are about to read is fact. It is also fiction. It is, by design, both fact and fiction. Allow me to explain.

When writing of the trial testimony in the case of *Texas v. Cameron Todd Willingham*, I have used the words of the witnesses, the attorneys, and the judge as I found those words in the trial transcripts. I concede that I have abbreviated much of what they had to say because attorneys tend to ramble and witnesses tend to stumble. I concede also that I have repaired some of the grammar and redacted many of the annoying speech mannerisms. I did so because unedited transcripts are fearsome to behold. Despite this editorial license, I tried to preserve the integrity of the testimony as it was presented in court. To the extent I have been successful, the trial testimony portions of this book are factual.

When writing of events taking place within the jury room, I leaned on my four separate experiences sitting in judgment of fellow Americans, each of them charged with a felony, one charged with first-degree murder. The jurors are my creations. I am entirely responsible for their conversation and their behavior. I have no unique insight into the deliberations of the actual jury. The jury deliberations presented in this book are fictional.

When writing of the aftermath to the trial, I once again attempt to accurately present facts as they occurred. Any fictions found in the Aftermath portion of this book are unintended factual errors.

<<>>

Corsicana is small town fifty-five miles south of Dallas. It was founded in 1848, named by Jose Antonio Navarro. Jose's father was born on the Mediterranean island of Corsica, and the island inspired the name of the town.

Despite its Latin heritage, only one-fifth of the population of Corsicana is Hispanic. Another fifth is African-American. People of other races and ethnic groups are not to be found there in substantial numbers. A fifth of the people live below the poverty line.

No one of particular celebrity hails from Corsicana. Aaron Allston writes *Star Wars* novels. John Larry Kelly, Jr. was a Bell Labs scientist best known for developing an algorithm for maximally investing money. In the 1950s, Lefty Fritzell sang such favorites as the now-suggestive "If You've Got The Money, I've Got The Time" and "I Love You a Thousand Ways." Both of those hits were on his album *Listen to Lefty*.

Corsicana was home to the first commercially-significant oil field in Texas, discovered accidentally by water prospectors back in 1894. That was nearly a hundred years before the small, wood-frame house at 1213 West 11th

Avenue burned, nearly a hundred years before three young girls were consumed there by fire.

With a population greater than 20,000, Corsicana is home to half the population of Navarro County. Only one other town in the county has a population greater than a thousand, and that one just barely.

Because of its disproportionate size, Corsicana is the natural county seat, and home to the stately Navarro County Courthouse. The courthouse is where we will hear the case of Cameron Todd Willingham.

It is also where we will sit in judgment of him, where we will decide whether to set him free or see that he is executed.

JURY ROOM: TEXAS v. WILLINGHAM
Thursday, August 20, 1992

The last of the jurors is just now entering. Once that door is closed, it will separate us from the rest of you who pass judgment on fellow human beings merely for sport. In here, passing judgment will literally become a matter of life or death. We are to decide if Cameron Todd Willingham should die for killing his three young daughters.

This jury somehow managed to settle on a foreperson before testimony was complete. It just seemed natural to most of my colleagues that Marti would be the one to lead us though our deliberations, though none of us had met or known her before this trial.

Marti is an attractive woman of middle-height and middle-age, one who listens as much as she speaks. She's not boisterous but she manages to make herself heard. She's assertive in an agreeable sort of way. She's seemingly perfect for the role.

With her blue eyes, bright grin, and golden locks, she looks somewhat like a slightly-aged version of Kate Capshaw from the movie *Indiana Jones and the Temple of Doom*. The resemblence is valid only for those few moments in the movie when Kate was not running hither and yon screaming.

Marti is seated at the top of the elongated table. To her left is John, a meek and hesitant man. His voice tends to increase in pitch as he speaks, frequently without breathing, and it tends to trail off as he nears the uncertain end of his thought. He reminds me of therapy patient Mr. Peterson from the original *Bob Newhart Show*. His bald pate and round glasses are uncanny.

John's diminutive personality stands in stark contrast to the man sitting next to him. Lee is large, strong, forceful, opinionated, and boisterous. He's personable enough, but when confronted with ideas other than his own, he tends to respond with volume rather than reason, persistence rather than persuasion. I fear I see myself in him, though I'm at least conscious of my failing. I make a mental note to practice restraint and subtlety.

Edie sits next to John, to his left. That places her in the middle of the five people sitting along that side of the table. She seems to be among the few very wealthy people of Navarro County. Everything about her is proper: her clothes, her demeanor, her speech, her education, her marriage, her station in life. She apparently was unable, however, to skirt jury duty.

Think of Edie as Eunice "Lovey" Wentworth Howell from *Gilligan's Island*, except with far more functional neurons. It's certainly reasonable to believe that Edie has played a substantial role in her financial success. She's precise and efficient with her speech, frequently numbering the points she wants to make. She separates the wheat from the chaff as quickly as anyone in the room.

Jack sits next to Edie, directly across the table from me. He's the youngest of the group, and he's nervous about it. This is his first time as a juror, and he tells everyone so, frequently. He wants to do his duty and do it well, but he fears he will fail.

He's not originally from Texas, nor am I. That's no secret to any of the other ten in the room. Jack was born and raised in Brooklyn. He has the hard look, hoarse voice, and bent nose to prove it.

Ed is the last person along the far side of the table. He is the most nondescript person in the room, absolutely normal in every regard. He would be impossible to pick from a line-up because he looks like every other nondescript man in the world. He would also be impossible to describe to a sketch artist. "Average height, weight and build. Hair is of normal length, as I recall, kinda sandy color, darker maybe, but not too dark, just kinda average. No, sorry, no distinguishing marks. Clothes? Pants and a shirt, if I recall. You know, just normal, I think."

Ward sits at the end of the elongated table and therefore faces foreperson Marti at the far end. Ward has better things to do than sit on a jury. More specifically, Ward hopes to be eating hot dogs and drinking beer at the Ranger game tonight. Nolan Ryan is pitching, and though Nolan's having his worst season as a Ranger, he's still worth the cost of a ticket. If he hits a batter with a fastball, it doesn't come out. Anyway, the Rangers are playing the Angels, and Ryan should mow them down, even if he doesn't have his best stuff.

Harriet sits just to my right. She's quiet and keeps to herself. She has a brunette wrap-around hairstyle that nicely frames her face, like Jane Fonda in *Klute*. Other than that she reminds me of no one else. She's a mystery woman, to me and everyone else on the jury.

Jorge sits directly to my left. He's a Cuban refugee, a product of the 1980 Mariel boatlift. He's obviously obtained his citizenship, or he wouldn't be sitting here with us. Good for him. He wears his juror tag as a badge of honor. He sports a distinguished moustache, a receding hairline, and dark, penetrating eyes. He speaks with a heavy accent and the wisdom of someone who has lived under a boot.

Ted sits next to Jorge. People avoid Ted. He has a knack for antagonizing someone the moment he meets them. Ted is an old, bitter, unhappy man. If he would look carefully at Lee, directly across the table, he would see the ghost of juror past. Similarly, if Lee would look carefully across the table, at Ted, he would see the ghost of juror future. For Lee, there is still time. For Ted, life has passed him by.

The final juror as we orbit the table is Robert. Robert is a mover and shaker of some sort: sales, advertising, something along that line. He looks as if he belongs in the board room of a mid-sized firm that's failing badly. He's the only one to wear a sport coat, or a coat of any kind. It's August in Texas, for goodness sake.

<<>>

There's a water cooler in the corner of the room behind Marti. Instead of those worthless conical paper cups, the wall-mounted cup dispenser holds reasonably-sized cups with flat bottoms. Most people have at least one of the cups sitting on the table in front of them. It's a warm and sticky day, and the air-conditioning is not holding up its end of the bargain.

Ward, the baseball fanatic, takes one of the empty cups, wads it into a crude ball, and tosses it in a high arc over his right shoulder. Without looking, based only on the sound of a paper cup landing in a metal trashcan, he whispers to himself: "Two points." He sneaks a peek to see if anyone has witnessed his amazing feat.

Marti takes her empty cup and taps it gently on the table. The yammering stops almost immediately. I don't know how she does it. Perhaps in a past life she was a third-grade teacher.

Marti: "Settle down please."

Ward: "Yeah. Batter up!"

Marti just looks at him, seemingly without expression. Ward sinks just a bit in his chair. She gives him an almost imperceptible smile.

"There are two ways we can handle this. We can jump right into the deliberations or we can take a preliminary vote to see where we stand."

Boisterous Lee: "Preliminary vote."

Sports fan Ward: "Second."

Marti: "Okay. All those voting guilty, please raise your hand."

Seven hands go up immediately. Several others follow more slowly. Everyone looks around the table. Marti counts the hands out loud, starting with Timid John at her left. She points at the hands as she counts them.

"One, two, three, four, five, six ..."

She pauses when she gets to Harriet. Harriet's hand is not up. Neither is mine. Marti continues her counting with Jorge.

"... seven, eight, nine ..."

Then she raises her own hand.

"... ten. Okay. How many not guilty?"

Harriet raises her hand.

I decline.

"That's ten guilty, one not guilty, and one abstention."

Ted: "That's just great. There's one in every crowd."

I presume he's speaking of Harriet.

Ward: "So what do we do now?"

Harriet: "I guess we talk."

Ted: "Boy, oh boy."

Lee: "You really think he's innocent?"

Harriet: "I don't know."

Lee: "You sat in court with the rest of us. You heard what we heard. The man's a child killer. You could see it. They proved it a dozen different ways. Do you want me to list 'em?"

Harriet: "No, thank you. Not right yet."

Lee: "Then what do you want?"

Harriet: "I just want to talk."

Sports Fan Ward: "You know he's guilty. We all know his guilty. Everybody in that courtroom knows he's guilty. Even his attorney knows he's guilty. You could tell. Do you really believe that little two-year-old girl actually wondered around the house pouring kerosene all over then went back and started a fire in each room? Seriously, do you believe that?"

Harriet: "It seems unlikely."

Ward: "So why the hell did you vote not guilty?"

Marti gently taps her cup on the table.

Harriet: "I want to talk about it before I send someone off to be executed."

Ward: "You think it's easy for me just because I voted guilty. I honestly think the guy's guilty."

Harriet: "I respect that and I think you should have the opportunity to make your case. I'm willing to listen if you're willing to talk. I just want to talk about the case first. Let's take a hour. We owe him that."

Ward: "We don't owe him jack. We sat and listened to the testimony. He had nothing to say. You were there. He refused to testify. You gonna testify for him?"

Ted: "And what's up with you. Why didn't you vote?"

He directed that last question, that accusation really, at me. I remind myself to keep my answer short.

"I took an oath. I'm obliged by that oath to deliberate before I reach my conclusion whether he's guilty or not. I'm not ready to vote either guilty or not guilty. I say we take a day. There were two days of testimony, and we're obliged to consider all of it. I say we take a day."

The room falls silent. They all seem to be in shock. It never entered their minds that we might be in here all day.

Ted: "You're crazy. This isn't going to take a day. We vote, we find him guilty, or we hang this jury. It's that simple."

High-Society Edie: "I don't see the value of arguing like this. It's unseemly and ineffective. We should be able to behave as ladies and gentleman."

Sports Fan Ward: "Yeah, the lady's right!"

The two are polar extremes. I'm laughing, but only on the inside.

Ad Agency Robert: "I may have an idea here. I'll run it up the flag pole and see if anyone gives it the old salute. What if we went around the table and each of took a minute or two to explain to them why this guy is guilty. If you don't like it, well, it was just a thought."

Marti: "And a good thought. Thank you. We'll work our way around the table. John, you're first."

Timid John: Oh. ... Well ... Lemme see. I guess I just think he's guilty. I mean nobody proved otherwise."

Harriet: "The defense doesn't have to prove anything. The burden of proof is on the prosecution. They have to prove he's guilty."

Marti: "And they must do so beyond a reasonable doubt."

John: "Sure, I know that. What I meant was -- well, anyway, I think he's guilty."

Boisterous Lee: "He's guilty. Guilty, guilty, guilty. Plain as the nose on his face."

He leans forward slightly and looks two seats to his left, towards Jack, as he adds the nose reference. Then he taps his nose a couple times. Classy guy.

High Society Edie: "Number 1, he confessed. Number 2, his behavior during the fire was not consistent with someone worried about his children. Number 3, two different fire investigators determined it was arson. Number 4, the doctor who examined him said he wasn't suffering the effects one would expect from someone who had been in a fire. For me, the State made a compelling case."

Lee: "I couldn't have said it better myself."

High Society Edie: "I believe you."

Marti: "Jack, what are your thoughts?"

Jack: "I'll pass."

Marti: "That's your privilege. Ed, it's Ed, right? How about you?"

Nondescript Ed: "For me, the testimony from the people in the neighborhood was pretty powerful. He didn't try to save his own kids. He was more worried about his car. I mean, I can't imagine that."

Marti: "Anything else?"

Ed: "No."

Marti: "Okay. Ward, how about you?"

Sports Fan Ward: "I don't know. She said most of it."

He points at Edie. She doesn't acknowledge him.

Ward wads up another cup, lobs it over his shoulder without looking, sinks it, and smiles.

"Swish."

Marti: "Harriet. It's your turn. You have the floor."

Harriet: "I didn't expect a turn. I thought you were all going to try to convince me. Wasn't that the idea?"

Bitter Ted: "Who cares what the idea was? You're the one keeping us here. You and maybe him. So spill it."

Harriet: "Okay. I heard what you heard, and it first blush, it seems as if it's an overwhelming case for the State. But there are a few little things that bother me, and I want to talk about them. I think there are a few holes in some of the witness testimony.

Bitter Ted: "Whadda ya mean, holes? They testified about what they saw. What can be complicated about that."

Harriet: "They could be wrong."

Ward: "Whadda you trying to say? Those people testified under oath."

Harriet: They're only people. People make mistakes. Don't you think they could they have been wrong?"

Ward: "Well, no, I don't think so".

Harriet: "Do you know for certain?"

Ward: "Come on, no one can know for certain, but they can't all be wrong."

Harriet: "That's one of the things we could talk about."

Boisterous Lee: "We are talking, aren't we? Aren't we? What about the confession?"

Timid John: "Excuse me. There's some people haven't talked. Shouldn't we go in order?"

Lee: "They'll get a chance to talk. Be quiet a second will ya? What about the confession? Let's talk about that."

TESTIMONY OF JOHNNY WEBB
Tuesday, August 18, 1992

Assistant District Attorney John Jackson will conduct the direct examination of Johnny Webb.

"Would you state your name, please?" >> Johnny Everett Webb.

"Johnny, I think it's apparent the place that you come from. Tell me where you live at this time." >> I live in Navarro County Jail, B-21 cell.

He calls him Johnny.

"How long have you been in the Navarro County Jail, Johnny?" >> Six, seven months.

"My understanding is that you're confined in the Navarro County Jail based on a robbery conviction, is that correct?" >> Yes, sir.

"How long have you been in jail on this robbery charge, Johnny?" >> Six or seven months.

"It's my understanding that you were convicted of the crime of robbery back in March of this year, is that correct?" >> I believe so.

"How old are you, Johnny?" >> Twenty-two.

"You have had a rather extensive criminal history, have you not?" >> Yes, sir, I have.

"You've been charged and convicted one time or another for stealing a car, is that right?" >> Yes.

"Of delivery of marijuana?" >> Yes, sir.

"Theft?" >> Yes, sir.

"Forgery?" >> Yes, sir.

"And of burglary, in addition to the robbery, is that right?" >> Yes, sir.

"Johnny, what is your problem as far as not being able to stay out of trouble?" >> Drugs.

"I take it you are off drugs now." >> Yes, I am, except for the medication.

"Okay. You have any trouble with mental impairment or anything like that, Johnny?" >> Not always.

Okay. That's a good one. I'm laughing inside.

"Okay. You have a good grasp of what is happening around you?" >> Yes, I do.

"Okay. What kind of education do you have?" >> About tenth grade.

I'm guessing "about 10th grade" is an approximate figure that eighth grade, tops. And probably not on the honor roll, either.

"All right. Johnny, while you were in jail, did you come in contact with a person named Cameron Todd Willingham?" >> Yes, I did.

"Is that the same Todd Willingham that is present here in this courtroom today?" >> Yes, it is.

"Is he here seated at the counsel table with his defense attorneys?" >> Do what?

Now I'm having trouble not laughing out loud.

"Is that the same Cameron Willingham seated here with his defense lawyers?" >> Yes, it is.

"What do you do at the jail, Johnny?" >> Housekeeper.

"Are you a trustee?" >> Yes, sir, I am.

"What does that mean?" >> It just means I get to go out, clean up, you know, in the morning and at night, just keep the floors mopped, swept.

"How did you happen to come in contact with Cameron Willingham?" >> Doing my normal thing, you know, just sweeping and mopping every day.

"Did you know what he was in jail for?" >> When I first met him? No, sir, I didn't. It took me a couple days before I found out what he was in jail for.

"How did you find out?" >> I was told by somebody else.

"Did he know what you were in jail for?" >> I'm not sure. I don't know if I told him or not. I imagine he does, though.

"Did you ever talk to him about why he was in jail?" >> Yeah, I did.

"All right. Did anybody ever ask you to go find out what Cameron Willingham knew about this crime?" >> No, sir, they did not.

"Were you working for any law enforcement agency when you talked to him?" >> No, I was not.

"Did anybody ever threaten you or coerce you?" >> No, sir, they never did.

"What did Mr. Willingham tell you about the incident of the fire at his house?" >> He said he had done it.

"Can you tell us what he told you about those events?" >> Yes, sir.

Defense Attorney David Martin objects. The Honorable Kenneth "Buck" Douglas overrules the objection. Johnny Webb continues with his answer.

He was telling me about something about he had came home or something, and he was, I don't remember exactly where he was at or what he was doing, but when he came in the house that one of the babies was injured or dead or something like that and he freaked out and --

"Did he tell you who had injured the child?" >> His wife.

"All right. Please continue." >> And he didn't know what to do. She was crying and going on, and he said he thought of a way to get them all out of it by setting the house on fire.

"Did he tell you what he did at that point?" >> Yes, he did. He said that he took some kind of lighter fluid, squirting around the walls and the floor and set a fire.

"Did he tell you anything else about how he attempted to shift the blame from him to someone else?" >> I'm not sure.

"Did he tell you anything about what he did with the children?"

Martin objects to the question as leading. Judge Douglas overrules the objection. Johnny Webb continues.

Yes. He said that he had burned one of the kids. I don't know which one, and I assumed at the time that it was --

Martin objects again, this time to the witness speculating. Judge Douglas sustains the objection.

"You can't tell us about your assumptions. Just tell us what he told you." >> That he took some paper, wadded it up, and lit a fire and burned one of the kids on their arm, on their forehead to make it look like they were playing with fire.

"What else did he say, Johnny?" >> That he ran out of the house to go call 911, and someone asked him to go get the kids. He said they were still in the house, and someone told him to go get them. He refused.

"Did he tell you why he wouldn't go back in the house?" >> Because he knew they would find out one of the babies was injured.

"Why did you decide to tell anyone about this conversation?" >> Because it got to bugging my conscience. I mean, three kids, you know? Someone tells you something like that, it's not something to be taken lightly.

"Did it worry you?" >> A lot, yeah.

"Who did you tell about it?" >> Robert Chapman.

"Based on your conversation with Mr. Chapman, did you elect to talk with me?" >> Well, in a way. Not exactly you, but, you know, I told him, I said, "What should I do 'cause I don't really want to get into it, but it's bugging me." And he said, "Well, yeah, it's true."

Martin objects to the response as hearsay. The Court overrules. Johnny Webb continues.

But Chapman said, "Now it's on my conscience, too." He said, "I don't think I can handle that on my conscience." So it went on about three weeks. He said, "Look, do you want me to tell someone?" I said "Yeah." That's when he said, "Okay. I'll tell them what you told me."

"Johnny, have I ever promised you anything in return for your testimony in this case?" >> No, sir, you haven't.

"As a matter of fact, I told you there is nothing I can do for you."

Martin objects to the question, the statement really, as leading. He's overruled again. Johnny Webb responds.

You said there was nothing that no one can do for me.

"Do you understand you placed yourself at risk by coming forward with this testimony?"

Martin objects.

"Your Honor, we object to that as leading, assuming some facts not in evidence. There is no evidence whatsoever that he has been placed at risk at all in any way."

Judge Douglas sustains the objection, but Jackson has made his point. He wants us to believe that Johnny Webb must be telling the truth because he put himself at risk somehow to testify.

Assistant Prosecutor John Jackson passes the witness to the defense for cross-examination.

<<>>

Defense Attorney David Martin will cross-examine inmate Johnny Webb.

"Mr. Webb, how long have you been in jail?" >> Six, seven months.

"And you were in jail this time for -- was it robbery or burglary?" >> Both. Burglary, robbery and forgery.

"Who did you rob? A woman?" >> Yes.

"Robbed her of her purse?" >> No, I did not.

"What did you take?" >> Nothing.

"You were charged with robbery, yet you did not take anything?" >> True.

"Tried to take something?" >> They say I did.

"But it's not true?" >> I don't know if it's true or not.

"You don't know whether you're guilty of robbery or not?" >> True.

"It was a fabrication on the part of the police?" >> I doubt that very seriously.

"Then you think it's true?" >> I could have done it, but I don't remember doing it.

"Because you were under the influence of drugs?" >> True.

"What kind of dope was it? Crack cocaine?" >> Marijuana and drink.

"You been smoking marijuana and drinking since you were nine?" >> About that, yes.

"And on occasion you have mental difficulties?" >> Yes, sir.

"You're on medication for that now?" >> Yes, sir.

"And what has the doctor diagnosed your mental problem as being?" >> Post dramatic stress disorder.

Okay. Another good one. I know this is serious business, but sometimes it's hard not to laugh.

"And what about the stress and the trauma?" >> I decline to answer that question in open courtroom.

"Well, I ask you to answer me immediately. What caused it?" >> I still decline.

The other defense attorney, Robert Dunn, asks the judge to inform the witness he must answer the question. Judge Douglas tells the witness he must answer.

I was assaulted in the penitentiary.

"And that was when?" >> '88.

"And how long were you in the penitentiary that time?" >> Thirty days shock probation.

"And you were sexually assaulted?" >> Yes.

"Raped by an inmate?" >> Yes.

"I don't mean to be indelicate, but you can see this is quite important, can you not?" >> Yes.

"And since that time -- and we sympathize with you, we do -- but since that time, you have suffered off-and-on mental difficulties?" >> Yes, I have.

"And would you tell us what the medication is that you take now?" >> It's Elavil, but I get the generic form.

"It's prescribed to you by a doctor?" >> Yes, it is.

"You've seen a psychiatrist?" >> Yes, I have.

"He's diagnosed you as having these mental problems?" >> Yes, he has.

"And how long had you used crack cocaine?" >> Probably four or five months.

"And did you steal to get money to buy crack?" >> Most people do.

"Is it possible for you to describe for us the strength of the addiction to crack cocaine? Would you say it is utterly overwhelming?" >> No, I wouldn't.

"Can you control your actions when you were under its influence?" >> Sometimes.

"And sometimes you cannot?" >> Right.

"The strength of the addiction is so strong that you will go out and rob people, correct?" >> Some people do.

"You do, do you not?" >> No, I did not.

"So, are you telling us that you did not rob someone or that you did or that you just don't know?" >> I'm telling you I did not rob someone for the money to get crack cocaine.

"Why did you rob them?" >> I don't know as if I did.

"But you pled guilty to robbing someone." >> Well, it seems pretty weird that someone would come up and say I tried to rob them when I didn't, don't you think?

"Are you telling us that you stood here -- was it in this courtroom that pled guilty?" >> Yes, it was.

"You were placed under oath just like you were now?" >> Yes, I was.

"Swore to the Court that you committed this robbery?" >> Yes, I did.

"But you can't remember whether you did so or not?" >> True.

"I suppose that you and Todd Willingham have been friends for a great many years?" >> No.

"You haven't been?" >> No, we haven't.

"You met him only when?" >> Jail.

"In jail this year. And do you remember when this year in jail?" >> January.

"And you were in the same cell with him, and you were friends with him and talked to him every day?" >> I was not in the same cell with him.

"You were not in the same cell, but you talked to him for hours at a time, no doubt?" >> Probably thirty minutes to an hour, yeah.

"When? Once a day?" >> Once or twice.

"And in some hidden spot there of the jail where no one else could hear you?" >> No. Anyone could have keyed a mike on the speaker system and heard exactly what I was saying.

"This occurred under a speaker in the jail?" >> Yes, it did.

"The deputies could have heard?" >> The deputies could have heard.

"Anybody else in the cell could have heard?" >> Yes.

"And what you are telling us is that Todd Willingham stood at his door and talked to you through the food tray slot, correct?" >> Correct.

There's other prisoners in there with him, correct?" >> I would assume so.

"Well, there were other people in there when you say you were talking to him, weren't there?" >> I believe there was.

"And so you are telling us that standing there at this food tray slot with these other people around, a person whom you did not know before you met them in jail confessed to you that he had murdered his three children?" >> True.

"Told you all about those details that you described?" >> Yes, he did.

"And you were dumbfounded?" >> I don't understand the word "dumbfounded."

"You were surprised that anybody would do such a bizarre thing?" >> Yes.

"First time it's ever happened to you, someone confess to you?" >> Yes.

"Never happened before?" >> Not with something like this, no.

"You took some notes?" >> No, I didn't take no notes.

"Can you write?" >> Yes, I can write.

"And read?" >> Yes.

"You took no notes?" >> No.

"This conversation occurred over the course of -- what did you tell us -- two or three weeks?" >> About a month.

"Over a month's time?" >> Yes.

"Bits and pieces picked up over thirty days or so?" >> No.

"How did it happen?" >> Well, I had been talking to him about everyday events, things. He was having a hard time sleeping and asked me if I would give him some of my medication. I said yes, I would.

"And you did?" >> Yes, I did.

"Had it in your pocket?" >> Yes, I did.

"Is it sleeping pills?" >> Yes, it is.

"Is that the only kind of medication you had?" >> No, it's not.

"You had some other medication on you?" >> Yes.

"And the people of the jail just let you wonder through the jail with medicine in your pocket?" >> No, they don't.

"But you had it with you?" >> Yes.

"Weren't supposed to?" >> Wasn't supposed to.

"How did you get it?" >> Through the nurse.

"Was she supposed to give it to you?" >> Yes, she was.

"What were you supposed to do with it?" >> Take it.

"But you didn't?" >> Yes.

"You just stuck it in your pocket?" >> Not all of it. I would give him, like, one pill every now and then to help him sleep because he said he was having a real hard time sleeping. He was telling me about the case the whole time, but he was always telling me that he didn't do it. Then one day, mainly, he just broke down and said, "I done it."

"Cried, no doubt?" >> Yeah.

"And everybody could see him there crying, confessing to you?" >> No. There was no one at the other doors. Everybody was watching TV.

"So, in other words, he talks to you about it for 30 days, says he didn't do it. Then all at once, much to your surprise, he confesses?" >> True.

"You go back to your cell. You write down what he said?" >> No.

"You just remembered it?" >> Yes.

"This occurred when?" >> About in April, I would imagine.

"And then you told us that you told Deputy Robert Chapman a month later?" >> No. About a week later. But, you know, I told him I didn't want him to tell what I knew. He said that he wouldn't, and I kept talking to him. He said, "Well, man," he says, " what are you going to do about that?" I said, "I don't know what to do. I really don't want to get involved in it." He said, "Yeah, but the man told you something that people really do need to know. I mean, if the dude done it, then you need to tell someone." You know, it got to bugging me.

"You didn't tell anybody for a week?" >> No. Robert, that's it.

"Then a week later your conscience began to bother you?" >> My conscience bothered me from the day he told me.

"You told the deputy sheriff that somebody had confessed three murders to you, and he asked you what you were going to do about it?" >> Well, you know, I considered him my friend. I said, "Look, can I tell you something without you telling anybody?"

"And for three weeks this secret was kept between you and him?" >> Yes, until he made the decision that it was the right decision. He just wanted me to do the right thing. That's what I tried to do.

"But you slept on it for a week?" >> Hum?

"You didn't tell anybody for a week?" >> No. Robert, that's it.

"Okay. But for the first week after this supposed confession, you didn't say anything to anyone?" >> No.

"Didn't tell anyone at all?" >> No.

"Then a week later your conscience began to bother you?" >> My conscience bothered me from the day he told me."

"You told the deputy sheriff that somebody had confessed three murders to you, and he asked you what you were going to do about it?" >> Well, you know, I considered him my friend. I said, "Look, can I tell you something without you telling anybody?"

"And for three weeks this secret was kept between you and he?" >> Yes, until he made the decision that it was the right decision. He just wanted me to do the right thing. That's what I tried to do.

"You know Joe Jackson?" >> Yes, I do.

"He was in the cell with James McKnight? Do you know the FBI agent, Mike McKlusky? You know him, don't you? You know any FBI agents at all?" >> No, I don't.

Mr. Webb, aren't you the same Mr. Webb that made a complaint to the FBI in May of this year that you were being physically abused in the jail?" >> No, I'm not.

"You called the FBI --" >> No, I did not.

"-- in Dallas. They came down here to investigate." >> No, I did not.

"You were interviewed by the FBI in May." >> No, I was not.

"Not at all? That's not true, not any of it?" >> No, sir, it's not.

"You never made a complaint to the FBI?" >> No, sir, I haven't.

"Joe Jackson?" >> He's a black guy that was in Cell 44.

"And how long was Joe in there?" >> I don't know, four, five months, maybe longer. I can't remember.

"How did you know him, just like you did Todd?" >> Just came around. You know, they ask us for bleach to clean their showers. We give them the stuff. That's about it.

"How did you learn his name?" >> Well, I've known him before from jail. I've been there. I know who he is.

"This wasn't the first time you met him?" >> No, it wasn't.

"Now, presently, you are under a sentence of fifteen years to do in the penitentiary?" >> True.

"Is that aggravated or non-aggravated?" >> Aggravated.

"How much time do you understand that you will stay at minimum in the penitentiary?" >> Three years, nine months.

"And when were you sentenced to that?" >> Late January.

"About seven months ago?" >> Yeah.

"Do you know why you're still here in jail rather than the penitentiary?" >> Basically, no. I think to testify on this, but I'm not sure.

"You should have gone to the penitentiary before now, but you you've been held over to testify here?" >> Not necessarily. There's another person in jail that's got thirty-five years aggravated. He's been there eighteen months. They're not really rushing to get anybody with aggravated time out because they got so much time to do.

"Would you tell us what the symptoms of your mental problems have been? Depression?" >> Yes.

"Loss of sleep?" >> Yeah, I've lost a lot of sleep.

"Mental confusion?" >> I wouldn't say mental confusion.

"You mean, you don't know that you robbed somebody, but you are not mentally confused?" >> I think I was so blitzed on drugs, you know, I blacked out.

"And how long have you been on medication?" >> Two years.

"Continuously for two years?" >> Not continuously.

"Just off and on?" >> Off and on.

"Have you been on medication for your mental problems the entire time you've been in jail?" >> Yes, I have.

"Been taking medicine every day for the entire time you've been in jail?" >> Yes, I have.

"It was prescribed to you by the jail nurse?" >> By the jail doctor.

"Can you tell us how many times you've been interviewed by the prosecutors in this case?" >> As in who?

"Mr. Jackson, Mr. Bristol." >> I've been interviewed about four times.

I'm guessing "about four" means "at least six."

"Did you ever make any notes about any of it?" >> No.

"Can you tell us when you are expecting to go to prison?" >> I expect to go whenever they make a list and put my name on it.

"Pass the witness."

<<>>

Deputy Prosecutor John Jackson with the redirect.

"Johnny, I believe you told Mr. Martin that this defendant was having a hard time sleeping, is that right?" >> Yes, it's true.

Interesting. He keeps calling him Johnny.

"He told you why he was having a hard time sleeping, didn't he?"

Martin objects to the question as leading. He's overruled and Johnny Webb answers.

Yes, he did.

"He told you he killed his children, didn't he?" >> Yes, he did.

"He told you he needed your sleeping medication to sleep, is that right?" >> True.

"You understand there's going to be lots of problems for you associated with giving this testimony, don't you?" >> I'm well aware of that fact.

"What happens to people who give this type of testimony in your situation?"

Martin objects to the question as calling on the witness to speculate. Also that the answer would be irrelevant. Also that the witness could have no personal knowledge. Jackson concedes the point before the judge rules.

"Let me rephrase that. Do you have personal knowledge of people who have given information about fellow inmates?" >> Not really.

"You have information of what's happened to you after you've given information about fellow inmates, don't you?" >> Yes, sir.

"What has happened to you?

Martin objects as irrelevant. Judge overrules. Witness answers.

My life has been threatened as well as my family's life. And if I make it to the penitentiary, then I'm going to be in deep trouble.

"Who has threatened you, Mr. Webb?" >> Two people, sir. Robert Lyles and Todd Willingham.

"What did Mr. Willingham say he would do?" >> He just pointed his finger at me. He did like this.

"Let the record show, Your Honor, that the witness has drawn his finger across his neck. Mr. Webb, you gave a written statement to a deputy sheriff in this case, I believe. Is that correct?" >> True.

"In that written statement, I believe you said Todd Willingham told you --"

Martin objects to the question as an improper attempt to bolster the witness statements. Jackson says Martin attacked the witness during cross-examination. Judge Douglas instructs Jackson to rephrase.

"Did Todd Willingham tell you he poured lighter fluid on the floor of the children's room in an X pattern?" >> Yes, he did.

"Did he tell you he removed one of the children to a different location in the house?" >> No, I don't think he said that.

"Okay. You made a statement at an earlier time, I believe --"

Martin objects to the question as another improper attempt to bolster the witness. He also says the question is leading. Judge Douglas is unimpressed by his objection and overrules it.

"In that statement you said, 'He then moved one of the kids from one room to another, then started the fire in the hallway.' Would that be a fair statement?" >> Yes, I believe it would.

"Are you scared of Todd Willingham?" >> Scared of what could happen through the people he knows, yes.

"Pass the witness."

<<>>

David Martin will re-cross Johnny Webb.

"Now, Mr. Webb, you told us twice that Todd didn't say anything to you about taking one of the children to another room. And then when the prosecutor showed you the script, you changed your mind. Now, which one is it?" >> I think he said -- you know, I can't remember exactly, but I think that's probably right.

"After being reminded by Mr. Jackson of what you said in the script he showed you, right?" >> Not just that. It's just, you know, that's probably right.

"Now, when Todd supposedly told you this, you didn't think too much about it, did you?" >> At first, no. It stunned me. I didn't really know what to think.

"Well, you said in the past that you didn't think too much about what he told you, did you?" >> I don't believe I've made that statement.

"Well, let me show you what Mr. Jackson showed you that he provided me. Didn't you say, 'In the past at first I did not think too much about what Todd told me?'" >> Probably, yeah.

"You said that, didn't you?" >> Yes, I did.

"Pass the witness."

<<>>

John Jackson is determined to get the last word. He has further redirect for Johnny Webb.

"Johnny, has Mr. Martin said anything that would make you doubt your testimony here this morning?" >> No, sir.

"Does it remain your testimony that Cameron Willingham said he killed his children?" >> Yes, it does.

DELIBERATION OF JOHNNY WEBB
Thursday, August 20, 1992

Harriet: "All right, Lee. Let's talk about Mr. Webb. Do you believe he was a truthful witness?"

Lee: "I don't see why not. He had nothing to gain and everything to lose. You heard that just like the rest of us."

Harriet: "Edie, how about you. Do you believe Johnny Webb told the truth."

Edie: "I think it's possible. He was there at the same time. He told a deputy months ago. He didn't just make it up right before trial. He hasn't been promised any time off, or anything else for that matter. So he has no motive to lie. He faces risks for informing on a fellow inmate, so he actually has a strong disincentive to testify. That suggests he testified because he was appalled by the crime and the admission, just as he said."

Harriet: "Why didn't we hear from the deputy sheriff he talked to?"

Edie: "I suppose it would have been hearsay. You're allowed to testify about what you said, but not what other people tell you."

Her voice trailed off as she was completing the last sentence. Perhaps it's because she has already spent too long sitting close to Timid John. Perhaps it's because she just realized she had set herself up.

Jack: "This is my first trial, so I don't understand all this hearsay and other stuff. But are you telling me it's okay for that prisoner, what's his name?"

Marti: "Webb."

Jack: "Yeah, Webb, it's okay for him to tell us what the guy who's on trial, what's his name?"

Marti: "Willingham."

Jack: "Yeah, him, it's okay for Webb to tell us what Willingham told him but not okay for the guard to tell us what Webb told him?"

That was painful, but his point is well taken.

Edie: "I'm assuming, I don't know for certain, that Webb was allowed to testify because Willingham made a statement against his own interest. It's an exception to the hearsay rule. So yes, I'm telling you there may be a perfectly legal reason why Johnny Webb was allowed to testify but Deputy Sheriff Robert Chapman was not."

She has good recall for names. That should help us get through this.

Jack: "I still don't get it."

Edie: "Remember the last witness the defense called. They only called two, so it should be easy to remember him."

Jack: "Yeah, they called a prisoner too."

Edie: "Right. His name was James McNally. He was a prisoner in the Navarro County Jail at the same time as Johnny Webb. McNally was in for tax evasion. He had a cell close to Willingham's. He was allowed to answer all the questions put to him until defense counsel asked what Johnny Webb had told him. Then the prosecution objected, we were all sent back here to wait while they argued about it, and when we went back, the defense attorney said he had no more questions. I assume the prosecution objected based on hearsay."

Jorge: "Pardon."

Jorge frequently begins by asking permission to intervene.

Jorge: "That is confusing to me as well. Why can only Mr. Webb tell us what someone told him. Why cannot Mr. McNally tell us what someone told him?"

Edie: "I tried to explain best I could. I believe it has something to do with an exception to the hearsay rule. I don't know for sure. I can't help you beyond that. I suspect though, if Johnny Webb had never spoken with Deputy Sheriff Chapman, the defense would have called him as their own witness. Chapman would have been allowed to testify that Webb never spoke with him. That would not be hearsay."

Jack: "I still don't get it, but I guess you're right. This is my first trial."

Sports Fan Ward: "So they didn't call this Chapman guy. So what? What you think he's going to say? 'Johnny Webb told me Willingham never confessed.' Is that what you expect?"

Harriet: "I'm not willing to a man executed based on the testimony of a police informant, that's all. I would like to have heard from the deputy. I don't know what he would have said, but I would like to have some sort of corroboration before I vote guilty based on the word of a snitch."

Boisterous Lee: "He's no snitch. A snitch is prisoner who lies on the stand about another prisoner in exchange for time off, or privileges. We got no evidence Webb is lying, and we have the word of the prosecutor that he's not going to get any time off, or anything else for that matter."

I decide to speak up.

"I'll give you two-to-one Johnny Webb is out in five years, no longer. He'll serve the minimum, maybe a bit more, but he won't be in fifteen years, not even half that."

Ward: "I'll take a piece of the action."

"Sorry. Offer's only good for Lee. What do you say? We get together five years from today. If your man Johnny Webb is still locked up, I write you a check for two thousand dollars. If he's been sprung, you write me a check for a measly thousand."

Lee: "Get outta here."

"I'm serious. Two-to-one."

Ward: "I'm serious. I'll take a piece of that action."

"This is between Lee and me. What do you say?"

Lee: "You'll never show."

"We'll set up an escrow account. Winner takes the proceeds and all the interest to boot."

Lee: "Give it a rest, will ya? Are you telling us the prosecutor was lying to us? Is that what you're saying?"

"They don't have to lie. They all know how the game's played. A wink here, a nod there, some hypothetical, off-the-record discussions, and somehow everyone's getting what they want, everyone that is except the poor schmuck who's only going to get needles in his arms."

Bitter Ted: "So now you're saying he's not guilty too?"

"Not saying that at all. I am saying that a snitch's testimony isn't worth a used roll of prison toilet paper. I'm saying that as far as I'm concerned Webb's testimony hurt the prosecution far more than it hurt the defense. The prosecution needs to prove to us beyond a reasonable doubt that Willingham did this crime, that a crime even occurred, and yet their very first witness is a jailhouse snitch. And we're supposed to believe him beyond a reasonable doubt?"

Ted: "You believe what you want, I'll believe what I want."

"Lee won't bet even a thousand dollars on him. Will you bet your life on the truthfulness of Johnny Webb?"

Ted: "That's a damn silly question."

Me: "But you'll stake Willingham's life on his testimony, won't you?"

Ted: "Forget I brought it up."

A weak voice makes its way through the ruckus.

Timid John: "I have a question."

Everyone is caught off guard. Everyone but Marti.

Marti: "Yes, John. We're all listening."

And somehow, we were.

John: "He said --"

Marti: "Johnny Webb?"

John: "Yes. Johnny Webb said he got confused when he wasn't taking his medications. So why shouldn't we believe him when he said that? He said he was confused at the time, so if we believe him on the other stuff, maybe we should believe him when he said he was confused."

Boisterous Lee: "You weren't listening. He said he got confused when he wasn't taking his medication, that's all. He was taking his medication."

John: "No he wasn't."

Lee: "How the hell do you know he wasn't?"

John: "He told us. He said he gave it to the defendant, to help him sleep."

Lee: "He said he gave him some of his medication. Not all of it. Some of it."

John: "Oh. That's right."

He lets it hang there for a moment.

John: "So maybe he was a little confused."

Beautifully done. I give him a slight smile and the hint of a nod. He notices it, smiles himself, then sinks back into his chair. Marti takes over.

Marti: "I think we've talked enough about Johnny Webb. We'll each decide for ourselves how much credence to give his testimony."

Now Marti lets it hang there for a moment.

Marti: "Personally, I don't think it's worth a used roll of prison toilet paper. Let's talk about the testimony of the Barbee family. They're a bit more believable."

TESTIMONY OF DIANE BARBEEE
Tuesday, August 18, 1992

"State calls Diane Barbee."

Assistant Prosecutor John Jackson will conduct the direct examination of Diane Barbee.

"Would you state your name, please, ma'am?" >> Mary Diane Barbee.

"And where do you live, Mrs. Barbee?" >> 1205 West 11th.

"Can you tell us where the Willingham house is or was with reference to your house?" >> Two doors down. East, I believe. I have a bad sense of direction.

<---- Barbee House, 2 Doors Down

"Let me direct your attention to December 23rd of last year. What you were doing around 10:00 AM?" >> I was babysitting. I was in the den. My two youngest daughters wanted to go out on the back patio because they was bored. I know it was around 10:00 because "The Price is Right" was coming on. I told them "You can stay out there just a little while," because it was cool.

"Can you tell us what, if anything, unusual happened at that point or shortly after that time?" >> They had been out there maybe ten minutes when Buffie, my eleven-year old, she come running through the back door and screamed that Sheila's house was on fire.

"Who is that?" >> Mrs. Daniels, sir, that lives right next door to us.

"In fact, her house was not on fire, though, is that correct?" >> That's right.

"And what did you do at that point?" >> I jumped up from the chair, and she was right behind me because it's a long room, the den area and dining room is together and she was right behind me, and we hit the screen door about the same time, and I just run out the front door.

"Can you tell us what you first saw when you ran out that door?" >> As soon as we got out the front door, I just immediately looked and Cameron was on the front porch screaming. He started screaming whenever we come outside.

"Had you heard any calls or screams from Mr. Willingham before you ran out the front door?" >> No, sir.

"Can you describe then what you saw when you ran out the front door?" >> He was on the front porch and he had both arms crossed like this and he was crouched down screaming, hollering.

"When did he start screaming?" >> When we come outside.

"So he had not been screaming before that point?" >> I had not heard any screams. Until we went out in the front yard, we didn't hearing any hollering.

"When you say he was crouched down, where was he crouched down?" >> In front of his front door, facing his front door on his front porch.

Location of Front Door

"Was the house engulfed in flames at that point?" >> No, sir. There was smoke coming out. It was coming out the front windows and the front door and the side windows of the front room. And it was coming down low. It wasn't a high smoke. It was low.

"Coming from a low point in the house?" >> Uh-huh.

"Based on your observation, did Mr. Willingham appear to be overcome by smoke, or was he coughing at that point?" >> Well, I wasn't up close to him. I didn't see him coughing. He was hollering. All he did was holler that the house was on fire and that the babies was in the house, and my kids, the three girls were, you know, was in there.

"At that point did you determine whether Mr. Willingham was injured or not?" >> Not at that time, I didn't. All he did was holler that, you know, the house was on fire and that the babies was in the house, and my kids, the three girls were, you know, was out there.

"Tell us what you did next." >> I said, "You stay here." I turned back around to go into my house when I realized that the phone wasn't working, and I just told my mother, "The babies are in the house. The house is on fire." I turned back around, just ran outside, started running. I ran back out the front door, told the kids to stay in the yard, stay there until I got back. I ran down the street until I found somebody to call 911.

"But how long would you estimate it took you to go down to the neighbor's house to call 911 and come back?" >> Well four, five, six minutes.

"Tell us what you did when you got back to the house that was on fire?" >> As soon as I ran back up to our house Cameron ran and met me about where my fence was.

"What did he do or say at that point?" >> I asked him where the babies was. I tried to get him to come into my house because I know when you are in shock and stuff, it can be critical. I didn't know how badly he was hurt or anything, and he was hysterical, hollering and all. I tried to ask him where the kids was and to get him to come in my house because I didn't know, you know, how bad it was, how badly hurt he was.

"What was the condition of the house next door at that time?" >> Still a lot of smoke coming out, just the front.

"Were you concerned about the children in the house?" >> I was hysterical. I got three daughters myself.

"Did you or anybody else ask Cameron to go back in the house or get the babies?" >> My daughter, that's all they were hollering. That's all they were hollering, screaming, "Go back in and get them."

"Did he make any response?" >> No.

"Did he go in the house with you?" >> Did he go in my house? No, sir, I could not get him to.

"What did he do?" >> Well, I asked him, I said, "Where are the babies?" He said that Amber had woke him up, and the house was full of smoke. She jumped off the bed. He couldn't find her, and he run out.

"Did he say where he ran out?" >> Run out back is what he told me, ran out back.

"He told you he ran out the back?" >> Out back .

"Okay. Tell us what happened next, Mrs. Barbee?" >> Well, the house was still smoking bad and my oldest daughter was out screaming for him to go back in, and he had gone back over to the house several times. We couldn't get him to do anything, couldn't get him to go in the house or anything. The fire truck still wasn't there.

"Was the back of his house involved in any flames or smoke?" >> No, sir.

"Just the front?" >> That's all I could see coming out the front room and the front door. So Mr. Long down the street, the other end of the street, had heard all the hollering and stuff. I seen him come out in the middle of the street, and he run down there and talked to Cameron, and it was about that time, I think, that the house erupted in fire. It blew up, blew out. Me and my oldest daughter started running back up toward the house when it blew up.

"Why were you running back toward the house?" >> Well, I was going to try to see if I could get in or, you know, see if we could see where the kids was. I didn't know the kids' room had been moved. I still thought that their room was across, and that was the living room where all the flames was. I didn't know they had moved their rooms. Then when it blew up, I knew there wasn't anything we could do. It was just, you know, it was totally engulfed in that front room and --

"You understood that you could not get in the house at that point when the fire actually broke out?" >> No. The heat was so intense. I was in the middle of Mrs. Daniels' yard, it just met me.

"And Mrs. Daniels' house is between your house and Willingham house, right?" >> Right.

"All right. Mrs. Barbee, tell us what you remember after the fire ignited in flames?" >> Well, Cameron hollered about his car and he run and pushed it back.

"Did he start the car up?" >> No. He pushed it back. I guess you have to put it out of gear to push it back. He pushed it back maybe five or eight feet, not far. It was on the side of his house up by the tree. He pushed it back down in the driveway.

"He was concerned about his car?" >> Well, he pushed it back.

"Did he ever go back in the house at any time you were present before the fire broke out?" >> No.

"Can you tell us how Cameron Willingham was dressed during these events?" >> He had on a pair of britches. That's all.

"Did he have on any shoes?" >> No, sir.

"No shirt?" >> No.

"No socks?" >> No socks.

"Did he have any injuries to his feet?" >> No.

"Did you have an opportunity to look at him to see later to see if he had any significant injuries?" >> I had my arms around him one time trying to get him into the house and to find out where the kids was, and his hands had black all on his arms and some on his back and his eye lashes and the top of his hair was singed was all that I seen. I couldn't tell. You know, I couldn't tell.

"Did he have any actual burns that you could tell?" >> I didn't see any, but his arms was black.

"What did Todd Willingham do after he moved his car?" >> He went across and sat in front of Mrs. Arnett's house right across the street from their house. That was about the time that the ambulances and fire trucks and police cars was all pulling up out there.

"Do you have any idea how long it was from the time Buffie first told you about the smoke and you ran out in the yard until the time the fire actually broke out?" >> Well, I would say it wasn't any more than ten minutes, if they were out there that long, and I think the fire trucks got there at 10:26.

"What did you do when the fire trucks got there?" >> Well, I was hysterical and we finally got two paramedics to get Cameron, and they couldn't get him to the ambulance. He went and sat on the back of the big fire truck that was right in front of their house and they was taking care of him, and they was trying to put out the fire.

"Were you there when the defendant, Mr. Willingham, was taken to the hospital?" >> Yes, sir.

"When was the next time you saw him or came in contact with him after that?" >> The next morning I seen him.

"Was there anything that drew your attention to him the next morning?" >> Well, I don't really know what time it was that morning, but I was in the kitchen and I was baking and, you know what boom boxes are? I don't know if that's the correct term for them, but any how, they go down the street all the time with these, kids, with these boom boxes. And I just thought one of the cars or something was -- well, it just kept getting louder and louder and I walked out of my kitchen, down into the den and you could feel the vibration of it coming off my walls, and I walked to the front door and looked out and there were some people over in front of the burned house.

"Who was there?" >> Cameron was there. I don't know who all was there. There was a small pick-up and another car out front. The little pick-up was parked in the driveway, and that's where the music was coming from, from the little pick-up.

"What were they doing?" >> They were out in the front yard talking. They were just all around talking in the front yard. When we went outside, they turned off the boom box.

"Did the party get quieter after that?"

Martin objects.

"We object to that as a misstatement of the testimony and assumption of facts not in evidence."

It was a cheap shot, that's for sure. Judge Douglas sustains the objection and instructs Jackson to restate his question.

"Did the gathering get quieter after that?" >> Yes, the music stopped.

"Do you have any idea how long that went on out there that morning?" >> I didn't stay outside long, but the kids stayed outside. Cameron and some other people was with him. They was getting stuff out of the house.

"Did you have an opportunity to see Cameron later on that day?" >> Well, Channel 5 come over to the house, I think, it was right at 6:00 o'clock that night. I seen them drive up, and it wasn't long afterwards that Stacy and Todd drove up, and they talked to Channel 5.

"Did Mr. and Mrs. Willingham come to your house at any time during that period of time?" >> After they got through with talking to them, they walked over.

"Did you have an opportunity to talk with Mr. Willingham or Mrs. Willingham at that time, that point?" >> Yes, sir. They come in, and that's the first time I had seen Stacy since it had happened.

"What was Todd talking about to you at that time?" >> Stacy sat down in the chair. I was trying to talk to her. She was crying, and I was trying to talk to Stacy and Cameron was talking to us about the neighbor who had took up some money and what they had went and bought for Amber, and he told her that when I ran down the street was when he went back into the house.

"You overheard Todd Willingham tell his wife that he went back into the house?" >> Yes, sir.

"To your knowledge did Todd Willingham ever go back in that house?" >> Not while I was out there.

"Do you have any reason to believe he ever went back in the house?

Martin objects to the question as calling for speculation. Sustained. Rephrased.

"You've had an opportunity to speak with your daughters, I assume, about what happened when they were there?" >> Yes, sir.

"Did it surprise you that Todd Willingham told anyone he went back in the house?" >> Yes, it did. My husband asked me why I didn't say something. I told him I couldn't.

"Why couldn't you?" >> Because Stacy had just lost them three babies. How could you tell somebody that? She was devastated.

"What was your reaction to hearing Todd say that?" >> I couldn't believe he said it.

"Pass the witness."

<<>>

David Martin will conduct the cross-examination of Diane Barbee.

"Mrs. Barbee, is it fair to say that during these events you described that you were hysterical?" >> Yes, I was hysterical.

"As was everybody else there?" >> Yeah.

"Is that the first time you've ever been that close to a house on fire?" >> That close, yes.

"And the first time you've ever been present when a house burned belonging to someone you knew?" >> Yes.

"Do you know what Mr. Willingham's wife calls him?" >> No, sir. I've always called him Cameron. I don't know.

"You have not been in their home?" >> I've been in that home but not since they -- I've been in that backyard.

"You would not consider yourself a close family friend of theirs?" >> No, sir.

"You told us that at some point during these events that Todd's car was parked near the corner of the house?" >> There's a tree that's about there. It was parked right by the tree.

"It was very close to the burning house?" >> Uh-huh.

"Just like a foot or two from the porch, probably?" >> Well, it was by the tree. I don't know how close the tree is. It's just right there.

"And when this happened, the house was burning, it was smoking. You could see it smoke. You knew it was on fire." >> You could see the smoke, yes.

"Now, when you first came out of your house over here, you ran around here and saw he was crouched down?" >> Yes.

"Had his arms folded across his chest?" >> Yes.

"You thought he had been injured? He looked like he had been injured?" >> Yes.

"Was that your first thought?" >> The house was on fire. I mean, the house was smoking. He was hollering. He was screaming the babies was in there.

"You saw smoke coming out from around the front window?" >> Come out the front door, down the windows, on the side windows.

"Smoke was coming out the side of the house, right?" >> Uh-huh.

"Smoke was coming out the front door?" >> Uh-huh.

"But you don't know whether the front door was opened or closed?" >> No, because I didn't run over there.

"You don't know whether the front door was open or closed at this time?" >> No. The girls said it was open.

"But you saw smoke coming out the front door?" >> Uh-huh. When I first come out, it was smoking, but it wasn't a black smoke. It was grayish, but it had not gotten black like it did right before it busted into flames.

"But you did not, at any time when you were out there before it burst into flames, see any actual fire on the front of the house, did you?" >> I didn't see any at first. I just seen the smoke.

"And then at that time you described something similar to an explosion?" >> Well, when we was running back up toward the house, it just busted out.

"Did the windows break out?" >> The windows, the electricity started crackling and popping, and the top of the -- well, I was facing the side of the house, and it just blew out. The flames just blew out.

"Did you first see flames coming out of windows?" >> Well, I was -- yeah, I seen them coming out of windows and the top. You know, I mean, it's just busted out. All the windows and the front room was engulfed. I guess what I'm trying to say, it was just engulfed.

"Now, you didn't go into the burning house, obviously?" >> No, sir. It looked as if you could not get in. It was burning.

"Now, you talked about the next morning you heard a loud radio in the yard?" >> Yes, sir.

"And was that coming from somebody's little pick-up?" >> Uh-huh.

"It was not Todd's pick-up, though, as far as you know?" >> No. His car was over in the yard.

"Okay. It was somebody else's pick-up playing the music, is that correct?" >> Uh-huh, right.

"Pass the witness."

<<>>

John Jackson has some redirect for Diane Barbee.

"Mrs. Barbee, you've talked about electricity popping. At what point did you first hear the electricity popping?" >> When it engulfed the house, when the fire broke out.

"When the flames engulfed the house?" >> Yes. It started, you know, cracking and sparking, all that.

"Had you heard any electrical noises before that?" >> No.

"When you had an opportunity to see Cameron the next day, could you tell that he had no serious injuries?" >> I didn't see any.

"Did he act like he had any serious injuries?" >> No.

"Have any bandages or anything like that at any point on his body?" >> No. He had on a sweater, britches and shoes and socks.

"Do you have any idea how long that house had been on fire when Buffie first smelled smoke and came into the house?" >> She went outside at 10:00 o'clock, and she smelled the smoke when she went outside, first went outside.

"You had not heard a cry for help during that time period?" >> No, sir, I did not.

"You did not hear a cry for help until you hurriedly went out the front door?" >> Until we went out the screen door, yes, sir.

"Was Stacy Willingham, the wife, at home at this time to your knowledge?" >> No, sir, she wasn't.

"Pass the witness."

<<>>

David Martin has some re-cross.

"Now, Mrs. Barbee, before you went outside, you were in your home watching television?" >> Uh-huh.

"And you believe that Buffie, your youngest daughter, had been outside smelling smoke for about ten minutes before she came in and alarmed you?" >> Uh-huh.

"Thank you."

TESTIMONY OF BRANDY BARBEE
Tuesday, August 18, 1992

John Jackson will conduct the direct examination of Brandy Barbee.

Would you state your name for the record, please?" >> Brandy Barbee.

"And where do you live?" >> At 1205 West 11th.

"I believe you are the daughter of Diane Barbee, is that correct?" >> Uh-huh.

"Let me direct your attention to the 23rd of December of last year, two days before Christmas. Do you remember that day?" >> Yes, sir.

"Let me direct your attention to the mid-morning hours of that day. Can you tell me, in your own words, what you remember about the events that took place shortly after 10:00 o'clock that morning?" >> After 10:00? Well, I heard my mom come back in the house screaming that there was a fire and that the babies were burning up. I had just gotten out of the shower. I threw something on, and I ran out there in the street.

"Can you tell me what you saw when you got out in the street?" >> Todd was standing in the yard when I got out there.

"Can you tell us or describe for us what part of the yard he was standing in?" >> He was standing by a tree. It was right by the driveway.

"And what was he doing when you first saw him?" >> He was screaming that there was a fire, that his babies were burning and for someone to help him, to call 911.

"What did you do at that point?" >> I was screaming for him to go back in the house and get the babies or tell somebody where the babies were, and my little sister was with me. I told her to go to the house next to his and call 911.

"Did he ever make an attempt to go back in the house when you asked him to go back in?" >> Not that I seen.

"Can you describe what happened after you asked him to go back in the house?" >> Well, he was screaming about the car a little while later and told someone to help him move it out of the driveway. The next thing I seen, he went across the street and sat down on the curb.

"Were you there present while your mother was going down the street to try to get help?" >> Uh-huh. That's when I run down towards his house.

"All right. And about how long did you stay there outside the premises of his house?" >> I was there until the fire trucks got there.

"All right. And you, at no time, saw him try to go back in the house?" >> No.

"Was he coughing during this time period?" >> No.

"Did you see him move his car?" >> Yes.

"Did he seem concerned about his car?" >> Yes.

"After the fire department got there, what did Todd Willingham do?" >> Well, he was still screaming about the babies, and by that time I had left.

"Were you acquainted with Cameron Todd Willingham and his wife, Stacy?" >> Well, I knew that they lived next door. I never really talked to them.

"Did you later have an opportunity to go to the hospital?" >> Yes.

"Can you tell us how you happened to go to the hospital?" >> Well, one of my friends, Stephanie, she babysat on Tuesday nights with Amy O'Shea, and she was hysterical. She couldn't believe the fire had happened and everything. She asked me to take her out there. I took her out there.

"What did you do when you got to the hospital?" >> We found out where his room was and went up to his room.

"Did you have an opportunity to see him when you got to the room?" >> Yes.

"Can you describe him when you walked into the room?" >> Well, when we first walked in, he was on the phone talking about caskets and --

"For the babies?" >> Uh-huh, I believe so.

"You overheard him making funeral arrangements?" >> Well, that's what it sounded like.

"This was how long after the fire?" >> It was probably about 2:30 or 3:00 that day.

"Fire was at 10:10, and this was about 2:30?" >> Uh-huh.

"What did he look like. Did he have any injuries?" >> Well, his eye lashes and eye brows was singed, but other than that, I didn't see anything wrong with him.

"Did he make any request of you or Stephanie at this time?" >> Well, we went downstairs, and then Stephanie said, "Well, let me call back up there to see if they want anything to eat." When she called up there, they wanted us to go --

Martin objects as to hearsay and speculation. Jackson rephrases the question.

"Based on a request from Mr. Willingham's room, what did you do at that point?

Martin objects again that Jackson is attempting to get hearsay in through the back door, that he's assuming facts not in evidence. Jackson denies it and Judge Douglas overrules the objection.

"What did you do at that point?" >> We went to *Jack In The Box* and got some food and then we came back to the hospital and I dropped Stephanie off and she took the food up to the room. I did not go back in.

"Were you upset at this point?" >> Yes, I was upset.

"Why were you upset?" >> Well, I couldn't believe that somebody would even think about eating after his babies had just burned up.

"Did Todd make any comments about the babies while you were there at the hospital?" >> I didn't really talk to him.

"Did he seem overcome with emotion when you saw him?"

That draws another objection from Martin, this time as a leading question. Judge Brown overrules.

"Was he upset in the room when you saw him?" >> He wasn't crying or anything.

"Pass the witness."

<<>>

David Martin cross-examines Brandy Barbee.

"Miss Barbee, you have never lost a family member in a fire, have you?" >> No.

"Never lost a close family member, have you, to accident or death?" >> I lost my grandmother, my great grandmother. I was small. I hardly remember it.

"So, my point is that this is the first time you've ever been around someone who has lost children in a fire or an accident, isn't that correct?" >> Yes.

"And so you wouldn't know typically how people would respond to that, would you?" >> No.

"You were not a party to the conversation that Amy O'Shea had with Todd in the hospital when she talked to Todd, were you?" >> No.

"Don't know what was said during that conversation?" >> No.

"Now, did I understand you to say that you ran out of the house and ran to where?" >> Toward his house.

"And how far did you get?" >> I was right beside him, where the small tree is.

"Okay. And this was after your mother had run back down the street the other direction?" >> She was down the street.

"Now, were you there to see Todd break these windows out the front of the house?" >> No.

"Had that already happened?" >> I didn't even know about it.

"You never saw that?" >> I never seen that.

"And when you came out, were the windows broken out on the front of the house?" >> I don't know. I never looked at the house.

"You just looked at him?" >> I was -- yes, I was looking at him.

"You were telling him to go back in the house?" >> Yes.

"But you didn't go back in the house?" >> No.

"Nor try to go into the house?" >> No. We made an attempt. We was running towards the house, me and my mother, we was fixing to go and try to get in, and that's when it was an explosion, the electricity and everything.

"You and your mother did this?" >> Well, we was on our way. We was in Mrs. Daniels' yard, and we was running up towards the house.

"Was this after the time you had first gone out there and talked to Todd?" >> Uh-huh.

"So, you had been out there talking to him, then you went back?" >> I didn't talk to him. I was pleading with him to go back in the house.

"But you didn't go in?" >> No.

"Because the house was smoking?" >> It was smoking.

"You could tell it was on fire?" >> I didn't see any flames but --

"But you did not feel it safe for you to go into the house, did you?" >> No.

"Because it was smoking?" >> Uh-huh.

"Because you recognized that it was on fire, but you didn't know how extensive the fire was inside, did you?" >> No.

"And from your vantage point here, you couldn't see down the hallway here, could you?" >> No.

"But you saw smoke coming out the front door and the front windows and the window on the side of the house?" >> Yes.

"Pass the witness."

<<>>

John Jackson has some redirect for Brandy Barbee.

"Were you present the next night when the Willinghams were at your house?" >> Yes.

"Did he make a statement about the babies walking in the hands of the Lord?" >> He said something like that.

"You didn't know where the children were in the house, did you?" >> No.

"The rear of the house was not involved in smoke and flames, was it?" >> No.

"Did it seem strange to you that Todd Willingham wouldn't go back in the house to try to rescue his own children?" >> At the time I didn't think about anything, but after awhile I started thinking about it, yes.

"Pass the witness."

<<>>

David Martin has some re-cross for Brandy Barbee.

"Well, Miss Barbee, did it seem strange to you that you didn't go rushing into a smoking house? That wasn't peculiar to you, was it?" >> No.

"Pass the witness."

<<>>

Now John Jackson has some further redirect.

"You think if you had children, you might have gone into a smoking house?"

Martin of course objects, and Judge Douglas sustains. Jackson passes the witness, Martin has nothing more, and Judge Douglas calls for a recess.

TESTIMONY OF BUFFIE BARBEE
Tuesday, August 18, 1992

"Call your next witness, Mr. Jackson."

"State calls Buffie Barbee."

Buffie Barbee is sworn in and John Jackson begins his direct examination.

"Would you tell us your name?" >> My name is Buffie Barbee.

"Buffie, I believe you are the daughter of Diane Barbee, is that correct?" >> Yes.

"Where do you live?" >> 1205 West 11th.

"Let me ask you to remember something for me. First of all, how old are you?" >> Eleven.

"Okay. Let me ask you to remember back to two days before Christmas. Do you remember then?" >> Yes.

"Well, do you remember the house catching on fire two doors down from you?" >> Yes.

"All right. Can you tell us what happened in your own words on that date?" >> My sister and me went out back to play, and we had a friend, and we were playing, listening to the radio and I smelled smoke. So it didn't really bother me the first time. Then I saw it, and then I said, "Oh, my God, the house is on fire." So I ran in and said, "Sheila's house is on fire" because there was so much smoke you couldn't tell which house it was. Me and my mom ran out the front door at the same time. And when we ran out the front door, he started hollering.

"Had you heard him hollering before then?" >> No, sir.

"You had been outside, hadn't you?" >> Uh-huh.

"Okay. Then what did you do?" >> He was hollering, "My babies are inside burning up. Help me." I said, "Go back in and get the babies."

"What did he do, Buffie?" >> He just stood there.

"Pass the witness."

<<>>

That was short. David Martin has some cross.

"Buffie, how old did you tell us you were?" >> Eleven.

"Do you think you were in the backyard about ten minutes or so before you ran in the house and got your mom?" >> Yes.

"You thought at first it was the house next door that was on fire?" >> Yes.

"Because there was so much smoke?" >> Yes.

"And you saw Todd break out the windows on the front porch of the house while he was there?" >> One of them.

"Pass the witness."

<<>>

That was brief. Now John Jackson has some redirect.

"Was the house on fire when you first went over there, or was there smoke?" >> There was just a lot of smoke.

"Pass the witness."

And before you can blink, Judge Douglas is instructing Jackson to call his next witness.

DELIBERATION OF THE BARBEE TESTIMONY
Thursday, August 20, 1992

Marti: "Let's talk about the testimony of the Barbee family. They're a bit more believable."

Bitter Ted: "Are we gonna have to do this for every witness?"

He turns his attention to Harriet and me.

Ted: "What do you think you're gonna accomplish? If you want to be stubborn and hang this jury, he'll be tried again and found guilty, sure as he's born."

Harriet: "You're probably right."

I'll let Harriet handle it. She's doing fine. I'm back to subtlety and restraint.

Sports Fan Ward: "So what are you gonna do about it? We can be here all night."

Harriet: "It's only one night. A man might die."

Boisterous Lee: "Well, whose fault is that? Did anyone force him to kill his kids?"

Ward: "Some of us have got better things to do than sit around a jury room all day."

Edie: "I can't understand a word in here. Why do we all have to talk at once?"

Marti: Edie's right. One at a time, please.

Ted: "Look, the mother and the two girls all said the same thing. He didn't start screaming and hollerin' until he saw them come out the door. They tried to get him to go back in there and save his kids, but he wouldn't. He cared more about his car. He tried to save that while his kids were burning up inside. Then he orders a burger from *Jack In The Box* and has a party at his burned down house the next day. What more do we need, you know what I mean? So let's get done and get out of here."

Jorge: "Pardon. I would like to say something."

Marti: "Go ahead, sir."

Jorge: "I have always thought that a man was entitled to have unpopular opinions in this country. This is the reason I came here. I wanted to have the right to disagree. In my own country, I am ashamed to say I do not.

Ted: "Whadda we got to listen to now? The history of your country?"

Ward: "Yeah, let's stick to the subject."

Marti gently taps a paper cup on the table. The room quiets down. She nods at Jorge.

Jorge: "Thank you. This lady --"

He points at Harriet.

Jorge: "-- chose to stand alone against us, all of us except this gentleman."

He points at me.

"That's her right. She doesn't say the man is not guilty. She just isn't sure. She just want's to talk about it. I respect that. I think he is probably guilty, but I would now like to talk about it some more too. I wish to withdraw my guilty vote. I vote not guilty"

Boisterous Lee: "You can't do that!"

Marti: "Of course he can. Right now the vote stands at nine guilty, two not guilty, and one abstention. I'd advise those who want so badly to get out of here that they facilitate rather than obstruct the discussion."

Ted: "Boy, oh boy."

Marti: "Let's get down to business. Who wants to respond to what Ted had to say about the Barbees?"

Young Jack raises his hand.

Marti: "Yes, sir."

Jack: "Maybe he moved his car because he didn't want it to explode right there by where the babies were."

Lee: "You don't know that."

Jack: "And you don't know that he was moving it just cause he cared more about it than he cared for his children."

Timid John: "You know, that makes more sense now that I think about it. If he didn't want his car burned up, he would have moved it before he set the house on fire. Don't you think?"

Lee: "No, I don't think."

Sports Fan Ward breaks into laughter. A few others giggle. I limit myself to a smile. Neither Marti, Edie, or Harriet change expression.

Young Jack: "And another thing. I didn't like when the older daughter --"

Marti: "Brandy."

Jack: "Yeah, when Brandy Barbee said she would never even think about food right after her babies had died. Didn't she and her friend think about food right after their neighbor's babies died? Didn't the girls offer to buy them food? That's what she said, right? She said they called back up to the room to see if they could get them some food, then they went to *Jack In The Box* and got them some food, just like they offered. Buffy's friend went up to the room to deliver the food, and Buffy stayed downstairs. Now she says she could never even think of food if her babies had just died. But they didn't think of the food, the girls offered to get them some food. They just said yes. Does that make them murderers? I'm sorry, I'm nervous. I've never done this before."

Harriet: "That's a good point, better than you may realize. Buffy said they offered to get them food. Plural. I suppose that means both Cameron and Stacy. And the food was delivered to both of them, at least as far as Buffy knows. So why are we supposed to think Cameron killed his children just because he accepted an offer of food, but we're not supposed to think Stacy killed her children simply because she accepted an offer of food. It seems like the prosecutor is just throwing mud every chance he gets, rather than presenting any real evidence the defendant is guilty."

She's on a roll. This subtle and reserved thing is working out great.

Ward: "If he didn't start the fire, who did?"

Harriet: "As far as I know, we're only supposed to decide whether or not he started the fire. We're not concerned here with how it might have started if he didn't start it."

Young Jack: "Maybe the little girl started the fire."

Ward: "You don't really believe that do you?"

Jack: "I said maybe. They were both smokers, right? Maybe she got hold of a match or a lighter. Maybe she was playing with a lighter, accidentally set something on fire, and then didn't do anything about it until it was too late. You know little kids. When they do something wrong, they don't run right in and tell their daddy. But maybe when the fire got scary, she went into his bedroom and woke him up, just like he told Diane Barbee she did. He goes to save the other two babies, but it's too hot and too late, and he escapes out his front door just as the Barbees are coming out theirs."

Ward: "You're guessing."

Jack: "But so are you, and so are the Barbees, and so is the prosecutor. You're all guessing at what went on in that house. Why is your guess right and my guess wrong?"

Edie: "It's simple. Number 1, someone poured lighter fluid on the floor of the children's bedroom, even under Amber's bed. Number 2, someone set that lighter fluid on fire. Number 3, someone then poured lighter fluid in the hallway and set that lighter fluid on fire. Number 4, someone then poured lighter fluid on the front porch and under the front door threshold, and lit that on fire. When the fire investigator explained that to us, he didn't need to tell me Amber didn't do all that. I knew it had to be Cameron. It's easy."

Jack: "I guess you're right. Sorry."

Marti: "Let's talk about that some. Let's talk about the firefighters' testimony."

TESTIMONY OF RONALD FRANKS
Tuesday, August 18, 1992

"State calls Ron Franks."

Ron Franks is sworn in. Assistant Prosecutor John Jackson conducts the direct examination.

"Would you state your name for the record, please?" >> My name is Ronald G. Franks.

"Mr. Franks, I think it's apparent to everybody, but how are you employed?" >> I'm a lieutenant paramedic with the Corsicana Fire Department.

"And how long have you been employed by the fire department?" >> Approximately six years, ten months.

"I'm assuming, then, you were employed in that capacity back on the 23rd of December of last year, is that correct?" >> Yes, sir, I was.

"Were you dispatched to a house fire in Corsicana during the morning hours of that day?" >> Yes, sir, I was.

"Can you tell us about where that was?" >> It was in the 1200 block of West 11th.

"Tell us what you observed when you got to that location?" >> I was the first unit in. I pulled up on the scene. It was a wood frame structure with fire totally involved in one room. The front porch was also involved with the fire, and there was some fire coming out the east side window of the structure.

"What procedure did you follow as soon as you got there?" >> I positioned my truck in front of the house to the west side of it. I immediately went to pull a line off to make an attack on the fire. At that time I was approached by a man that said that his babies were inside the house. I asked him where in the house and how many. Then I proceeded to charge the line and attack the fire.

"Can you describe how you did that?" >> I pulled the line off the back of the truck, charged the pump panel, then I approached the front porch, which was fully involved with fire. I tried to knock it down, tried to direct the stream in the room that was fully involved, and knocked it down. Then the smoke rolled out of the house and I turned around, looked at Chief Fogg. "We need some men with air packs on." He advised me to go get air packs on. He took my line.

"Could you tell where the fire was coming from or which portions of the house were most involved at that time?" >> The area just behind the front porch. It was fully involved. The front porch was involved with fire. The fire was rolling over the top of the front porch. It was fire coming out the window on the east side.

"Was fire burning low or middle on the walls or high?" >> The fire was burning all the way down on the porch.

"All right. Were the floors of the house involved in the fire?" >> Yes, they were.

"Were you able to equip yourself so that you could enter the house?" >> Yes. Once I turned the line over to Chief Fogg, I went back and put on air packs. Then I took the line back and attempted to go into the room that was fully involved. And as I entered it, knocking some of the fire down, another line came in from the west side of the house and the stream struck me. So I backed out of that room, came back out, went back in and made a primary search of the house.

"When you first entered the house, how did you enter?" >> I entered through the front window of that room that was involved on the front porch.

"You later came back through that window?" >> I came back out the window. Then I entered the front door.

"Was the floor burning in that room when you entered it?" >> Yes, it was.

"What did you do at that point?" >> I left my line with another man outside. Then I went in for a primary search through the front door, down the hallway to the back of the house, worked my way back up to the front.

"What did you find when you got inside the house as far as fire involvement?" >> The fire pretty much had been knocked down by the other crew going in, but there was a lot of heat, a lot of smoke. There were few areas of fire still burning all through the hallway through the room that was fully involved. At first I went back to the back of the house. There was a lot of heat, a lot of smoke. I went to make a search of the house where the kitchen was and tried to open the back door for ventilation, and there was a refrigerator in front of it.

"Was it possible to exit through the back of the house?" >> No, sir.

"Tell us why." >> Because there was a refrigerator in front of the back door.

"What did you do from that point?" >> I moved on around to the other room, searching each room and making sure there was nobody in each room.

"Did you determine where the children were, where the fatalities of the fire were?" >> When I pulled up on the side, Mr. Willingham approached me. I asked him where the children were at. He pointed to the room that was fully involved. He told me the number of children. Then it's still customary that we search every room to insure that nobody is in each room.

"After the fire was knocked down, you had an opportunity to inspect those rooms. Did you learn at that time where the fatalities of the fire were located?" >> Yes, sir, I did. I saw the twins.

"Where were they?" >> They were just -- as you step inside the front door, there's a door going left into the bedroom, and they were right there by the door, just right near the front window where I walked in.

"Was that room damaged significantly?" >> Heavy damage.

"Were the children burned beyond any possible survival?" >> Yes.

"I'm sure you have had an opportunity to see people who suffer from smoke inhalation, have you not?" >> Yes, sir, I have.

"You had a chance to observe the defendant, Cameron Todd Willingham, on this occasion, is that correct?" >> Yes, sir, I have.

"Did he appear to be a person who was suffering from any type of smoke inhalation problems or coughing?" >> Not at that time. I didn't notice any. He was really excited. And once he told me there were children in the house, I proceeded to attack the fire.

"Let me direct your attention to an occasion a few days later, the 27th of December of 1991. Did you have an opportunity to return to that fire scene?" >> Yes, sir, I did.

"Can you tell me the reasons why you returned to the fire scene on that day?" >> Yes, sir. I was to assist the fire marshal with the drawing of a sketch of the house.

"What type activity had you been engaged in just prior to returning to the fire scene?" >> I had been to the children's funeral.

"Okay. Did you have an opportunity to observe him there at the fire scene on that occasion also?" >> Yes, sir, I did.

"Did Mr. Willingham attempt to engage you in conversation at this point?" >> Yes, sir, he did.

"Did he, in fact, speak to you on this occasion?" >> Yes, he did.

"Did you initiate any questions with him?" >> No, sir, I did not.

"What did Mr. Willingham want to speak with you about on this occasion?" >> Initially, he had asked about a dart set that was in there. He asked to escort him inside so that he might look for it. As we were going through, he proceeded in the bedroom where the children were burned.

"Can you tell us what other type conversation he engaged you in when you entered into the children's bedroom?" >> He asked me if I knew where the fire started or how it started?

"Did he make any statement to you about his knowledge of the fire?" >> Yes, sir. He said that when he came into the room, it was burning. He pointed over to an area of the room along this wall and on the ceiling.

"So he indicated to you he came into the room, is that correct?" >> Yes, sir, he did.

"Did he seem to be upset about his dart board?" >> Yes, sir, he did.

"Did he make any conversation with reference to samples being taken by the police or fire department?" >> Yes, sir. As we were coming out of the house, we met the fire marshal toward the front door of the hallway. He made the statement to the effect that if any more samples were taken of the floor, he had poured some cologne on the floor because the children had liked the smell of that cologne. He poured it from the bathroom to where the children were burned.

"Let me make sure I get this right. He told you he poured it from the bathroom through the hall into the children's room?" >> Yes, sir.

"The cologne?" >> Yes, sir.

"And mentioned this in reference to samples that were being taken?" >> He said if there were any more samples taken, the cologne would probably show up in the samples.

"Pass the witness."

<<>>

David Martin cross-examines Lieutenant Ronald Franks.

"Mr. Franks, when you first saw Todd at the scene, you were not examining him for the purpose of diagnosing smoke inhalation, were you?" >> No, sir, I wasn't.

"You were in hurry?" >> Yes, sir, I was.

"He was hysterical?" >> Yes, sir.

"Your attention was on the other matters?" >> Yes, sir.

"Now, it is not uncommon for people to return to their home after a fire to claim property, is it?" >> No, sir, it's not.

"You would expect them to do that, would you not?" >> Yes, sir.

"And if anyone had poured anything on the floor of the residence that was being investigated, you would want to know that, would you not?" >> Yes, sir.

Martin passes the witness. Jackson has no further questions. It's ten minutes to noon. Judge Douglas calls for a lunch break and instructs us to return by 1:00 PM.

TESTIMONY OF STEVEN VANDIVER
Tuesday, August 18, 1992

"State calls Steven Vandiver."

Steven Vandiver is sworn in. John Jackson with the direct examination.

"Would you state your name, please?" >> Steven Keith Vandiver.

"Steve, how are you employed?" >> Corsicana Fire Department.

"Steve, let me direct your attention back to the morning hours of December 23rd, 1991. Do you remember that day?" >> Yes.

"Can you tell us what type duties you were engaged in on that day?" >> We had just had a house fire on North 36th, and we were back at the station cleaning up, getting the trucks ready to go back into service.

"Can you tell me what location, approximately, you were dispatched to on that morning?" >> The call come in as 1200 block of West 11th.

"Did you proceed to that location?" >> Yes, sir.

"Can you tell us what you found when you arrived?" >> When we arrived, there was a frame residence, it was pretty well involved in fire. There was fire coming out the front windows and pretty well the whole front porch was involved in fire.

"Did you learn that there were children who might be present in the house?" >> Yes, sir. There was people out in the street and stuff saying there was still kids in the house.

"What action did you take at that time?" >> We laid a line from the hydrant at 19th street, and we were hooking it up and I put on an air pack, went around to the front of the house. They already had a line pulled off the other truck and Lieutenant Charles Dennison and I started going into the house.

"What did you notice when you went into the house?" >> A lot of fire, you know, in the front of the house and to the left front room. To the left there was a lot of fire.

"How did you make entry into the house?" >> We went in the front door and knocked down the fire.

"Where was the fire concentrated?" >> The front of the hallway into the first room to the left.

"Was the floor on fire?" >> Yes, sir.

"Do you find that rather unusual in house fires?" >> Yes, sir. Most of the time the floor will be the safest place to be because there won't be any fire there. It will be cooler. It won't have as much heat and smoke on the floor.

"Did that create a problem for you in this particular fire?" >> Yeah. It slowed us up a little bit. We had to really put a lot of water on it so we could, you know, go further into the house.

"When you got the fire knocked down and got into the house, what did you do?" >> We went all the way down the hall and to the kitchen, and I let go of the hose, went to the right, the first room to the right, and started doing a search on the floor and went through the room.

"What were you looking for?" >> Well, just feeling around mainly. You can't see anything. You are just feeling around to feel somebody or something. I went through the first room there and then didn't find anything in there. And kind of by accident, I went through the door into the bedroom, and I started checking in there.

"Can you tell us what happened when you got in there?" >> I felt a bed. I couldn't really see the bed. I started feeling around on it, and about that time they got what we call an exhaust fan set up in the front door. They turned that on. It started blowing some of the smoke out, and I could make out a body laying on the bed.

"All right. What action did you take at that point?" >> There was another fireman next to me, and I tapped him on the shoulder as I grabbed her so he could help lead me back out of the house. I picked her up and we made our way out in the front yard.

"Can you tell me where on the bed she was lying?" >> She was lying about in the middle of the bed face down, and her head was probably where the pillows would be at the top of the bed.

"Had she apparently been the victim of some burns?" >> All I could really see on her was some what I would call soot. It was kind of around her mouth and stuff. That's all I could see because I still had my mask on and stuff. It was kind of hard to see.

"Could you tell whether she was alive at that time?" >> I couldn't tell.

"Did you have an opportunity to see a person identified to you as Cameron Willingham on that day?" >> No, sir, I never did.

Jackson passes the witness. Martin has no questions, and just like that we are through another witness.

TESTIMONY OF DOUGLAS FOGG
Tuesday, August 18, 1992

"State calls Doug Fogg."

Doug Fogg is sworn in and John Jackson proceeds with the direct examination.

"Would you state your name for the record, please?" >> Douglas Fogg.

"Mr. Fogg, how are you employed?" >> Assistant Fire Chief for Corsicana Fire Department.

"How long have you been a part of the fire department?" >> A little over 22 years.

"Did you have an opportunity to be present at a structure fire on 11th Avenue in Corsicana on the 23rd of December last year?" >> Yes, I was. The alarm came in. We were at another structure fire on North 36th. The alarm came in as a structure fire on West 11th with children in the house. I responded from there.

"What did you find when you got to the house?" >> Heavy fire, heavy smoke on the front of the house.

"Did you see a gentleman in the front yard later identified as Mr. Willingham?" >> Yes. Mr. Willingham was saying, "My babies are in the house." I asked Mr. Willingham to step back in that there was some electrical lines that broke away from the house. They were still popping in the front yard. George was there out by the engine. I asked him to get with Mr. Willingham. I went around and relieved Lieutenant Franks on the nozzle so he could get his air pack on and proceeded to put water on the fire through the porch, through the window, and through the front door.

"What was the part of the house that was most heavily involved in the fire that you could see?" >> Across the front porch, fire coming out of the front doorway, and the double window on the front of the house.

"Did you remain there at the fire scene until the fire was extinguished?" >> Yes, I did.

"Can you tell us what procedure you followed after the fire was extinguished?" >> After the fire was extinguished, the remaining two bodies were discovered. We called for a justice of the peace to come to the fire scene. And after the two remaining bodies were removed, we started investigation as to the origin and cause of the fire.

"Can you tell us, just for the benefit of the jury, just how you go about a fire scene or arson investigation?" >> Normally, we work from least damaged to most damaged of the fire scene itself. Then we go to the areas of heaviest fire that we saw while we were there to start the investigation.

"Can you go through with us the step-by-step process that you employed in attempting to determine the origin and the cause of this fire?" >> Initially, we started looking in the front hallway and front bedroom area of the house. That was the area of most fire damage. Initially, we started looking for accidental causes of the fire. We started eliminating those in the front bedroom. One of the first things we look for was the space heater. The space heater was located in the southeast corner of the bedroom. The stop along the east wall or gas outlet along the east wall was found to be in the "off" position. We eliminated that space heater. We started looking for electrical shorts from wiring which was visible in the bedroom. We found no electrical shorts in the bedroom. From there we went to the hallway, which was just outside the doorway of the bedroom. The low burn, heavy burn ended immediately south of the doorway. And in that area there were no gas outlets. There was a light switch by the front door facing. The wires were intact. No evidence of electrical short. And as we started removing debris then from the floor, as we had low burn, we started finding configurations of puddling effect, pouring effect of a liquid or what we would consider a liquid being used to accelerate a fire.

"Do you feel that you eliminated gas as a cause or an electrical cause as the origin of this fire?" >> Yes. We even had the gas company come out and do a leak test and bar test where they punch holes, checking for gas leaks, which they found none. The electrical, you look at the electrical wiring for evidence of shorts from the outlets, from fixtures, so forth. There again, those were eliminated.

"Tell us what you proceeded to do at that point." >> From there we started going to the deep burn or lowest burn areas in the hallway and followed them into the bedroom where the two twins were found. We removed some of the debris. We had to punch holes in the floor to allow some of the water to drain out. As the water drained down, more patterns -- we call them pour patterns. Puddling effects were evidenced on the floor. We started removing debris from the floor and additional areas of low burn. Floor level burns were noted.

"Did this cause some suspicion in your mind with regard to the cause of this fire?" >> Yes, it did.

"Can you articulate what the cause of suspicion was at this point?" >> After eliminating the accidental causes, you start suspecting a deliberately set fire. And with deaths involved, you have to go a lot further before making a statement as to a deliberately set fire. We have to settle in our own mind that we have eliminated all accidental causes, which we did. Not only did we attempt to connect the low burn on the floor configurations, it actually ended up starting on the front porch, through the threshold of the front door into the hallway, very minutely linked to the bedroom. Then the patterns in the bedroom were interlinked.

"I would like you to describe the pour patterns or puddling patterns in that structure." >> Okay. In the floor covering of the bedroom was carpet tile, under the tile was quarter-inch plywood. Then there was felt or tar paper. Then the original oak flooring. Most of the carpet was gone, but the tile remained. The areas where liquid had been poured is very evident where the tile remained. As the fire burned on down through the other coverings into the original oak flooring, we see the interlinking of the pour patterns on the floor.

"Once you found that, did you proceed with what you believed was an arson investigation?" >> Not at that time. We had to take a look at all of the contents that were in the room to determine whether they could have left this impression.

"Did you proceed to do that?" >> Yes, we did.

"Can you tell us how you did it, what your findings were with regard to any other explanations?" >> As you go through the debris, removing the debris off of the floor, we found clothes, we found some toys, plastic toys on the floor. To eliminate the plastic toys melting and running, we looked at the area around the remains of the plastic toys to determine whether they had ran and produced these patterns, and we found that they had not.

"Can you tell us now what the next step of your investigation was?" >> We continued removing debris. The fire marshal took some samples to be carried to the lab for analysis to confirm what I had determined at the scene. A call was put into the State Fire Marshall's Office for an investigator to double check everything that I had found, just to be sure that we were not calling it a deliberately set fire when it was not.

"I assume you wouldn't want to make any hasty decision of that nature, is that correct?" >> That's correct.

"I'm going to ask you to identify this photograph for me, if you can." >> This is the threshold of the front door with the concrete front porch to the bottom of the picture. The remains of the threshold were removed for laboratory analysis.

"All right. Is that picture otherwise significant, do you think?" >> It is. There is burning down on the seal of the foundation of the house, underneath the threshold plate. Liquid had dripped down as it was poured, ran down under the threshold plate.

"Does that photograph exhibit an unusual burning characteristic?" >> Yes, it does. When a fire normally burns, it burns up. As heat rises flames go up. This burning characteristic had fire going under the threshold plate, which is very unusual in that it should have been protected from flame itself under that base plate.

"To what do you attribute that?" >> Liquid being used to accelerate the fire. It's showing the burn patterns from the hallway across the threshold plate, even melting part of the aluminum, and out on to the concrete floor. Also on the concrete floor, the staining left is very characteristic of a liquid burning on the concrete.

"When you refer to accelerant, what is an accelerant?" >> An accelerant is something that is used to accelerate a fire or to make a fire burn faster.

"Do you find evidence of an accelerant in this fire?" >> Yes, we did.

"I believe you said earlier that you had an opportunity to associate with the State Fire Marshall, is that correct?" >> That is correct.

"And at what point did you decide to involve him?" >> Christmas day I made the decision to go ahead and call them. It was December the 26th that I actually placed the call.

"And did you later meet with him?" >> Yes, I did.

"Did you and he make a journey to the fire scene?" >> Yes, we did.

"And can you tell us what you and the State Fire Marshall did at that point?" >> Initially, he came down here December the 27th. We visited the fire scene. I stayed back, and he walked through the fire scene. Then we got together and matched my findings to what he saw and came to the same conclusion that we had a deliberately set fire.

"All right. Pass the witness."

<<>>

David Martin will cross-examine Assistant Fire Chief Douglas Fogg.

"Chief, any arson investigator must be very careful when he encounters what he believes to be a puddle pattern, is that correct?" >> That's correct.

"Because it's not just accelerants that can cause those, right?" >> That's correct.

"In fact, anything that is in that area of the floor that causes the fire to burn hotter might mistakenly lead you to that conclusion, is that correct?" >> That's correct.

"That's why, for example, you've examined whether it was a plastic toy that caused it, right?" >> That is correct.

"Now, did you know that this house is about 40 years old?" >> Later on after the investigation, yes.

"But you determined that being the case, it was built sometime in the '50s?" >> Yes, sir.

"And originally had an oak tongue and grove floor?" >> Yes, sir, it did.

"And on top of that was tar paper?" >> Yes, sir.

"We call it tar paper because it's got tar in it?" >> That's correct.

"And tar burns?" >> That's correct.

"On top of that was linoleum tile?" >> No, sir. On top of that was quarter-inch plywood.

"And on top of that was the tile?" >> Yes, sir.

"Was the plywood all over the floor?" >> To my knowledge it was. I did not see an area where it was not.

"And the tile was all over the floor?" >> To my knowledge it was, yes.

"And what is the tile connected to the floor with?" >> It would have been an adhesive.

"Glue?" >> Glue.

"Glue burns?" >> Some glue does, yes.

"Tar paper?" >> Yes.

"Linoleum burns?" >> Yes, it does.

"Plastic toys will run when they are hot and melt?" >> Some do and some do not.

"Some clothing?" >> Some clothing will.

"And some other items that we may not be able to think of right now?" >> Yes, sir.

"But there are things that will do that, right?" >> Oh, yes, sir.

"Now, the reason that you find a pattern in the floor that is burned deeper than elsewhere is basically two reasons. One, you suppose the fire is hotter there, and, two, the floor is thinner there in some instances?" >> That is correct.

"For example, a house that has been lived in for 40 years has had a lot of foot traffic. Can we suppose that?" >> Yes, sir.

"And in certain areas of the house, like where you walk through a door, there is more foot traffic than elsewhere, isn't there?" >> That's correct.

"These areas of the floor are thinner because they have been walked on a lot?" >> That's a possibility, yes.

"Those areas will burn faster and deeper than a area with less foot traffic?" >> Commonly so.

"Aren't you cautioned in the arson investigation books that you read and refer to that you must be careful to distinguish those areas?" >> Yes, sir.

"It says in these books that heavily traveled areas will burn down deeper than less traveled areas, generally speaking?" >> Sometimes, yes.

"Now the areas that we see that are burned down are burned below the tile, correct?" >> Correct.

"And glue on the bottom of tiles will burn in a fire, won't it?" >> Yes. It will if it can receive the heat and the air.

"And you don't think that the glue burned in this case, do you?" >> Surely some of the glue had to burn.

"Because some of the tile was burned?" >> Yes, that's correct.

"Glue can be an accelerant as well, can't it?" >> That's correct. It can be.

"And in areas where the glue burns, it will burn hotter than just in an area where the tile burns, correct?" >> Sometimes, yes.

"And in every case where you found some kind of pattern on the floor, there was glue and tar paper as far as you can tell?" >> That's correct.

"And so what you found is that in most areas, the carpet that was on top of here burned up, right?" >> That's correct.

"And that the tile burned up and some of the wood burned up?" >> That's correct.

""And all the plywood was covered with glue because it was all under the tile, correct?" >> Yes.

"Now, you didn't perform any tests yourself on any of these samples that you took, did you?" >> No, sir, I did not.

"And you say that you found some areas on the porch that you thought had had some accelerant on them?" >> That's correct.

"Like charcoal lighter fluid?" >> That's correct.

"And, as far as you can tell, someone could have been barbecuing on the front porch, spilled lighter fluid and made the same kind of stain?" >> That's correct.

"And the threshold before it burned was painted or do you know?" >> I could not say for sure.

"So, you don't know whether it was painted or not right off?" >> I don't remember seeing any painting on it.

"But paint burns?" >> Yes. Some paint does.

"If you have a piece of painted wood, the painting will burn off of it?" >> If it's an oil base paint, yes. If it's water base, it will not.

"Well, isn't it common that exteriors of houses painted with oil base?" >> Some cases. Most of it is water base.

"But if you had a piece of wood like this jury rail or if it had oil base paint, had finish on the bottom and caught fire, you would expect the bottom of it to burn?" >> Not that much. More or less it would blister more than char burn.

"Would it be uncommon to find paint that would burn off of a piece of wood?" >> Oil base painting will, yes.

"When it does so, it leaves an indication on the wood that there's been a fire on it?" >> Not a char burn or a deep burn but a discoloration type burn, yes.

"Well, in other words, Chief, if the threshold is painted and the house catches on fire, heavily involved in fire, wouldn't you expect the paint to burn, to be some indications on it, on the threshold?" >> Yes.

"Now, when you say that you eliminated all the causes of the fire, you are speaking really of the electricity and the space heaters, aren't you?" >> That's your most common type accidental fires, yes.

"Because, for example, a child could have started a fire with a cigarette lighter or match?" >> Not unless they set it outside and went back in.

"Was there anything about the fire that eliminated the possibility that a child started the fire?" >> A child could have done it.

"You have investigated fires that were accidentally set by children, have you not?" >> Yes, I have.

"And it's not uncommon in human experience for a child in a home where people smoke to get a hold of a cigarette lighter and light it, is it?" >> No, that's not uncommon.

"And it's not uncommon around any home to have accelerants in a place where children could reach them, is it?" >> No, that's not uncommon.

"It has been your experience in these past twenty years to find fires where a child, for example, has gotten ahold of an accelerant and sprayed them or poured them or some other way got them on the floor then accidentally set it on fire?" >> That's correct.

"It happens?" >> It happens.

"It could have happened in this case as far as you know, couldn't it?" >> In my opinion, no.

"I'm not asking about your opinion now, and I know you have one. I'm asking about what you found at the scene. This is my real question: Why could not have the child, Amber, for example, two years of age, have inadvertently or accidentally got the charcoal lighter fluid or sprayed the lighter fluid and inadvertently set it on fire There wasn't anything that you discovered about this fire that would have eliminated that as a possibility, was there?" >> I could not say that she did not set the fire.

"That's my question. Pass the witness."

<<>>

Jackson has some redirect for Chief Fogg, who he refers to as simply Doug.

"Based on your opinion, do you believe that babies set this fire, Doug?" >> In my experience from other fires where children have accidentally set them and where they have ignited an accelerant type or liquid type, there was one area. It did not go from, in this case, the front porch into the hall and into the bedroom. No, I've never seen one like that.

"In your opinion would that be implausible?" >> It could happen, but the possibility would be very remote.

"Doug, Mr. Martin asked you lot of questions about how glue burns and how paint burns and how tar paper burns. Did glue or paint or tar paper leave those puddle patterns on the floor in this room and the burn trails in this house?" >> In my opinion, no. Glue will burn some. Even water base type glue will burn, but in order for it to burn, it's got to get some air. The glue being sandwiched between the tile and the plywood did not have the opportunity for the air to get to it until after the tile loosened from heat that was coming from another source, and then you are talking about a very thin layer of glue that is sandwiched between the tiles and the plywood. So I don't think the glue would have had anything to do with the puddle configurations.

"In the face of the questions that were asked you by Mr. Martin, do you still find this was an intentionally set accelerated fire?" >> Yes.

"Pass the witness."

<<>>

Martin has some re-cross for Chief Fogg.

"Well, Chief, this room that we are talking about had clothing in it, wooden furniture, plastic toys and other things that burned, didn't it?" >> That's correct.

"And when those things burn, they get hot, do they not?" >> They do.

"They will burn through the floor. And it could easily set the glue on fire under the tile, couldn't it?" >> Not until after the tile had been loosened.

"Is that a picture of tile in the bedroom?" >> Yes.

"It shows the glue was burned?" >> It shows a small area where we picked up a piece of the tile, yes.

"Could you answer the question that I asked you?" >> I cannot say that the glue itself burned. It could have been where the liquid burns, and it got up under the tile and burned.

"Or it could be where the glue burned, couldn't it?" >> It's possible. The other glue on the back of the tile did not, though.

"Do you recognize this as a picture that was taken of the front porch of the house?" >> Yes, I do.

"And do you recognize the white object there as being a disintegrated portion of a charcoal lighter container?" >> Yes, I do.

"This was on the front wall of the front bedroom, correct?" >> That's correct.

"Do you recognize this as a newspaper photograph taken while the fire was burning?" >> I did not see that in the paper.

"Do you recognize this as the front of the house we are talking about?" >> It appears to be, yes.

"Do you see behind this fireman an upside down charcoal grill?" >> Yes, sir.

"And do you recognize this picture as the pile of debris outside the front room window?" >> Yes.

"And that was all of the things that were shuffled, raked swept out of that bedroom, is that correct?" >> That's correct.

"There is no reason why the brown stains you described on the front porch couldn't have come from that charcoal lighter fluid container, is there?" >> No.

"It's not uncommon to find a charcoal lighter fluid container around a charcoal grill, is it?" >> No, it's not.

"Are you familiar with those charcoal lighter fluid containers that HEB used to sell, generic lighter fluid?" >> Yes, I am.

"Do you know they had easily accessible lids children could get into?" >> Yes.

"Are you aware of the fact HEB pulled those from the shelves because the number of the children opening them and starting fires or injuring themselves?" >> No, I was not.

"Pass the witness."

<<>>

Jackson has some further direct examination for Chief Fogg.

"Is it still your testimony in your opinion this was a deliberately set, arson fire." >> Yes, it is.

"Based on anything Mr. Martin has asked you, can you visualize a situation where some child went through the house pouring these puddle patterns, leaving a trail out through the hall and into the front of the house as you have described in your testimony? Does that seem logical to you?" >> No, it does not.

"Pass the witness."

<<>>

Martin has some further cross-examination for Chief Fogg.

"Nothing in your investigation would make it impossible that a child took a container of some flammable liquid and inadvertently or otherwise spilled or poured it on the floor and set it on fire, correct?" >> That's correct.

"There wasn't anything you found that would show that could not have happened, correct?" >> That's correct.

"Pass the witness."

Jackson has no further questions. Judge Douglas calls for a ten minute recess. When we return, the judge instructs Jackson to call his next witness.

TESTIMONY OF JAMES PALOS
Tuesday, August 18, 1992

John Jackson conducts the direct examination of James Palos.

"Would you state your name for the record, please?" >> My name is James Palos.

"James, how are you employed?" >> I'm the Fire Marshal at the Corsicana Fire Department.

"Let me direct your attention back to the 23rd of December, two days before Christmas last year. Did you have an opportunity to be present at a structure on 11th Avenue in Corsicana that was damaged by fire?" >> Yes, I was.

"Did you have an opportunity to participate in a fire scene investigation with Mr. Fogg and others?" >> Yes, I did.

"In the course of that fire scene investigation, did you take certain samples of materials and other items?" >> Yes, I did.

"I will show you this photograph and will ask you to identify it for me, if you can." >> That is at the front door, the wooden threshold.

"Was that an area that was utilized by you as a sample in this case?" >> Yes, it was.

"Can you tell us the reason you obtained a sample from this area?" >> Yes. I obtained a sample from this area because of the unusual burn characteristics on the wood.

"Would you explain what that photograph depicts?" >> This area here is the front porch, at the side of the house, and this was the remains of some type of plastic which was collected as evidence also.

"Were both of these samples taken to laboratories?" >> Yes. All of them were taken there.

"What was the purpose that you took samples in this particular structure fire?" >> The reason I take samples in a fire investigation is to identify any possible accelerants that could have been used in a fire.

"With regard to the threshold, was this obtained from an area which you believed had been accelerated?" >> Yes, I do.

"All right. Pass the witness."

<<>>

David Martin will cross-examine Fire Marshal James Palos.

"But those were the only samples you took?" >> No, sir.

"You took many others?" >> Yes, I did.

"You took samples from the hallway of the house?" >> Yes.

"And from the bedroom at the front of the house?" >> Yes.

"You took samples from any area that you thought was suspicious?" >> Yes.

"And sent them to the lab, did you not?" >> Yes, I did.

"You also you took some glass. Where did you get the glass?" >> I retrieved fragments of glass from the front bedroom below the east front window of the north wall.

"And then you took carpet and glass samples?" >> Yes.

"What else?" >> There was a sample from the bottom of the south side door facing from the doorway into the front bedroom.

"And then there was some more wood." >> It was base board underneath the south window in the front bedroom.

"And some metal?" >> It was an aluminum threshold taken from the front door.

"You sent these to a lab?" >> Yes.

"You concentrated your collection on areas which were most suspicious to you?" >> Yes.

"And then sent them off and asked the lab to detect whether there was an accelerant in those samples?" >> Yes, I did.

"And the only accelerant that was detected was here, the container for the charcoal lighter fluid?" >> Yes.

"And here, the threshold of the door?" >> Yes.

"But none others, correct?" >> That's true.

"All else was negative?" >> Right.

"All right. Are you familiar with this kind of kerosene lantern that I have here? You have seen these before?" >> Yes, sir, I have.

"And they are used by filling them with kerosene and lighting the wick, are they not?" >> True.

"And kerosene that will work in this lamp is the same kind of kerosene that were found in your samples, correct, or do you know?" >> Yes, it is.

"The lab reported to you, did it not, that what was recovered from the threshold and also from the charcoal lighter container was straight run petroleum distillate known as mineral spirits of kerosene, correct?" >> Yes.

"In other words what we can buy at the gas station and call kerosene. Is that the way you understand that?" >> Yes.

"I mean it's just kerosene?" >> Kerosene.

"And this kind of distillate can be found as a fuel in some charcoal starters?" >> That's true.

"Or as solvent for paints and specialty products?" >> Correct.

"The kind of kerosene we might light this lamp with if we wanted to?" >> Yes.

"Pass the witness."

John Jackson has no redirect for Fire Marshall James Palos. That's a first. Judge Douglas instructs Jackson to call his next witness.

DELIBERATION OF THE FIREFIGHTERS' TESTIMONY
Thursday, August 20, 1992

Marti: "Let's talk about the firefighters' testimony."

Bitter Ted: "I don't see how anyone could have sat in that courtroom, listened to what those guys said, and think that this guy is not guilty. He was more worried about his dartboard that he was his kids. He goes back there, has a party on the remains, and complains about someone taking his dartboard. Know what I mean?"

Harriet: "There's no evidence of a party after the fire. None of the witnesses used that word. The prosecutor said it was a party, then acted as if he made a simple mistake. The firefighter said that it wasn't unusual for people to return to their home after it burned down. I've seen images of people on TV picking through burned out homes hunting for anything that might have survived. So what if he mentioned a dartboard?"

Ted: "But not everyone is laughing and play loud music and having a good time."

Harriet: "There was no evidence they were laughing and having a good time. And the evidence was the music wasn't coming from his car."

Ted: "You just don't get it, do you?"

Harriet: "Why isn't Stacy on trial?"

Silence falls across the room. Briefly.

Ted: "You're crazy. You're outta mind. You know that don't ya?"

Boisterous Lee: "You mean instead of this guy? She wasn't even there."

Harriet: "She was there all right."

Lee: "Whadda you talking about, she was there?"

Harriet: "The Barbees said that the next day, when the truck was playing the loud music, both Todd and Stacy were at the house."

Lee: "But she wasn't there when the house burned down."

Harriet: "If you say so, I guess she wasn't. I was talking about the next day. Best we can tell from the evidence, she was behaving same way as he was, just talking. The prosecutor is telling us that behavior proves Todd set the fire, so why doesn't the same behavior prove Stacy set the fire."

Lee: "Cause she wasn't even there when the house --"

Harriet: "If you say so, but she was there at the hospital when the teenage girls offered to buy them food. I don't recall any testimony that the girls only bought food for Todd, or that Todd was the only one to eat the food. So why didn't they arrest her? If eating food after your children die is evidence of arson, why didn't they arrest them both? If visiting the fire scene while music is playing in a truck is evidence of arson, why didn't they arrest them both?"

Good one.

Bitter Ted: "Because you have to be at the fire to start the fire. Know what I mean?"

Harriet: "No one testified where she was when the fire started. Maybe she was in the children's bedroom setting it on fire. She would have had plenty of time to leave, at least according to the Barbees. The girl playing in the back yard claimed she smelled smoke for ten minutes before she decided to do anything about it."

Lee: "No mother would do that?"

Harriet: "But a father would?"

Young Jack: "That's another thing I was wondering about. I thought they had to prove motive. No one ever testified why he might have wanted to kill his children. I don't know. I've never been on a jury before, so I was just wondering?"

Edie: "No, they don't have to prove motive. Not required."

Lee: "And they did prove motive, didn't they? The prison guy, what's his name Webb, he said that this guy told him he killed them because he was protecting the mother."

Everyone in the room stares at him.

Lee: "Whadda ya all looking at? What?"

He's squirming badly now.

Lee: "He didn't mean he was protecting her because she set the fire. That's not what he said."

Beads of sweat are forming on his reddening forehead.

Lee: "He said she had hurt the kids, that's why he killed them. He did it to protect her."

Time for me to violate my self-imposed subtlety oath.

"That's the best reason of all to arrest her, assuming they believe Webb. But they don't believe Webb. They're using him to get what they want, and he's using them to get what he wants. We all know that, at least most of us do. So I'm going to double my bet, and I'll give you even better odds. If Johnny Webb gets out within five years, you write me a check for one-thousand. If he's still in, I write you a check for four."

Sports Fan Ward: "I want a piece of that."

"This is between me and Lee. Isn't it, Lee?"

Lee: "I don't know what you're talking about, this between you and me stuff."

"If the prosecutors believed Johnny Webb, Stacy would be sitting right there next to Todd. And if they really believed the evidence about the music or the food or all other crap they threw at us, if they believed any of that was worth a plugged nickel, Stacy would be sitting beside Todd. The prosecution doesn't believe its own evidence, but they want us to."

That's probably enough for now.

Ward: "So you really think he's innocent?"

I need to return to my subtle, restrained alter ego.

"I thought we were deliberating whether the State proved its case beyond a reasonable doubt. I was merely pointing out that I have some doubt about some witnesses and some issues in the State's case. That's all."

Ward: "But you think he's innocent?"

"Too early to say. I like that we're talking about it, though."

Ward: "Too early! You think we haven't talked enough?"

Young Jack: "This is my first time on a jury --"

Edie: "You mentioned that."

Jack: "-- yeah, sorry. Anyway, I was wondering. Shouldn't they have secured the crime scene?"

Harriet: "It's up to us to decide it if was a crime scene. But you're right. It seems they should have secured the scene until they were through investigating it. Let me think. The fire happened on the day before Christmas Eve, so that would be the twenty-third. And the fire chief, Fogg, and the state fire marshal, Vasquez, didn't go through the house together until the twenty-seventh. That's four days. It seems to me as if the house should have been secured the whole time."

Bitter Ted: "Boy, oh boy. This is gonna go on forever. I remember someone said they put that yellow tape around the place, or something like that, so what's your point?"

Jack: "I guess the tape wasn't good enough. People were shifting through the house the next morning. Maybe they should have posted a guard."

Ted: "And if they had, then this guy wouldn't have been able to contaminate the crime scene by pouring cologne all over it."

Jack: "He didn't contaminate it. They had already tested their samples."

Ted: "But he didn't know it."

Jack: "I think he did. He warned them about the cologne in case they planned to take any more samples. I'm pretty sure that's what he said. If he talked about talking more samples, he must have known they had already collected samples. And if they hadn't taken all the samples, why didn't they leave a guard?"

Ted: "Cause I told you. They used that yellow crime scene tape."

Timid John: "I guess that just makes his point. They should have left a guard. If they can go to all this trouble to try him and maybe execute him, it doesn't seem too much to ask to leave a guard, so ..."

And his voice drops off below audible level.

Marti: "Harriet, let me ask you. Why do you think he poured cologne on the fire scene?"

Harriet: "I presume because he wanted it to smell like cologne rather than whatever it smelled like. I've never been in that situation, so I have no idea how it might have smelled there, but I don't have any trouble believing it was unpleasant, to say the least. I think it's possible it was a sincere gesture, but realistically there's not much anyone could do for their children in that case. Maybe he was trying to cover up evidence, but it doesn't seem so to me. It's certainly not the type of evidence on which to base a guilty verdict."

Jack: "And they should have secured the scene."

Harriet: "Yes. They should have secured the scene."

Lee can't let go of Johnny Webb. He speaks to no one in particular.

Lee: "You know that thing I said about him trying to protect her, I didn't mean that she might have set the fire."

Marti: "Yes, Lee. I think we all understood you."

He points an accusing finger in my direction.

Lee: "He was just trying to bait me."

Edie: "He did a pretty good job."

Lee doesn't understand that he just can't win on this one any longer. The jury has grown to distrust Webb. Lee won't be able to rehabilitate him. He should let matter drop.

But, of course, he won't.

Lee: "Webb was right about the little girls, wasn't he? He said this Willingham guy carried one of them into another room, and that's just how they found 'em. The baby twin girls were in the front bedroom and the older girl was in his bedroom. Just like he said. You've got an answer for everything. Whadda you say about that?"

I remind myself: subtlety and restraint.

"I don't believe he's a credible witness."

Lee: "How would he get that information?"

"I believe that's obvious."

I restrained myself from adding "at least to everyone except you."

Lee: "Whadda ya mean obvious?"

What the hell!

"You really don't get, do you? They fed him the information. They spoon fed it to him, bit by bit. They didn't just meet with him once and hear his story. They met with him over and over, at least four times that Webb would admit to.

"Webb only has hear the story from Willingham once, and to tell the story to the guard just once, but he has to tell it to the prosecutors four times? Of course not. He tells them a story, they go back and compare notes, and then they come back a few days later. 'Did he say how he set the fire? Did he say anything about spreading lighter fluid all over?' And then Webb, who knows as well as any other snitch how the game is played, says something smart, like 'Uh, yeah, what you said. He used lighter fluid.'

"They go away and come back a couple weeks later. 'What about the little girl? Did he say he moved her from the bedroom or did he just leave her there with the other two?' To which Webb answers, "Uh, he left her with the others.'

"That's a disappointment to the prosecutors of course, but they've run into this before. It's easy to fix. They just ask 'Are you sure?'

"Webb knows those are the code words for 'try again', so he tries again. 'I mean, he said he moved one of them to another room. That's what he said.'

"And those little meetings keep happening over and over until Webb is telling the story that the prosecutors want to hear. Then they give him a wink and a nod and say 'All we want is for you to tell the truth. We can't promise you anything, understand.' And Johnny Webb, professional snitch, winks at them and says 'I understand.'

"Now they could have recorded every single one of their interviews with Johnny Webb, and they could have played every one of them for us during the trial. But they chose not to, and I'll tell you what. If you can lay your hands on any one of those recordings, I'll be pleased and honored to write out a check for my five thousand dollars, right there on the spot. You don't even have to put any money up."

Ward: "Now I'd really like some of that action."

"Give it a rest, Ward. None of you are going to find any of those tapes because they never made them. The last thing they want is for anyone to see what goes on in those little secret meetings. They just want you to believe their snitch when he gets on the stand and talks about how awful he thought it was and how terrible he felt and how he just had to do the right thing.

"The problem is they talked to him so many times he can't keep his story straight. So when he gets there up on the stand and ask him if Willingham said anything about moving the little girl, he says 'No. I don't believe he said that.'

"It's just like my little make-believe story of what happened in those secret meetings. He gives them the wrong answer, except this time he's on the witness stand, right in front of us. While that's a little embarrassing for the prosecutors, they never flinch. They just hand him a piece of paper and ask if he now remembers it differently. Supposedly the paper is a statement he signed, but it may have just as well read '15 years is a long time.'

"Suddenly, and if by magic, Johnny Webb changes his testimony right there on the spot and tells us that Cameron Todd Willingham said he moved one of the girls from the children's bedroom to somewhere else. So I'm sitting there in the jury box, and I sure as hell know Johnny Webb is lying his ass off. The interesting question to me now is: how did he learn that the girls were in different locations?

"Then I give myself a metaphorical slap on the forehead and realize the information has been fed to him, and I have a pretty good guess on who did the feeding. Then I decide, right then and there, that if the prosecution is going to begin their case with this lying, son-of-a-bitch snitch, I'm going to be damn suspicious of everything they try to feed me.

The room seems to be in shock. I realize I had exhibited neither subtlety or restraint, so I try to cover it.

"I guess what I'm saying is that I'm pleased we're all discussing this case together."

Yeah. That'll do.

Timid John raises his hand.

Marti: "Yes, John."

John: "I'd like to change my vote to not guilty."

Marti: "The vote is now eight to three guilty, and one abstention."

Lee: "Whadda ya mean, not guilty? How can you change your vote like that?"

John: "I don't have to defend my decision to you. I'm beginning to have doubts. If we can't trust the prosecutor, how can we vote guilty?"

Jack: "And I want to change my vote. Same thing. I don't understand how we're supposed to put a man to death based on this kind of evidence."

Marti: "That's seven guilty, four not guilty, and one abstention. John, Jack, Harriet, and Jorge voting not guilty. And the excitable gentleman abstaining."

Edie: "Before everyone gets too excited about changing votes, I suggest we look at the hard evidence of arson. I agree that all these miscellaneous issues of music, food, dartboards and cologne are silly. I'm not concerned particularly how he behaved after the fire. I have no idea how I would behave in such an awful circumstance. And for what it's worth, Lee, you probably don't want to use Johnny Webb any more to bolster your arguments."

Lee: "You have no right to talk to me like that."

Edie: "Yes I do. The hard evidence for arson, on the other hand, is substantial and it is compelling. Chief Douglas Fogg ruled out possible sources of accidental fire. He checked the space heater and it was off. Then he checked the electrical wires and outlets, and they were fine. Everyone with me so far?"

Bitter Ted: "Everyone listen to this woman. She knows what she's talking about."

Edie: "Please don't help me. On the other hand, there's the evidence of arson. There were puddles all over the bedroom and hallway floors. Those puddles indicate a combustible liquid was poured there. Chief Fogg said the floor was hotter than it should be, that the fire burned from the floor up, and that's evidence of arson. Finally, the door threshold tested positive for an accelerant, and the Chief said the fire spread from the front door, through the hallway, and into the bedroom. That sound about right?"

Harriet: "Not quite. Vasquez was adamant that the fire started in the bedroom, went to the hallway, then out the door. That's just the opposite of what Chief Fogg testified to."

Edie: "You're correct. We haven't really talked about Deputy Fire Marshal Vasquez' testimony yet, but on this issue, I guess I would defer to Vasquez. After all, he's the state expert that Chief Fogg called in to help."

Harriet: "So which way do you think it burned."

Edie: "I'm not sure it matters. Either way, it looks to me as if the fire was set."

Marti: "And I would like to withhold discussion of the Vasquez testimony until last. He was the state's star witness, and he testified way longer than anyone else, so let's just hold that for a bit longer while we discuss the medical testimony."

TESTIMONY OF ETHEL BAPTIST
Tuesday, August 18, 1992

"Call your next witness."

"State would call Ethel Baptist at this time."

Ethel Baptist is sworn in. Assistant Prosecutor John Jackson will conduct the direct examination.

"Would you state your name, please, ma'am?" >> Ethel Baptist.

"Can you tell us what kind of work or occupation you are engaged in?" >> Nursing supervisor, emergency room.

"How long have you been a nurse at the emergency room?" >> Twenty years.

"Are you a licensed nurse or registered nurse?" >> Registered nurse.

"Were you on duty at the emergency room on the 23rd of December of last year?" >> Yes, sir.

"Were you on duty when certain persons, apparently the victims of a fire, were brought to the hospital?" >> Yes.

"Did you have an opportunity to come in contact with a person by the name of Cameron Willingham at that point?" >> Yes, I did.

"Can you tell us the context or the circumstances in which you came in contact with Mr. Willingham?" >> Actually, I was in my office when we got the call that they were coming in. The nurses needed assistance, and I came out. They were taking care of another child. So I went to his room and took care of him.

"All right. Can you tell us what you observed insofar as Mr. Willingham was concerned?" >> Well, he was doing a lot of crying and a lot of talking about the fire and how he should have died with them, that it should have been him instead of them and that he was asleep at the time and heard one of the children calling him.

"Did he make any comments about where he observed the fire in the house?" >> Well, he started talking about how hot it was. Then he said the ceiling was on fire. At one point he said the ceiling was on fire.

"Was Mr. Willingham's wife present there in the hospital?" >> She entered later, I believe.

"Did Mr. Willingham ask to see her on one or more occasions?" >> Yes, he did.

"Did she immediately enter the room?" >> No.

"Did you find that unusual?" >> Yes, and he had asked several times where she was. I believe one of the ladies in the room was maybe a family member of hers that was telling him why she wasn't there. So I thought it was really unusual. Then, finally, they just kept telling him she would be here in a few minutes. I thought it was unusual.

"Was your impression that she didn't want to see him?"

Martin objects to the question as calling on the witness to speculate. Of course it does. Judge Douglas sustains the objection.

"Do you believe based on what you saw that she did not want to see him?

Same objection. Same result. Sustained.

"Did she finally come into the room with him?" >> Yes.

"Did he seem agitated with her failure to come in sooner?" >> Yes.

"In what way did he seem agitated?" >> Well in that he -- when she came to the room, he wanted her -- he kept begging for her. She wouldn't approach the bed where he was laying, and he kept telling her, "Come on up here. Come up here to me," and she kept kind of standing back. Finally, he said, "Come on up to me. What's wrong with you? Why are you acting like that?"

"You have an opportunity to observe people under very traumatic circumstances, I'm sure?" >> Yes.

"Based on what you observed, did this seem unusual behavior for a person to exhibit in the face of circumstances like these?" >> Yes.

"I will pass the witness."

<<>>

David Martin will cross-examine Ethel Baptist.

"Ms. Baptist, did you know that at the time you saw Stacy she had been informed that her three children were dead?" >> I believe she had.

"Did you know that she was in the room with Amber, and that's why she didn't come in there with Todd during the time you are talking about?" >> The lady told him that.

"You don't find it unusual that a mother would go to the bedside of the dead or dying child first, do you?" >> No, I don't.

"You recognize that under these kinds of circumstances, people act differently and they act strange, don't they?" >> Yes.

"Pass the witness."

<<>>

John Jackson has some redirect for Ethel Baptist.

"By the same token, you would still characterize Mr. Willingham's behavior as strange?" >> Yes.

"Did you observe any injuries insofar as Mr. Willingham was concerned?" >> Couple of small burns.

"Would you characterize these as inconsequential injuries?" >> Yes.

"Did he seem to be suffering from any type of smoke inhalation?" >> No.

"Pass the witness."

<<>>

Now David Martin has some re-cross for Ethel Baptist.

"Mrs. Baptist, you weren't the treating physician, were you?" >> No.

"And did you render any medical care?" >> Yes.

"And what did you do?" >> I assessed his injuries, his vital signs, and I stayed with him and gave him medicine.

"And did you clean the burn on his shoulder?" >> No. I only put cold compresses on those burns.

"So, he had burns?" >> Yes.

"He had burns on one of his hands and burns on his shoulders?" >> Yes.

"His hair, his eye lashes and eyebrows were burned?" >> I think that's right.

"And, in fact his nasal hairs were singed, weren't they?" >> I don't recall.

"Do you know that he had soot in his nasal cavities and pharynx?" >> No.

"How do you get soot in there?" >> From inhalation of smoke.

"Pass the witness."

<<>>

John Jackson has some additional redirect for Ethel Baptist.

"But still I believe your earlier testimony was that he did not seem to be suffering from smoke inhalation, is that correct?" >> That's right.

"Did he have any injuries on his feet?" >> Not that I recall.

"The burn on his shoulder, I believe, was characterized as inconsequential. You characterized it as about an inch or two long, is that correct?" >> Yes.

"He had a blister on his hand?" >> That's right.

"Pass the witness."

<<>>

David Martin, of course, has some additional re-cross for Ethel Baptist.

"Were you there when the doctor examined him?" >> Yes.

"Which doctor was that?" >> Dr. Shaw.

TESTIMONY OF GRADY SHAW
Wednesday, August 19, 1992

"The State calls Grady Shaw."

Grady Shaw is sworn in and takes his seat. John Jackson will conduct the direct examination.

"Would you state your name, please?" >> My name is Grady Carlton Shaw.

"And, Dr. Shaw, how are you employed?" >> I'm an emergency physician in Navarro Regional Hospital. I practice emergency medicine only. I work in an emergency room. I see all kinds of medical problems that come into the emergency room. My special expertise is in the treatment of acute conditions that make somebody acutely, seriously ill, or injuries.

"Let me ask you to direct your attention to the 23rd day of December of last year. Did you treat or attempt to treat a child by the name of Amber Kuykendall?" >> Yes, I did.

"Can you tell us how you happened to come in contact with that child?" >> Amber Kuykendall was brought into the emergency room by ambulance from the scene of a house fire.

"And can you tell us the procedures you followed in treating her at that time?" >> Yes. She had been rescued by Fire Department personnel. She was not breathing, nor was her heart beating. She was treated at the scene by paramedics from East Texas Medical Center Emergency Medical Service. They inserted a tube into her windpipe and began to breathe for her and brought her to the hospital. When she arrived there, her heart was not beating. She was not making any attempt to breathe. We established an intravenous line and gave her medications to stimulate her heart. I called her pediatrician to help me in the attempt to resuscitate her. We continued to do CPR, to artificially compress her heart so that her blood would flow. Our attempts were unsuccessful and she was pronounced dead some fifteen minutes after arrival at the emergency room.

"Did she ever exhibit any vital signs, Dr. Shaw?" >> No.

"Can you describe her appearance when she was brought to the hospital and during the time that you treated her?" >> She was burned extensively about the head and face. The skin was not charred, but was burned, especially on the face and neck and on the arms and hands and on one foot. There was a sock on the other foot, the burns had spared that foot. She had some soot-staining of her trunk and sparing of most of her chest and abdomen from burning. She had on a pair of underpants and that area covered was spared of soot-staining and burning.

"Will you take a look at these photographs and tell me if these are true and accurate depictions of how that child appeared to you at that time?" >> Yes, they are.

"I notice what appears to be some extensive burning on the head and the neck. Is it possible to tell whether those burns were inflicted from super-heated air inside the house or from open flame?" >> No, it's not really possible to tell on those type burns. Either one of those mechanisms could have caused those burns.

"When did it become apparent to you that the resuscitation efforts would not or could not be successful?" >> As soon as she was connected to a cardiac monitor it became clear that it would be unlikely that we could resuscitate her. After we gave her the first set of drugs her heart did exhibit a little bit of electrical activity, but that was not associated with the pulse, which is another bad sign. And then things just went downhill from there after that.

"Is it possible to render a child unconscious without leaving any exterior indicators of the means by which the child was rendered unconscious?" >> Yes, it is.

"Would it be safe to say that you cannot tell whether this child was conscious or unconscious prior to the starting of the fire that inflicted these injuries?" >> No, I can't tell that.

"On this same day, did you have an opportunity to examine a person by the name of Cameron Todd Willingham?" >> Yes, I did.

"Can you tell us how you came in contact with him?" >> Mr. Willingham was brought into the emergency room near the end of the attempted resuscitation on Amber Kuykendall. I did not see how he arrived at the hospital and that is not noted on our records, so I don't know if he came by ambulance or another type of vehicle. But when I first saw him, he was in Trauma Room 2 of the emergency room.

"Can you describe his appearance?" >> Mr. Willingham had burns. The hair of his head was singed somewhat. He had first degree burns of his face and neck.

"Can you describe what first degree burns are?" >> First degree burns are burns that cause a reddening of the skin, without any blisters or peeling, like a sunburn.

"Okay." >> He had a second degree burn on his right shoulder, which was about one centimeter by six centimeters or approximately four-tenths of an inch by two and a half inches long. One of the middle fingers of his left hand had some blisters. I don't remember if it was the long finger or the ring finger. Particular examinations that are done from fire victims revealed some other evidence. Some of the hair in his nose was singed and there was some soot present in his nose and the back of his throat.

"Did he appear to you to be suffering from any type of smoke inhalation?" >> The presence of the soot in the nose and throat indicated the possibility of smoke inhalation.

"Did he exhibit any outward symptoms, such as coughing or nausea, or anything like that, that would suggest any significant smoke inhalation?" >> There was some cough.

"Would you characterize his injuries superficial, Doctor?" >> The burns were superficial, yes.

"Did he have any burning of his feet?" >> No.

"Was any testing done with reference to carbon monoxide levels?" >> Yes. A set of arterial blood gases was done on Mr. Willingham while in the emergency room, timed at 11:40 AM. Carbon monoxide level is a part of that examination.

"Could you tell us what that carbon monoxide level indicates with that test?" >> The level was three percent.

"Could you tell us how that level compares with people walking around on the street, not subjected to fire?" >> This is a normal level for a patient who smokes or lives with a smoker.

"Pass the witness."

The defense has no questions for Grady Shaw.

TESTIMONY OF JUAN LUIS ZAMORA
Wednesday, August 19, 1992

"Would you state your name, please?" >> My name is Juan Luis Zamora.

John Jackson will examine Juan Luis Zamora.

"Can you tell us what your occupation or profession is, Dr. Zamora?" >> Yes. I am a physician employed by the County of Dallas as Medical Examiner.

"Do you perform autopsies on a regular basis?" >> Yes, sir. Part of my duties at the Office of the Medical Examiner is to perform autopsies in the bodies who are brought to the office. I would say that on a busy day, we have fifteen to twenty bodies. On an easy day, we have five to six.

"Do you have any idea how many autopsies you've performed during the past two years, Doctor?" >> I would say that over the past two years I have performed about fifteen hundred autopsies.

"Let me let me direct your attention back to December 24th of last year. Did you have an opportunity to perform autopsies on children from Navarro County, one by the name Karmon Willingham, the other by the name of Kameron Willingham?" >> Yes, sir, I performed autopsy on both children that were presented to me as Karmon and Kameron Willingham.

"Tell me what procedures you went through insofar as these particular autopsies were concerned in arriving at conclusions and opinions that are stated in those documents." >> The routine of work in order to examine the body is to perform an external and an internal examination. And I did both in these two bodies. The external examination showed in these two bodies that the action of fire was on the surface of the body identified by charring of the most part of the bodies. The mouth gave me the indication of identification. I could identify four lower incisors in one of the children and two lower incisors erupted in the other child. And I conveyed this information to the mother, through the investigators, and she identified the bodies based on that finding.

"How about the internal examination?" >> The internal examination showed me that the organs are pretty much preserved. The skin and the muscles of the surface of the body protects the internal organs as to the char. I found them normally developed and normal babies. The airways show some amount of soot, indicating that the babies may have aspirated the soot in the fire, as I was told that the babies were rescued from the house fire. And the findings didn't have any discrepancy with the history of those babies in a fire.

"Did you test the blood?" >> Yes. I looked at the amount of carbon monoxide present. In Karmon, the amount of carbon monoxide is eight-six percent separation. Normally, the separation for carbon monoxide is in the level of up to five percent in normal individuals, or it is twelve percent in individuals who smoke cigarettes. Kameron had about thirty-six percent separation of carbon monoxide in blood. These are lethal levels in a normal individual.

"Can you tell us, then, what your opinion is as to what caused the death of these children?" >> In my opinion, these two children die of smoke inhalation, or carbon monoxide.

"Thank you, Doctor. With respect to the exterior examination of these children, I believe you said that there was significant burning and charring, is that correct?" >> Yes, sir. The bodies have extensive charring and scorching of the surface.

"I assume that it would be very difficult or impossible for you to determine whether these children had any external evidence of injuries which may have occurred before the fire." >> Yes, it is difficult to identify any injury present in these children because the charring may obscure any injury, if present.

"I pass the witness at this time."

<<>>

David Martin will cross-examine Medical Examiner Zamora.

"Now, Dr. Zamora, you did not find any such injury, did you?" >> No, sir. I didn't find any injury that I could identify as such.

"And you performed a comprehensive autopsy?" >> Sorry, I don't know what you mean with "comprehensive."

"Well, I don't know what one is, either, but I don't guess you do any superficial autopsies, do you?"

Good one.

"Do you do all of those things required to satisfy your mind as to the cause of death?" >> Yes, sir. I do.

"You performed that kind of autopsy on these children that we're discussing?" >> Yes. I performed a complete, thorough autopsy in these babies.

"And your conclusion was that the cause of their death was carbon monoxide poisoning." >> Yes, sir.

"These autopsies were performed on the 24th of December, correct?" >> Yes, sir. It was on Christmas Eve.

"I notice that on the last paragraph of your report you conclude that the death is to be classified as a homicide, correct?" >> Yes, sir.

"And you say that that is based upon the information provided by the regional state fire marshal. Would that have been Mr. Manuel Vasquez?" >> It was through his office, yes, sir.

"So he's the person you're referring to there?" >> No, sir, I'm referring to the entire regional office. We met with several personnel from that office.

"Your report says the regional state fire marshal. Are you referring to Mr. Manuel Vasquez in that sentence?" >> Yes, sir, to Mr. Vasquez and to his personnel. I'm referring to the office of the fire marshal.

"So your conclusion is based upon what he told you in that regard?" >> Yes, sir. The manner of death, in several cases, is based upon the information provided. That has to match with the findings at the time of the post-mortem examination.

"Because you can't tell from an examination of the body whether it was an accidental fire or otherwise, can you?" >> No, sir. It's not possible to determine, based on the examination of charred bodies, if the fire could is an accident or a criminal act.

"So, in this case, your opinion about it being homicides was based upon what Mr. Vasquez and the people associated with him told you?" >> Yes, sir. It's based on that, the information provided by that office.

"Because you did the autopsy on the 24th, and Mr. Vasquez didn't even go to the house until three days later, did you know that?" >> I think that they came up after the fire was extinguished. I don't know how long it took them to go over the house.

"There wasn't anything in your autopsy examination that indicated one way or the other whether it was accidental or otherwise, did you?" >> No, sir. As I said before, the examination of the bodies do not give many clues of whether the fire was a criminal act or it was an act as a result of any play or anything.

"And you found both of these infant bodies to be well-developed and normal in every respect other than the injuries caused by the fire?" >> Yes, sir.

"And all of the children were obviously alive when the fire broke out and they breathed smoke and fumes for some period of time?" >> Yes, sir. As indicated by the amount of carbon monoxide and the presence of soot in the airways that identify that these children were alive when the fire start.

"One of the indicators of smoke inhalation is soot in the pharynx, is it not?" >> Yes, sir.

"Pass the witness."

<<>>

John Jackson has some redirect. I predict Martin will have some re-cross afterwards.

"Dr. Zamora, I asked you a question, or perhaps more than one question, about how the charring of the exterior bodies prevented you from determining whether there were any external injuries. Do you remember that question?" >> Yes, sir.

"I ask you to take a look at this photograph. Let me ask you: Does that photograph clearly and accurately depict the infants who were the victims of this crime? Excuse me, let me retract."

I'm confident his use of the term "victims of this crime" was only a slip.

"The infant victims of the fire, I mean, based on the autopsy and the examination you've done?" >> Yes, sir. This picture pretty much depicts the status of the bodies that I received at the time of the post-mortem examination.

"Is this condition of the body illustrative of your earlier testimony that exterior injuries to the body were impossible to determine, based on the charring of the bodies?" >> Yes. The status of the body pretty much precludes the identification of the injuries that may be present. Pretty much all the surface of the body is charred, leaving just small parts intact, therefore, injuries, if present in any of the charred parts, are not possible to identify. They should be present in the intact part, which is the lesser part of the body, in order to be identified.

"Pass the witness."

<<>>

Martin has further cross-examination for Medical Examiner Zamora.

"In order for an injury of the skin or the underlying tissue to cause death, it has to have an effect on the internal organs in some way, doesn't it?" >> Yes, sir. Blunt force injuries -- a blow or a fall or any other injury -- necessarily has to left some mark inside from the neck down. Not in the head. The head sometimes shows no evidence of injury, even if the person has died of a blunt-force injury of the head.

"But you didn't find any broken bones in the children's bodies?" >> No, sir.

"You didn't find a fractured skull in the children's body?" >> Not a fracture that I may attribute to forces other than the fire energy.

"So you didn't find any blunt force trauma to the bodies, did you?" >> No. I didn't identify any injury, other than the fire problems.

"And the charring impeded your examination of the skin and its underlying tissue, but the other organs and body parts were present for your examination, were they not?" >> The fire didn't impede me from examining them.

"You had a body intact to a sufficient degree to determine whether there was a blunt force trauma or other cause of death that you could attribute the death to?" >> Yes, sir. I didn't identify any cause of death other than the fire action.

"Pass the witness."

<<>>

Oh good. Jackson has some more redirect examination.

"Doctor, a child may be rendered unconscious by forces that leave no identifiable marks on the body of the child. Would that be a fair statement?" >> Yes, especially children or incapacitated adults may be rendered unconscious or even dead without leaving any mark by the assailant.

"Pass the witness."

<<>>

Oh joy. Additional re-cross by Martin.

"But, Dr. Zamora, what makes you go unconscious?" >> Lack of oxygen to the brain through a press of the neck or impeding the entry of air to the nose, or even shaking from using some subtle damage to the brain that, especially in children, may render them incapacitated or even dead.

"But in this case you examined the bodies carefully, did you not?" >> Yes. I did.

"And you did not find any sign of the cause of death other than the carbon monoxide poisoning, did you?" >> Yes, sir.

"Pass the witness."

<<>>

Jackson can't let it be. More redirect.

"Certainly a child could be rendered unconscious before a fire began and the fire could be the cause of death and you'd never know what rendered that child unconscious. Would that be also a fair statement?" >> Yes, sir.

"Pass the witness."

<<>>

Martin won't let it rest, either. More re-cross.

"But you found no evidence of that, did you?" >> No, sir.

"Pass the witness."

<<>>

Jackson gets snippy.

"That's what I just said, Your Honor. Pass the witness."

Perhaps a Freudian slip there. Perhaps he meant "That's what I just asked." It's almost as if he thought he was the one testifying.

DELIBERATION OF THE MEDICAL WITNESS TESTIMONY
Thursday, August 20, 1992

Marti: "From the medical testimony, from Ethel Baptist more specifically, we heard an indirect and extremely condensed version of Willingham's explanation of what happened that night. She said, as I recall, that Willingham told her he had been sleeping when he heard one of the children calling him. He said the ceiling was on fire. That's all I recall her saying about Willingham's story. Edie, could you give us run down of his injuries?"

Edie: "Bits and pieces from different witnesses. Singed hair and eyebrows; blistering burns on his shoulder and one finger; first degree burns on his face and neck; soot in his nasal passages and his throat, as well as on his face and arms. His carbon monoxide level was normal for a smoker. The wounds were described as superficial."

Ward: "Now doesn't that seem suspicious? Seriously. His daughters were burned to a crisp, and he gets a sunburn. Tell me that's not suspicious."

Harriet: "Two of the daughters, the twins, were badly charred. The older girl, Amber, the one who could walk, was burned on her head and neck, arms, legs, and one foot. One foot had a sock and was spared. She wasn't burned beneath her underpants either. It seems she hadn't -- forgive me, this is very difficult -- it seems as if she hadn't actually been in the fire itself, as had her sisters. Her burns were due to radiation from the hot air or nearby flame. The only comfort from the testimony was that they all died of carbon monoxide poisoning rather than burning."

Ad Agency Robert: "I understand that's how most people die in a fire. They suffocate. They never wake up. I hope that's what happened here."

Jorge raises his hand.

Jorge: "Pardon me. I have made some notes here."

He rises and begins referring to a sheet of paper he holds in his hand.

Jorge: "I would like to say something please. From what was presented at the trial, the man looks guilty on the surface. But as we go deeper, it seems we always find something that makes us wonder about what we have been told. I have been thinking about the clothing that the little girl Amber had on, and I think it tells us something important."

Sports Fan Ward: "What clothing? She had on a pair of underpants and one sock."

Jorge: "This is my whole point. I have here that this fire happened on the day before Christmas Eve, so it would have been cold outside. Mrs. Barbee told us it was cold outside. She told her children they could play outside but only for a little while because it was cold."

Boisterous Lee: "She said it was cool outside."

Edie: "Lee is correct. Diane Barbee told her children they could play outside because it was cool outside, not cold.

Jorge: "But not so warm that they could stay outside for long, even when they were fully clothed, even when they were eleven years old and not two years old like Amber."

Edie: "Fair enough."

Bitter Ted: "Whadda ya getting at?"

Jorge: "I look at the pictures of that house, and it seems old and perhaps not so warm inside without a heater. But the fire chief Mr. Fogg -- I like that name -- Mr. Fogg tells us that the space heater was not turned on. That makes me wonder why the girl had on so little clothing."

That's a good question. Very perceptive.

I wish I had thought of it.

Ad Agency Robert: "I have a thought. So why don't I just throw it out on the stoop and see if the cat licks it up."

That causes smirks and laughter among most the jurors. I give it a smile. Even Jorge smiles. Harriet finds no humor in it.

Marti: "See if the cat licks it up?"

Robert gives her the shoulder shrug then throws his idea onto the stoop.

Robert: "Perhaps she was covered with blankets."

Lee: "There you go."

Jorge: "I don't think so. The nurses and doctors told us she was not sleeping under a blanket."

Edie: "I don't recall that."

Jorge: "Not in those words, no. But she was burned on her arms and legs."

Edie: "And her head and neck."

Jorge: "Yes, and on one foot. But the doctor told us the other foot, the one covered with the sock, that foot was not burned. He said also that she was not burned beneath her underpants. Now it seems to me that if a sock can keep her from being burned on her foot, then blankets would have kept her from being burned on her arms and legs, anywhere that would have been covered."

Jorge lowers the paper and looks around the room. He's proud of himself. Harriet gives him a smile, he gives her a slight nod and takes his seat.

Marti: "That's an interesting observation. Anybody have any thoughts?"

Robert: "Let me run this one around the gym. Maybe she was sleeping under blankets, was awakened by the fire, and got up and ran into her father's bedroom."

Jorge: "You mean just like Mr. Willingham told the nurse and the neighbor?"

Robert: "I guess."

Furrows suddenly appear on Robert's brow. Jorge sees them and knows what they mean.

Jorge: "So now you have some reasonable doubt."

Robert looks confused.

Robert: "I don't know. Maybe I do."

Jorge: "Because if you are right, there is no need for us to talk any longer. If it happened just as the Mr. Willingham said it happened, then we should all vote not guilty and this gentleman --"

He's pointing at Sports Fan Ward

"-- can go to his baseball game."

Ward: "Get outta here. This mumbo jumbo with the clothes doesn't mean anything."

Jorge: "Maybe you don't fully understand the term reasonable doubt?"

Ward: "Whadda ya mean I don't understand it? How do you like this guy? I'm telling ya they're all alike. They come over here running for their life, and before he can even take a deep breath they're telling us how to run the show. Boy, the arrogance of this guy!"

Marti: "Enough! Who's got something constructive to say?"

Edie: "You don't think she was covered with blankets, do you?"

Jorge: "No, I don't."

Edie: "You think the space heater was on?"

Jorge: "Yes, I do."

Edie: "And you believe Amber unintentionally started this fire putting something in or close to the space heater?"

Jorge: "Yes."

Edie: "How do you explain Chief Fogg's testimony, and that of Fire Marshall Vasquez, that they discovered the heater to be turned off."

Jorge: "I don't know."

Edie: "You raise some interesting issues, but in the face of overwhelming evidence of arson, I still believe he is guilty."

Jorge: "Beyond a reasonable doubt?"

Edie: "Beyond a reasonable doubt."

It's time for me to add a little fuel to the fire.

"Chief Fogg didn't say the heater was off. He said the gas valve was in the off position. As soon as I heard him say that, I thought the distinction was interesting. I still do. The heater itself probably had a dial that allowed you to set the temperature somewhere between its highest and lowest settings, or to turn it off completely if you wished. But he didn't mention the temperature control dial on the heater, or an on-off switch of some sort. He said the gas valve was in the off position. And he said they had the gas company come in and check the gas line for leaks, so they were clearly worried about leaking gas."

This gets Young Jack excited.

Jack: "You're right! It's a gas heater, so it has to be connected to the main gas line somehow. And he said there was a gas outlet along the wall, and the space heater was connected to that. He said the gas outlet was in the off position. I remember that now. He didn't say the heater was off, he said the gas valve was in the off position."

He's getting there. He just needs a little nudge.

"So if you were a firefighter, one of the many who were there, and after you put down the fire, you walked through the house and you found --"

Jack: "-- and I found the gas valve in the on position, I'd reach down and turn it to off. Then I'd check every other gas valve in the house, and turn them all off. Then I'd go to the gas meter, and turn it off. Then I'd go to the electrical box and flip the circuit breakers or pull the fuses. That's what I'd do."

Edie: "And would you then tell your fire chief that you had done so, or would you keep it a secret while he told a jury that the heater could not have been the source of the fire because the gas valve was in the off position?"

Jack: "Uh, uh, I don't know. I guess so."

Edie: "You guess you would have told him?"

Jack: "Yeah, maybe."

Jorge: "Pardon me."

He's directing his question at Edie.

"I hope this is not rude, but if you had been the mother, would you have left your two-year-old daughter dressed only in a pair of underpants and one sock in a cold house with no heat?"

Edie: "Certainly not, but the mother is not on trial here. The father is on trial for murdering his three children. And if he murdered them, and I still believe he did just that, I doubt that he would take the trouble to see they were properly dressed."

Jorge: "And that is the other point I wish to make. I believe the little girl Amber's medical condition tells us that the defendant did not murder her. And if he did not murder her, then I don't believe he murdered any of them. I am no longer voting not guilty just because I want us to discuss this case before we vote. I am now voting not guilty because I have reasonable doubt that he killed any of them."

Marti: "Please explain how you believe Amber's medical condition proves her father did not murder her."

Jorge: "Of course. I have made notes on that as well."

He rises to make his case, as he did before.

"All of the girls died of carbon monoxide poisoning. Two of them, the youngest ones, the twins, were found in the front bedroom where the fire was the worst. One of them, Amber, was found in Mr. Willingham's bedroom, where no fire had been set. So it is simple. If he wanted to murder her, he would have made sure she was in the front bedroom with the other two or he would have set fire to his own bedroom. They tell us that he poured lighter fluid where he wanted the fire to burn, but there is no evidence of anything being poured in his bedroom."

Ward: "Well maybe he figured she would suffocate, just like she did."

Jorge: "Then there would be no reason to set the fire in the children's bedroom either. He could have simply set the hallway on fire and let them all suffocate."

Ad Agency Robert: "But we don't have to believe he murdered all three of them, remember? We can convict him if we believe he murdered just two."

It hits me like a ton of bricks. Harriet sees it as well.

Harriet: "Marti, would you please read those two jury instructions to us."

Marti rummages through the box of evidence and paperwork and pulls out the instructions. She flips to the third page.

Marti: "Now bearing in mind the foregoing instructions, if you find from the evidence beyond a reasonable doubt that on or about the 23rd day of December 1991, in Navarro County, Texas, as alleged in the Indictment, the defendant, Cameron Todd Willingham, did then and there intentionally murder more than one person during the same criminal transaction, to wit: The said Cameron Todd Willingham did intentionally cause the death of an individual, Karmon Willingham, by starting a fire within a habitation occupied by the said Karmon Willingham, and the said Cameron Todd Willingham did then and there intentionally cause the death of an individual, Kameron Willingham, by starting a fire within a habitation occupied by the said Kameron Willingham, with the express intent to cause the death of the said Kameron Willingham, and the said Cameron Todd

Willingham did then and there intentionally cause the death of an individual, Amber Kuykendall, by starting a fire within a habitation occupied by the said Amber Kuykendall, with the express intent to cause the death of the said Amber Kuykendall, you will find the defendant guilty of capital murder."

Ward: "Huh?"

Edie: "It says if he intended to kill all three of his children, Karmon, Kameron, and Amber, and succeeded in doing so by setting his house on fire, then he is guilty of capital murder."

Ward: "Oh."

Harriet: "And the next one?"

Marti: "Now bearing in mind the foregoing instructions, if you find from the evidence beyond a reasonable doubt that on or about the 23rd day of December 1991, in Navarro County, Texas, as alleged in Count 2 of the Indictment, the defendant, Cameron Todd Willingham, did then and there intentionally murder more than one person during the same criminal transaction, to wit: The said Cameron Todd Willingham did intentionally cause the death of an individual, Karmon Willingham, by starting a fire within a habitation occupied by the said Karmon Willingham, with the express intent to cause the death of the said Karmon Willingham, and the said Cameron Todd Willingham did then and there intentionally cause the death of an individual, Kameron Willingham, by starting a fire within the habitation occupied by the said Kameron Willingham, with the express intent to cause the death of the said Kameron Willingham, you will find the defendant guilty of capital murder. Unless you so find beyond a reasonable doubt or it you have a reasonable doubt thereof, you will find the defendant not guilty of capital murder."

Edie doesn't wait for Ward to express his confusion.

Edie: "It says if he intended to kill two of his children, Karmon and Kameron, and succeeded in doing so by setting his house on fire, then he is guilty of capital murder."

Harriet: "They knew Amber was the weak point in their case. They were afraid someone such as Jorge might figure out that Willingham didn't kill Amber, at least not intentionally, and if we followed the instructions carefully, we would vote not guilty on a charge that he intentionally murdered all three. So they put in the second count, the one where we could still find him guilty of capital murder if we decided he didn't mean to kill Amber.

Marti: "Go ahead."

Harriet: "So now the motive is more confused than ever. The only motive they offer is from the lying lips of Johnny Webb, who says that the mother hurt the girls and Willingham intentionally killed all the children, not just two of them, to cover it up. They don't believe their own witness anymore than we do."

She pauses to give Boisterous Lee a chance to defend Johnny Webb. Lee wisely takes a pass.

Harriet: "They don't arrest the mother and put her on trial, at least not that we can tell from here. Instead they try to get the doctors to tell us the children might have been injured and the injuries were hidden by the burns. But those doctors conceded on cross-examination that they found no broken bones or no damage to internal organs, and that the fire couldn't mask those sort of injuries.

Marti: "In other words, they don't want us to convict him on the medical evidence, they want us to convict him on the lack of medical evidence?"

Harriet: "Exactly."

Marti: "Interesting."

Time for another intervention. It has to do with Johnny Webb, so I'll have to try extra hard to restrain myself.

"It's worse than that. A lot worse."

Marti: "Go ahead."

"Certainly. I want to talk again about the inside knowledge that Johnny Webb seems to have. If he didn't get it from Willingham, I'm guessing he got it from the prosecutors during one or more of their many get-togethers."

Boisterous Lee: "You don't know that! You can't know that. Nobody can know that. Now you're not only claiming he lied, you're claiming they set him up to lie."

He just can't help himself.

"That's exactly what I'm saying. Are you just now figuring that out? Sure they asked him to lie. Sure they fed him the information. I already talked about how he screwed up on the stand and couldn't remember his lines about Willingham moving Amber from one room to another. He said he didn't recall Willingham saying that, they showed him the mystery paper, and he changed his tune.

"But that's not the only thing he forgot about. He forgot he was supposed to cover their ass in the off chance one of the jurors wasn't completely brain dead and figured out Amber started the fire. So Assistant Prosecutor John Jackson asks him if Willingham said anything about trying to shift the blame to someone else. And what did Johnny Webb say?"

There's a pregnant pause.

"He said, and I believe this is an exact quote, he said 'I'm not sure.'

"Well that answer didn't cut any mustard with John Jackson, so Jackson asks him specifically whether Willingham told him anything he did with the children.

"Martin is objecting left and right that Jackson is leading the witness, because that is exactly what Jackson is doing. He's leading the witness by a fifteen-year-long nose. Judge Douglas overrules the objection, either because he couldn't recognize a leading question if it bit him on the ass, or because he just assumes Willingham is some kind of dirt bag who deserves whatever he gets.

"And while all that objecting and overruling is taking place, Mr. Webb realizes he just screwed the pooch. So he changes his story again, and he tells Jackson just what he wanted to hear, just as they rehearsed it. Johnny Webb says, with a straight face mind you, that Willingham told him he burned one of the kids to make it look they were playing with fire, that he wadded up some paper, set it on fire, and burned his own child on the arm and on the forehead with that burning piece of paper.

"But it gets worse, even worse, because now it's not just some low-life snitch behaving badly, it's the people who are supposed to protect us that are bending and twisting the truth so that they can see one of us strapped to a gurney and shot full of chemicals.

"They are so afraid one of us will figure out Amber started that fire, and thereby blow their precious case to kingdom come, they not only feed the story to a low-life snitch, they involve a well-trained, well-paid professional in the charade. Jackson asks him if he could determine whether the burns on Amber's body had been caused by super-heated air or an open flame. The doctor said he couldn't tell.

"So that's it. Case closed. We're supposed to figure Webb's story might actually be true. Marti said it exactly right. They want us to convict on the lack of evidence.

"But if Jackson really wanted to get to the bottom of it, if he wanted us to understand what really might or might not have happened, he could have asked somewhat more penetrating questions. For example: 'Doctor, did you find any wounds consistent with a flaming, wadded-up piece of paper applied directly to the victim's forehead?'

"And I'm guessing the good doctor would have said 'No.'

"Then he could have asked, "Doctor, could these generalized burns on the victim's face, neck, arms, legs, and one foot be caused by a flaming, wadded-up piece of paper held close to her skin?'

"And I'm guessing the doctor would have said 'No.'

"But Jackson didn't ask those questions or anything like those questions because he didn't want us to believe that Amber might have started this fire. And just in case one of us turns out to be clever enough to figure out that she may have, we're supposed to remember that Willingham told upstanding citizen Johnny Webb that he framed one of his little girls for the crime.

"So you tell me: who's the one more likely being framed here? Amber or her father?"

Ward: "And we go into extra innings."

Ted: "I'll tell you what I think. We're going nowhere here. I'm ready to walk into court right now and declare a hung jury. There's no point in this going on any more."

Ward: "I go for that, too. That's all you're doing here, getting a hung jury. You're not going to save this guy. He wouldn't stand a chance with another jury, and you know it. You're just don't want to do the dirty work yourself."

Harriet: "Maybe you're right."

Ward: "You know I'm right."

Edie: "I've been exceptionally patient listening to all of you argue over everything except the evidence that really matters. We should be discussing the testimony of Manuel Vasquez. We should have discussed his testimony first, but there's nothing we can do about that now. So Marti, please, do you think we can move on the real evidence in this case?"

Marti: "If there are no objections, let's talk about the testimony of Manuel Vasquez."

DIRECT EXAMINATION OF MANUEL VASQUEZ
Tuesday, August 18, 1992

Manuel Vasquez is called to the stand and sworn in. The second prosecutor, Alan Bristol, conducts the direct examination.

"Deputy Vasquez, could you state your name and occupation, please." >> My name is Manuel Vasquez. I'm Deputy State Fire Marshal. I've been employed with the State Fire Marshal's Office for six years, nine months, last Saturday.

"What are your duties as Fire Marshal, Manuel?" >> "My duties are to investigate fires and determine the origin and cause of the fires. I determine whether the fire is accidental or incendiary

"What does incendiary mean?" >> Incendiary means that a fire is deliberately set intentionally.

As compared to deliberately set unintentionally.

"An arson?" >> That is the crime of arson, yes, sir. And if I cannot prove either accidental or incendiary, then the fire is undetermined.

"And how many fires have you investigated since becoming a certified fire arson investigator?" >> Perhaps in the range of twelve-hundred to fifteen-hundred fires.

"Of these twelve-hundred to fifteen-hundred fires, how many turned out to be arson in your opinion?" >> With the exception of a few, most all of them.

"How many arson fires that you investigated involved injuries or death?" >> Unfortunately, fires injure a lot of people, kill a lot of people. It's about fifty percent.

"Let me direct your attention specifically to your investigation of this case. How did you become involved in this investigation?" >> We make all investigations upon request by the community in the area. This request was received on December 26th, 1991, made by Assistant Fire Chief Doug Fogg.

"When did you first come to Corsicana?" >> I arrived in Corsicana the next day, December 27th, close to noon.

"What is this?" >> It's a diagram that I, myself, drew of the structure where the fire occurred.

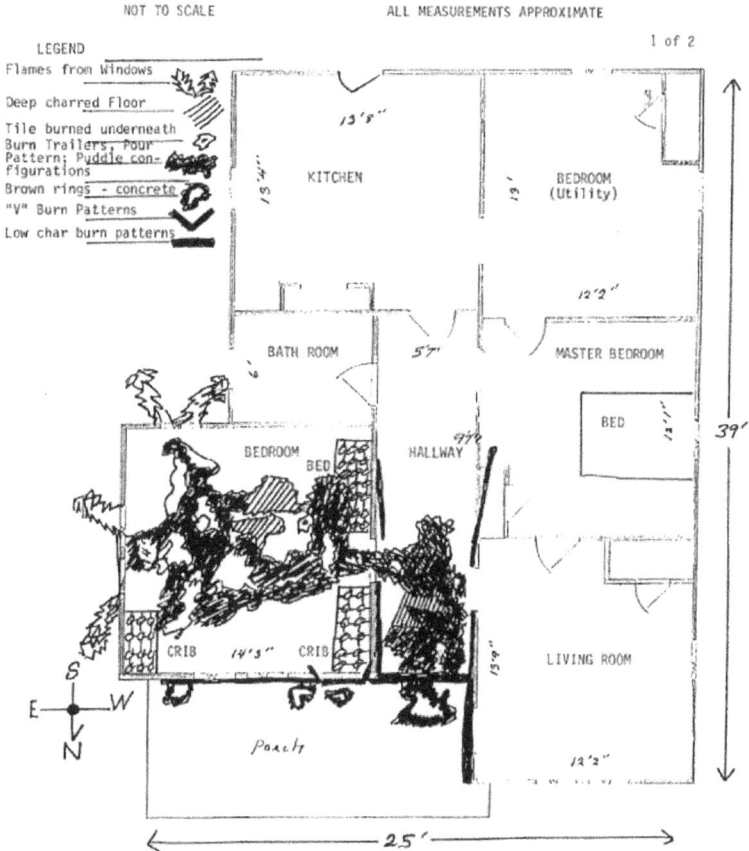

CASE: #923-037-12   DATE OF INCIDENT: 12-23-91   INVESTIGATION DATE: 12-27-91
INCIDENT LOCATION: 1213 W. 11th Ave., Corsicana, Navarro County, Texas

NOT TO SCALE   ALL MEASUREMENTS APPROXIMATE

1 of 2

LEGEND
Flames from Windows
Deep charred Floor
Tile burned underneath
Burn Trailers; Pour
Pattern; Puddle con-
figurations
Brown rings - concrete
"V" Burn Patterns
Low char burn patterns

KITCHEN   BEDROOM (Utility)

BATH ROOM   MASTER BEDROOM

BED   39'

BEDROOM   HALLWAY   LIVING ROOM

CRIB   CRIB

Porch   25'

"Will this diagram help you explain your testimony to the jury?" >> Yes, sir.

"Could you just go through and describe your investigation of the scene?"

As an expert, Vasquez will be allowed to narrate his testimony rather than simply respond to questions put to him by the State. He stands beside a large poster displaying his fire scene diagram and describes his investigation.

As you look at the diagram, the bottom part of the diagram is the north. The top part of the diagram is south.

I went to the south part of the structure. Above the kitchen door, there was smoke where the smoke had vented out. There was no flame, just smoke, when I entered the structure here.

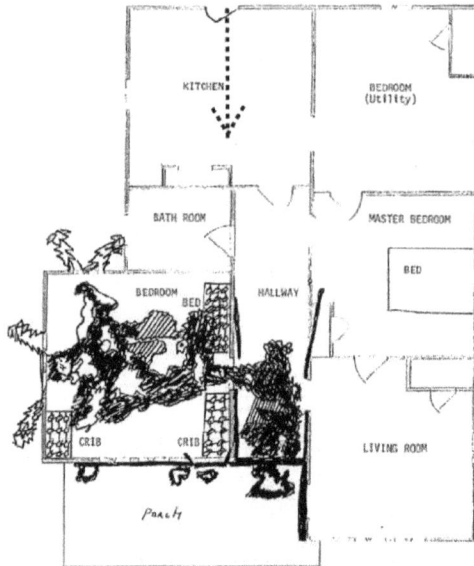

It was just a little area for me to squeeze in. There was a refrigerator blocking the door. The person who moved the refrigerator was the Assistant Fire Chief Doug Fogg during fire fighting operation. There was no fire in the kitchen, just a lot of smoke.

I went into this bedroom, which is the utility room.

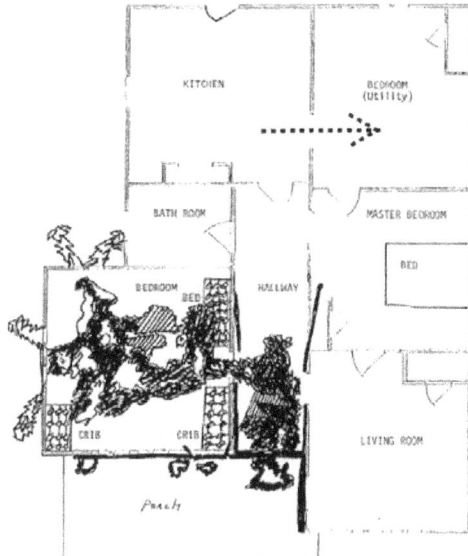

The only thing I found was a lot of soot, smoke on top of everything. There was some pictures on the wall that I took, and these are some of the pictures. This one here is on this wall on this corner right here, on the southeast corner on this wall right here, it's this picture. It's the grim ripper.

I presume he means "reaper."

It's got some other weird things. And this other picture's again indicating -- weird pictures in there on this wall right here. Also in this room we found a piece of carpet, and I know you have seen this carpet on the wall with the dogs playing poker. Okay. When we unrolled it, there was a bunch of blond hairs inside this roll of carpet. So we just rolled it back up. I don't know what significance it had. I don't know, but we got it.

From here I went into the master bedroom.

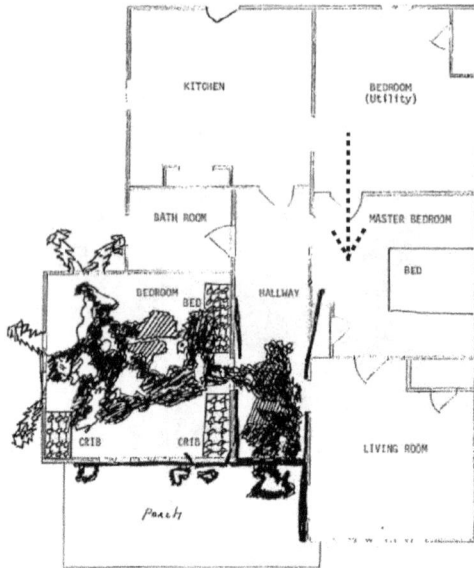

The master bedroom is at the center of the house, and this is the bed right here. When you walked in, you could see the burn patterns on the doors. The heat had come from the hallway. That was the main thing that I noticed from here. It had almost the same burn patterns that the kitchen door had. So it told me that the fire came from somewhere in the hallway.

I went into the living room.

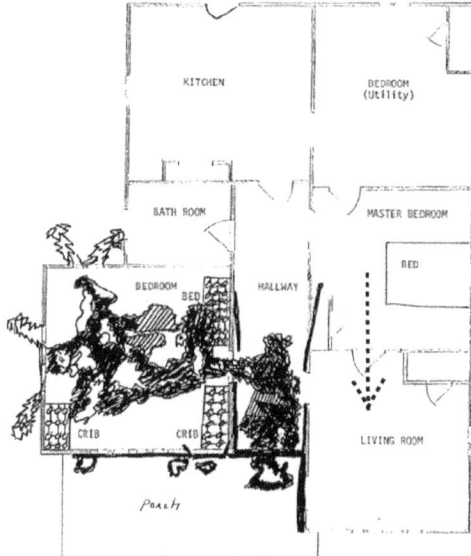

This room here had burn damage on the doors, and there was a lot of heat in this I think here. The heat line is because heat rises up, and when it comes down the wall it leaves a mark just like a water mark, but the water marks from the bottom up the heat mark comes from the top down. So that's what it had there.

One of the things that I noticed there was a Christmas tree right here next to this closet, but during the fire fighting operations, it got knocked down.

The significant part about this living room, ladies and gentlemen, was that there was no fire in here. There was a lot of heat damage on this side, but in this room there was no window here. The window was gone, but the heat came from the outside. And this window here, the heat came from the inside. And on this window in here, the heat came from the outside. So, you know, right now I'm just collecting information. I'm collecting facts. I have not made any determination. I don't have any preconceived idea. That's my job, to collect the information and analyze.

From here I went back into the bedroom, and into the hallway.

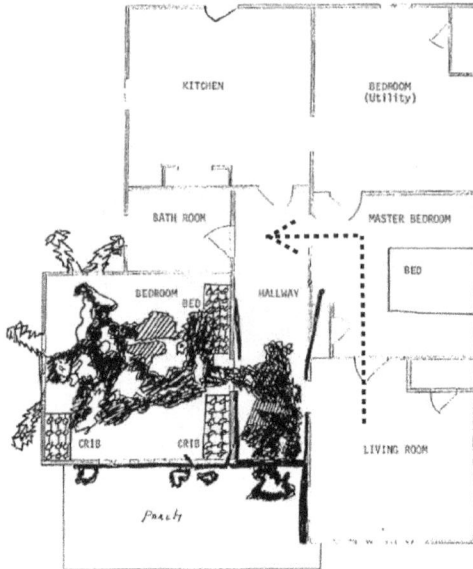

This hallway had a lot of damage. There's a lot of debris on the floor. There's a lot of insulation falling down here. I noticed right here a burn pattern from the floor in a 45 degree angle going up. That is one of the indicators of the origin of a fire. It's a V-pattern. So I get an indication for the first time that I'm inside that possible fire origin. It's in this area, but I won't know this until we clean this area up to make sure.

The next thing I noticed looking north is that the door is totally gone.

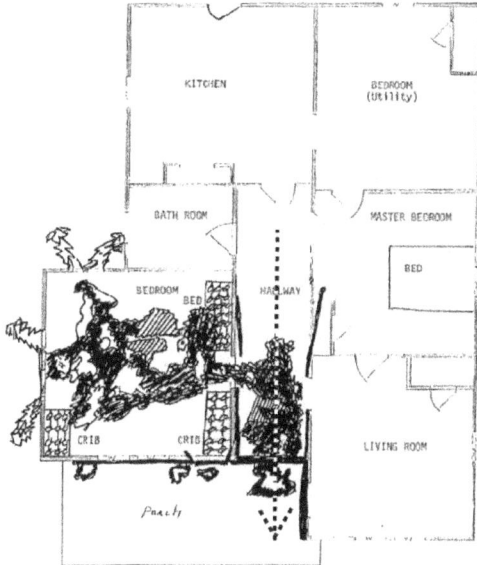

There is no door. It's completely burned. It had burned totally. And that was also unusual. I have seen fires in a bedroom and kitchen, and portions will burn on the door, but portions of the door are left. So, you know, my curiosity is up. Why is this burnt?

I went back into the hallway.

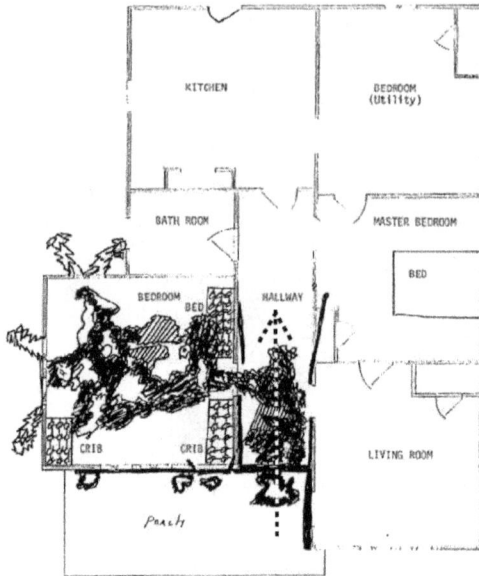

And when I walked in, I looked at the walls and I looked at the ceiling. I noticed that this wall right here had very intensive damage from a fire right here. And the fire line was two or three feet from the floor.

In the hallway, there was a space heater right here near the V-pattern. But the V-patterns goes over the heater. The heater got some damage from heat, but the fire went right over the heater. Because of the patterns around the heater, it is my determination that this heater was a victim of the fire, was not the cause of the fire.

Let me explain these markings. Burn trailers are a burnt path. A pour pattern is where somebody put some liquid on the floor. Of course when you pour liquid, then it creates a puddle. Liquids create puddles. When it rains, you get puddles. When the baby drops its milk, you create puddles. If you ever drop a Coke, you create puddles. All this area has burn trailers and pour patterns. These are indications that somebody poured something there.

This is the door to the front bedroom.

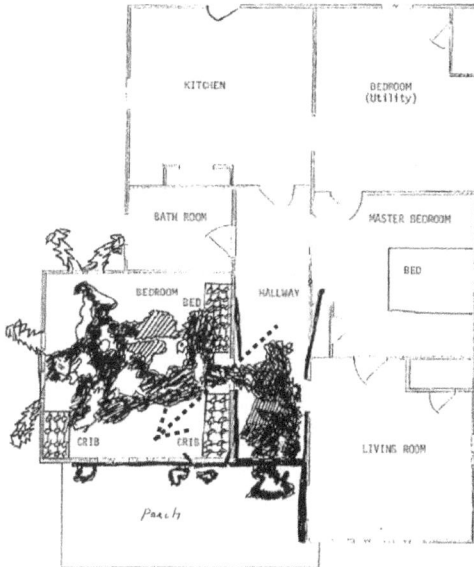

It's got a wire along the edge of the door. The significant part about that is the wire is not broken. It's not beaded. All the coating is burned off, which indicates that the wire is a victim of the fire. This wire did not contribute to the fire.

There is a lot of burned area on the wall right above the bed.

The significant part about this bed is the frame. Notice that the metal frame on the near side is white and the far side is rusty colored. This indicates that the white part was subjected to intense heat. Metal reacts to heat. You don't burn metal, but it leaves the mark there. That's intense heat right there. And there was more intense heat on the near side than on the far side of the bed.

My determination is that this bed was at one time on fire. Consequently, the heat radiated next to the wall and left that burnt pattern on there. The springs were on the floor, just completely burned. The springs were burned from underneath. This indicates there was a fire under this bed because of the burn underneath that bed.

I've always known that there had been two bodies found in this bedroom and I asked the assistant chief Doug Fogg to mark on the floor where the bodies were found in the debris when they first put out the fire.

And one body is right here laying 18 inches from the door. The other body is a few feet down here from the crib, according to the markings.

Then there's the crib, right here, next to the entrance to the bedroom. If you reach out from the hallway, you can touch the crib, the springs, because I tried it and my arm is not very long. Again, there is the burn pattern on the wall where the intense heat from that crib was on exhibit.

We cleaned up this floor with a pressure hose, and you can't mistake it. A lot of this room was saturated with a liquid. At this time I don't know what kind of liquid it is, but it is a liquid.

By this time, I am seeing something that I am not very happy with. I am seeing burn patterns on the floor. When a liquid hits the floor or any flat area, it goes to the lowest level. When it does, as it goes it soaks in. If you pour something on this floor here, then the liquid is going to look for the lowest level. Then it puddles so when it burns, it burns in the same way that it went down. This is a strong indicator of a liquid.

Let me say this: The fire is telling me this. The fire tells a story. I am just the interpreter. I am looking at the fire, and I am interpreting the fire. That is what I know. That is what I do best. And the fire does not lie. It tells me the truth.

There is a space heater in this front bedroom, in the far corner. I examined this space heater because if it was an accidental fire, the space heater caused the fire.

Interesting.

Again the heat pattern behind this space heater is from above. There is nothing but debris around this space heater, and the top part and the front part of the space heater has received a lot of heat damage. There is no way that this heater could have started the fire. So that was eliminated. If I may say so, one of the things that I need to find out: Was the heater on or off? The heaters were off.

After I finished with this front bedroom, then I made a closer look at the porch. That's the entrance to the house. Again, there is no door.

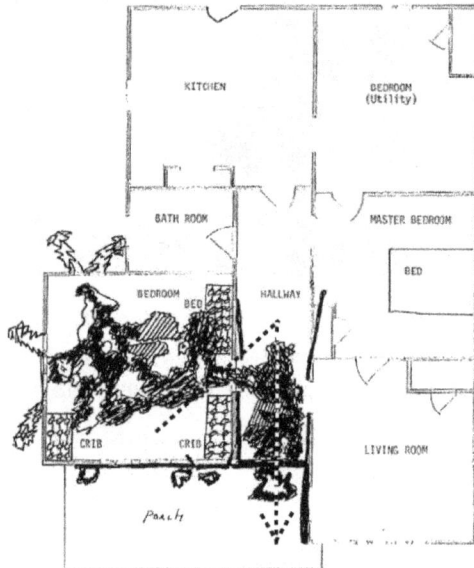

I found that the baseboard is charred. I mean, it's very black and charred, burned. That's a very low fire. Why did it burn so low?

This is the aluminum threshold. Aluminum melts at 1200 degrees normal. A wood fire does not exceed 800 degrees. So to me, when aluminum melts, it shows me that it has had a lot of intense heat. The only thing that can cause that is an accelerant. You know, it makes the fire hotter. It's not normal fire.

I noticed some brown stains in front of the door. These brown stains are consistent with a combustible or flammable liquid that's poured on the concrete. The concrete is porous, but this liquid did not have time to soak into the concrete, so it leaves a stain. So there is a difference. This liquid here on the porch that burned didn't have time to soak in. The liquid in the bedroom did.

These pour patterns indicate to me the intent of why the fire was set here. And the intent was to prevent people from coming in through that place to delay entrance of persons, thereby creating a fire that would impede entrance, a fire barrier.

I'm looking at the board here at the door, underneath the aluminum threshold. I noticed that it's charred underneath. And the only thing that makes that char pattern is a liquid. So we cut that piece out and sent it to the laboratory. And when the report came back is when I found out what kind of liquid it was.

Now I know why the door burnt. The door burned because it was incinerated with that liquid outside and inside. It ran down the door before it was ignited. It got under the base board. It got also in the front of the boards there on the concrete. That's why it burned down.

There's a brown stain all along the base and the char burning on the concrete. Also there is a glob down here that's fused to a wire. We looked at it, and we could see what the glob was. This little glob here was charcoal lighter fluid. That's why the wall burned. There is no V-pattern. It just burned completely up because that's the way -- that's why there was a fire outside.

<<>>

"I believe when we were all together, you told us that flashover occurred in the bedroom in which the twins were found, is that right?" >> Yes, sir.

"Could you explain to the jury what the term 'flashover' means?" >> Yes, sir. Flashover is, like this room right here, and you've got a small fire. And every fire, of course, creates heat. And as the fire builds up, the heat builds up. The fire is expanding and gets hotter and hotter and hotter. Eventually, everything in this room will reach ignition temperature simultaneously. And then everything will ignite at the same time. And that's a flashover. And you will hear a whoosh sound. A lot of people mistake that for an explosion, but it's when the fire catches fire. The whole thing.

"If some witnesses said they thought they heard an explosion, possibly the flashover is what they heard?" >> Yes.

"In your investigation, what did you determine upon completion of the examination of the house?" >> First of all, if this fire had been a combustible material fire, like a pile of clothes or a pile of paper, then you would have a point of origin. But when you have a liquid, you no longer have a point of origin. You have an area of origin. That's the whole bedroom is a point of fire origin. Also the hallway is another area of fire origin. So inside the interior I have determined two points, two areas of origin: in the hallway and in the bedroom. And then the examination of the porch, the front of the door is another area of origin. So there were three areas of origin. That's what we call multiple areas of origin.

"What does multiple areas of origin indicate?" >> Multiple areas of origin indicate that they were intentionally set by human hands.

"There has been testimony that there was accelerant found underneath the metal plate at the bottom of the door and underneath the wood sample taken from there. Why would there be accelerant in that area in that sample and not in any other samples that were taken?" >> There's two ways that that liquid got under there. One was that that liquid was poured or sprayed on the door and it ran down before it was ignited. And the other is that it was directly poured at the base of the board.

"Why would there be accelerant found in one area of the fire, say like was found underneath the entrance to the door, and not found in the bedroom?" >> Well, that accelerant will burn up. And so there won't be anything left. It will burn up. The only thing left is a burn pattern. The fire, itself, leaves the evidence of what was there.

"Why did the liquid underneath the door not burn?" >> The reason, and it happens in all fires, when it soaks into the wood, it will burn right outside the wood and it will char the wood, but it won't burn through the wood.

<<>>

"Can you tell me from your investigation or do you have an opinion as to the order in which these fires were started?" >> Based on my experience and from what I observed at the fire scene, the first fire was in the bedroom, the front bedroom.

"The bedroom that the twins were found?" >> Yes, sir. Then the second fire was in the hallway, and the third fire was on the front door on the porch.

"Can you explain the term 'incendiary indicator' to the jury?">> Yes, sir. The first incendiary indicator is the auto-ventilation. The inconsistency of the fire going out of window and the fire going out of the door. That's inconsistent with fire behavior. That's an indicator that it's a possible incendiary fire.

Also puddle configurations, pour patterns, low char burning, charred floor, the underneath burning of the base board, the brown stains on the concrete, the fire right underneath the bed, the puddle configurations in that area, and the total saturation of the floor as indicated by the pour patterns. That's some of the indicators that I came up with.

All I'm doing is looking at the facts, at the evidence. That's all I'm using.

"Could you explain the difference in the burning of the floor versus the burning on the ceiling?" >> Yes, sir. Heat rises. So when I found that the floor is hotter than the ceiling, that's backwards, upside down. It shouldn't be like that. The only reason that the floor is hotter is because there was an accelerant. That's the difference. Man made it hotter or woman or whatever. A human being made it hotter.

"Could you explain how the puddle configurations were created?" >> Yes, sir. The liquid in the bedroom was poured but not ignited immediately, because it soaked through floor to the hardwood floor. It had time to soak. It took at least five minutes or more for that liquid to soak.

<<>>

"Deputy Vasquez, during your investigation, did you interview witnesses, including the occupants of this house?" >> Yes, sir. I've talked to the occupant of this house, and I let him talk and he told me a story of pure fabrication.

"Okay. What, if anything, did he tell you?" >> I listened to him. I never questioned him. I never asked him any questions. He just talked and he talked, and all he did was lie. Pure fabrication.

"What did he tell you?" >> The inconsistent thing that he said right away was that his little girl had awakened him by saying, "Daddy, daddy," twice. Then he went from the bedroom to the hallway on through the door and then went straight south into the porch and out.

"Why is this particular story implausible?" >> What he said he had done is inconsistent with the burn patterns in the house.

"Mr. Vasquez, you have been made aware of Mr. Willingham's injuries, the injuries he suffered?" >> Yes, sir.

"Are they consistent with the story he told you?" >> No, sir.

"How are they inconsistent?" >> In my opinion, they are self-inflicted.

"What kind of injuries would a person have sustained if his story had been true?" >> The little girls died from smoke inhalation and carbon monoxide poisoning. He did not exhibit any symptoms of smoke inhalation. I have experienced smoke inhalation personally. You want somebody to put a gun to your head and shoot you because it's excruciating. You want to puke your guts out. Furthermore, it takes a long time for you to clear the smoke out of your system. The blood has an infinity for carbon monoxide.

Perhaps he meant "affinity."

"Based on the story Mr. Willingham told you, would you, in your opinion, expect him to have injuries on other parts of his body?" >> On his feet. There was fire on the floor.

"Based on information that he was simply wearing blue jeans, no shirt, no shoes, would you have suspected there to be more injuries?" >> Yes, sir. If he was inside a hot, very hot house, he would certainly receive some injuries.

"Based upon all your investigation and interviews and experience as a fire or arson investigator, do you have an opinion as to the person or persons who started this particular fire?" >> Yes, sir. The occupant, Mr. Willingham.

"Based on your experience, is it possible that one of the children started the fires?" >> No, sir. First of all, which of the children went around pouring a liquid into three areas of the house then ignited three different areas. If they had done that, the occupant would be dead right now. He would have died in the fire.

"If a child or some other person had started those three fires that you previously testified about, Mr. Willingham, if you believe his story, would have had to go through that fire, is that right?" >> Yes, sir. He never would have woken up.

"In your opinion, could Cameron Todd Willingham have gotten out of the house from the bedroom that Amber was found in, after the fire started, without sustaining injury?" >> No, sir.

"Without sustaining smoke inhalation?" >> No.

"Was it necessary, as far as your investigation was concerned, that the fire scene be secured or guarded in any way?" >> No.

"Why is that?" >> Because, like I said, the fire leaves the burn patterns. You can't alter the burn patterns. You cannot pollute the fire scene. You can try, but you can't.

"Based on your experience, your training, your investigation, examination of the scene, do you have an opinion as to whether this particular fire was arson or incendiary in nature?" >> Yes. It's a set fire. It's an incendiary fire, and consequently is a crime of arson.

"Pass the witness."

DELIBERATION OF MANUEL VASQUEZ
Thursday, August 20, 1992

Edie: "Thank you. I believe Cameron Todd Willingham is guilty as charged because of the testimony of Deputy State Fire Marshal Manuel Vasquez. He was the only person to testify who was qualified as a fire investigation expert. He assured us multiple times that the fire resulted from arson and that no thing and no person other than the defendant was responsible.

Bitter Ted: "You listen to this woman, I tell you. Just listen and maybe we can get out of here."

Edie: "Excuse me. I didn't interrupt you when you were speaking and I would appreciate the same courtesy."

Ted takes it hard, mumbles something about "How do you like that?", folds his arms over his chest, and turns away. Edie takes no apparent note of his petulant behavior. It's unlikely any of us will interrupt her further.

Edie: "He backed up his assurances with detailed observations based on his six years and nine months experience with the State Fire Marshal's Office. He walked us room-by-room through the remains, pointing out the overwhelming evidence of arson.

"The most significant evidence, in my opinion, are the patterns burned into the floor in the front bedroom and the hallway. He called them pour patterns. He explained that they are formed by a combustible liquid poured on the floor and then set ablaze. That poured liquid causes the fire to burn low over large areas of the floor, and that is unusual since heat rises and fire tends to climb towards the ceiling. Chief Fogg, if you will recall, commented on the floor being unusually hot. I submit his observation is consistent with and corroborates the testimony of Manuel Vasquez in this regard.

"Deputy Vasquez explained not only that a combustible liquid was used to start separate fires in the front bedroom, hallway, and front porch, he identified the specific liquid used. It was charcoal lighter fluid. A sample of the door threshold had been sent to a laboratory for chemical analysis, and the laboratory identified the presence of mineral spirits of kerosene. In other words, lighter fluid.

"He explained all of this. And damning as all that is, he provided even more evidence of arson. He described the patterns he found in the hallway. Those patterns are created when something on the floor is set on fire. The fire climbs the wall while spreading out in a V-pattern.

"And still he provided even more evidence of arson. He found brown stains on the porch, near the base of the front wall just outside the children's bedroom. These stains, he explained, were caused by the lighter fluid when that fluid was squirted on the ground.

"But the defendant was not satisfied with merely setting the front wall on fire. He set the front door on fire to prevent anyone from rescuing the children. He poured so much lighter fluid on the front door that the door was completely consumed and that, according to the only expert fire witness to have testified in this trial, is exceptionally rare.

"Mr. Willingham spread so much fluid around that the fire burned with enough intensity to melt the aluminum threshold, something a normal fire without an accelerant could not do.

"In fact, Mr. Willingham spread so much fluid that the fire burned hot enough to reach flashover, a phenomenon in which everything in the room ignites at once. The flashover happens so rapidly that those who witness it describe it as an explosion, and that's exactly what the Barbees saw: a flashover that they interpreted as an explosion.

"And when the fire flashed over, it expelled flames through the front window and front door. In the words of Deputy Vasquez, it auto-ventilated. The auto-ventilation is yet another indicator of arson.

"Even with all this evidence, he didn't jump to a conclusion of arson. He took the trouble to eliminate the other possible sources of the fire. He explained that all the space heaters were turned off and no flaws could be found in any of the electrical wires or pull boxes he examined. And he specifically ruled two-year-old Amber out as a possible source of the fire.

"The defense would have us believe that Amber started this fire by pouring an accelerant in her bedroom, and the hallway, and presumably the porch, and then lighting each of those areas on fire, one at a time, then telling her father to wake up, and then dying in his bed. Deputy Vasquez took time to explain why such a theory is untenable, but I won't. I can't imagine any of us would entertain such an improbable thought.

"And finally, Deputy Vasquez explained that the defendant's injuries were inconsistent with his story of being awakened by Amber in the midst of the fire, and being able to escape barefoot down the hall without suffering burns to his feet or smoke in his lungs.

"So you may if you wish, and I suspect you will, continue arguing the minutiae, but that will not influence my belief that the defendant is guilty beyond all doubt, not just reasonable doubt, beyond all doubt. Unless someone can explain away this arson evidence, and I consider that an unlikely scenario, I am obliged to vote guilty."

The room falls silent. Not even Ted dares to cheer her performance. And what a performance it was. She compressed hours of rambling, often incoherent testimony into a lucid two-minute summation that might spell the end of Cameron Todd Willingham.

She waits patiently for someone to attempt a rebuttal. No one so far has taken the challenge. I have something in my back pocket, but it's unlikely to sway everyone. I decide to hold on to it a while longer.

"Pardon."

We all know who that is.

Jorge: "I do not care for this man. He is too positive about himself, even when the liberty of another man is at stake. I have seen many people like him, people in authority who will not listen."

Sports Fan Ward: "Of all the nerve! You come here from some backwoods town in a backwoods country, I'm guessing you know absolutely nothing about fire like that man does, and you have the nerve to talk about him like that. You don't argue with anything he says, because you can't. You just don't care for him, he makes you feel uncomfortable. I've had enough of this."

Bitter Ted: "Boy, oh boy."

Jorge: "I was quite surprised to hear that he had investigated so many cases, more than a thousand, and decided all but just a few were caused by arson. I'm afraid he makes up his mind before he arrives, before he even looks at the evidence. And if he does that I don't know if I should trust him when I am deciding if another man should live or die."

Boisterous Lee: "Whadda ya mean he makes up his mind beforehand? We all heard him lay out the evidence. He didn't just make up the evidence. He had pictures and diagrams. He had test results. And he testified, under oath, that he didn't make any decisions about what caused the fire until he had collected all the evidence. You heard him, we all heard him."

Jorge: "Yes, I heard him say that. But I think he is not telling the truth."

Lee: "You're calling him a liar. How can you say that?"

Jorge: "Because he didn't examine the scene until two days after Christmas."

Uh, oh!

Lee: "So he didn't examine it until then? So what?"

Jorge: "Don't you remember what Dr. Zamora said?"

Uh, oh!

Lee: "Dr. Zamora? Who can keep 'em all straight?"

Jorge: "He is the one who did the autopsies on the twins the day before Christmas.

Uh, oh!

Lee: "So?"

Jorge: "Do you not remember? Dr. Zamora listed the cause of death as 'homicide' because Mr. Vasquez told him to. That was three days before Mr. Vasquez ever arrived at the scene, before he ever saw the evidence."

CROSS-EXAMINATION OF MANUEL VASQUEZ
Wednesday, August 19, 1992

David Martin will cross-examine Deputy Fire Marshal Manuel Vasquez. Martin has no intention of allowing Vasquez to narrate.

"Mr. Vasquez, tell me whether you agree with this statement, please. 'The point is that deep charring or a complete burn-through of the flooring is not, per se, indicative of an accelerant. Investigators have concluded and testified in court that intense burning of a certain section of flooring meant unequivocally that an accelerant was present in the area. This is not necessarily so. And the investigator must eliminate other possible causes of the deep charring and/or burn-through, such as falling burning material.' Do you agree with that?" >> Yes, sir.

"And have you ever been wrong in a conclusion that you make?" >> Not to my knowledge.

"So you're always right?" >> I said not to my knowledge.

"But your opinion is that you're always right and have always been right?" >> I have interpreted the burn patterns correctly.

"Now I want to talk to you about the opinions that you expressed yesterday. Do you recognize that there is available on the market a fluid like this lamp fluid, which is used in these kinds of lamps? Coal-oil lamps, we call them, or kerosene lamps." >> Yes, sir.

"This fluid is not like gasoline. When you put a match to it, it doesn't blow up in your face, does it?" >> That is correct.

"A person in a small closed room who douses the floor with gasoline and lets it soak, as you mentioned yesterday, and is in there and lights a match, what will happen in the room?" >> He will also receive burns.

"Because the fumes will catch on fire, won't they?" >> The fumes will ignite simultaneously throughout the whole area.

"Things like coal oils, though, or lamp fluids have different properties, don't they?" >> Yes, sir.

"You could pour them on the floor and go back in there later and catch it on fire, couldn't you?" >> You've got to have an open flame.

"You recognize this as a picture of the hallway, do you not?" >> Yes, sir.

"Can you recognize that as the globe to an oil lamp similar to the one I have on the table?" >> No, sir, because I didn't examine it.

"You didn't take a look at that, did you?" >> No, sir.

"Do you recognize the remnants of shelves in the hallway?" >> No, sir.

"What do you think that is leaning over there? You don't think that's the remnants of a burned shelf?" >> It looks like a ladder to me.

"Well, look at it carefully. That looks like a ladder to you? It may look like a ladder if not carefully examined, and I'm asking you to carefully examine it." >> It's an item that's leaning against the wall.

"You don't know what it is?" >> No, sir.

"Now, Mr. Vasquez, everything that you say happened could have occurred by somebody having a lamp similar to this with a combustible fluid in it and splashing this out in some manner, both in the hall and in the bedroom, right?" >> Yes, sir.

"It's a possibility that comports with the facts that you found, isn't it?" >> Yes, sir.

"And then that having been done, the fire could have started in the bedroom and could have been burning in the bedroom while the hallway was not on fire, correct?" >> It's possible, sir.

"And you told us yesterday that you believed that the front bedroom caught fire first, correct?" >> Yes, sir.

"And then the hallway caught fire, right?" >> Yes, sir.

"And then the front porch caught fire?" >> Yes, sir.

"In that order?" >> Yes, sir.

"And there were no connecting puddles between the hallway and the bedroom, was there?" >> There were no connecting puddles. There was a discernible path, but it was not enough to be a connecting path.

"All right. So, in other words, do you believe that the bedroom caught the hallway on fire, or at least that the hallway caught on fire second?" >> The fire in the bedroom did not ignite the fire in the hallway.

"You think it was two separate causes?" >> Yes, sir. Two separate fires.

"In other words, you think there was a combustible liquid on the floor in both locations, don't you?" >> Yes, sir.

"But you don't think that the fire in the bedroom could catch the hall on fire?" >> Yes, eventually it would have.

"It could, couldn't it?" >> It could have burned the whole house eventually.

<<>>

"This is the way in which you found it when you went there, did you not?" >> Yes, sir.

"With a lot of debris on its floor?" >> Yes, sir.

"In fact, much of this debris was shoveled by the firemen out onto the ground, wasn't it?" >> No, sir. This debris came from the bedroom. That's in the hallway.

"Debris in the bedroom was shoveled out on the ground?" >> Some of it was.

"The debris in the hallway was shoveled out somewhere, wasn't it?" >> I didn't see it.

"Were you standing there when somebody cleaned up the debris?" >> They were working cleaning up. I was looking. I don't know where the debris went.

"Did you know they used shovels and similar hand tools?" >> I don't remember seeing that when I was there. They must have used them before I got there.

"It's common, isn't it?" >> Yes, sir. It's common.

"And they used shovels in this case, didn't they?" >> Apparently, they did.

"I mean, the debris didn't leap out the window of the room, did it?" >> No, sir.

"All right. The point being that they used hand tools, scraped along the floor, to remove the debris, correct?" >> Yes, sir. They had to.

"And you can tear tile with a shovel or you can tear it with a hoe, you can tear it with a high-pressure water hose, can't you?" >> Yes, sir.

"And some of the tile on the floor in the hallway and the bedroom was torn in that manner, wasn't it?" >> No, sir.

"None of it was." >> Some of them might have been, but not all of it. See, this is jagged --

"My question is: Some of it was, wasn't it?" >> Yes, sir. Some of it was.

"And that accounts for some of the tile to be missing, doesn't it?" >> Yes, sir.

"Burning debris on a floor can cause marks and patterns in areas that could be mistaken for a place accelerant was poured, could it not?" >> I took that into consideration.

"Could it not?" >> Not in this case.

"Could it not? Is it a possibility? Does it happen? I know what your opinion is, Mr. Vasquez, but this is a capital murder case and I'm more interested in the fact of the matter." >> That's what I'm interested in, too, sir. Repeat the question, please.

"And the fact of the matter is, as the training books warn us, that falling and burning debris laying on a floor can cause patterns and marks in areas that could be mistaken for accelerant puddles and trails." >> That is correct. And I am very careful about that.

<<>>

"You determined that the fire began here in the front bedroom, right?" >> Yes, sir.

"And so that it is possible that a person could have gone down the hall at a time when it was not on fire and the bedroom was on fire, right?" >> It's possible.

"And you're swearing to us that a person who was in the bedroom where Amber was found couldn't possibly have gotten out of the house alive. Is that what you're telling us?" >> No, sir.

"It is possible, isn't it?" >> He would have received injuries, but it is possible.

"All right. Because, as we've seen, the carpet in the bedroom area caught fire first, correct?" >> Yes, sir.

"And then that fire could have spread to the hallway. I understand you think somebody else dropped a match in it, but it could have spread to the hallway and caught the hallway on fire, correct?" >> Yes, sir.

"And you're telling us that, while the fire burned in the bedroom, that nobody could have come out the hallway because it would be burning and he'd have burns on his feet, is that right?" >> No, sir, I didn't say that.

"Okay. That could have happened, couldn't it? The bedroom was burning at one point when the hallway was not, wasn't it?" >> Yes, sir.

"Now, Mr. Vasquez, with the fire beginning in the bedroom, smoke will go as far through the house as it can get, won't it?" >> It will go throughout the whole house.

"It begins high and goes low?" >> Yes, sir.

"And there is some point at which a person in the center bedroom will not be breathing smoke because it'll be above him, correct?" >> He's supposed to not to breathe smoke, that's correct.

"There are various points in time in which a person in the center bedroom is below the smoke, correct?" >> He's in a tolerable level of smoke.

"In a house fire, the smoke gathers toward the ceiling first, doesn't it?" >> It rises.

"As the house fills with smoke and you can see the smoke line coming down the wall, correct?" >> Yes.

"And, just like the water mark that you talked about yesterday, you can tell where the smoke went to by its marks on the wall, can't you?" >> Yes, sir.

"Because it's black?" >> Yes, sir.

"And as you described yesterday, the coolest and the safest place to be during a fire, normally, is on the floor, isn't it?" >> Yes, sir.

"Because the smoke is up here and you don't want to breathe it, do you?" >> That's correct.

"You'd rather be on the floor while the smoke is above you?" >> Yes, sir.

<<>>

"Now Mr. Vasquez, did you see this picture that we introduced yesterday of the charcoal grill on the front porch? See it there behind that fireman?" >> I see something, sir, but I couldn't tell you what it is.

"Well, yesterday Doug Fogg said it was a charcoal grill that was on the porch." >> Well, apparently. Yes, sir.

"But my point is that grill was not there when you investigated the fire, was it?" >> No, sir.

"You didn't have the opportunity to know that people had been barbecuing on the front porch, did you?" >> I don't know that, sir.

"Well, you don't remember anybody telling you that, do you?" >> No, sir.

"And they didn't say, 'Deputy Vasquez, oh, by the way, there was a charcoal grill on the front porch'?" >> No, sir.

"Now, the bottle remnants that we have here was found somewhere right behind this fireman, wasn't it?" >> Yes, sir.

"We see on the concrete floor the brown stains of where some charcoal lighter fluid has been, don't we?" >> It's been squirted on there.

"Could you answer the question I asked?" >> Yes. I'm sorry.

"Now, when the bottle melted, and we don't know how much was in there, but at one time it had some in there, didn't it?" >> I would presume. It's an empty bottle now.

"And the fluid inside of the bottle went somewhere, didn't it?" >> It was either burned up or it flowed away and dried up.

"Or it flowed away and burned up." >> Possible.

"Or it flowed away down here to the threshold and burned up. We don't know, do we?" >> That's a long way for it to flow.

"We know that the charcoal lighter fluid, though we don't know how much was in there, was in the plastic container, correct?" >> Yes, sir.

"Which melted, right?" >> Yes, sir.

"And that the fluid in the plastic container went somewhere, didn't it?" >> Yes, sir.

"It's going to flow some distance, isn't it?" >> Yeah, but it's also going to soak.

"Well, let's talk about the porch." >> Yes, sir.

"It was number three to catch on fire, wasn't it?" >> Yes, sir.

"The front door, you didn't examine it because it wasn't there, correct?" >> That's correct.

"And you don't know whether it was a hollow-core door or a solid-core door, do you?" >> No, sir.

"A hollow-core door is much thinner and burns more rapidly and more completely than you would expect a solid-core door to burn, doesn't it?" >> No, sir.

"Why not? One is solid wood and one isn't." >> But they don't burn, the patterns are not the same, sir.

"Will you just respond to the question I asked? You mean to tell us that you think a solid-core door burns as quickly as a hollow-core door?" >> No, sir.

"A hollow-core door has less wood in it, doesn't it?" >> Yes, sir.

"Generally speaking, less wood, under the same conditions, will burn up more quickly and more completely than more wood will, won't it?" >> Yes, sir.

"And you don't know whether the front door was hollow-core or solid core, do you?" >> That's correct.

"You don't know whether, during the fire, the door was standing open, which would mean it was flung to the inside, or whether it was closed, do you?" >> I did determine that the door was closed.

"Well, let's explore how you determined that. I know that's what you think, but the door wasn't there, was it?" >> No, sir.

"Let me ask you whether you recognize that as a picture taken of the front door jambs?" >> Yes, sir.

"And in this picture we see the hinge where the front door once hung, do we not?" >> There was a door hung in there, yeah.

"Can you answer the question I asked? We see the hinge where the front door was hung, don't we?" >> I don't know if it's the front door or not, sir. It's a door, yes.

"It is a door on the inside of the jam, isn't it?" >> I can't tell. Honestly, I cannot.

"Is it a picture that you took?" >> Yes, sir.

"Do you recognize this on the left-hand side of the picture as the door jamb?" >> It's a door jamb. Yes, sir.

"Do you recognize it as the front door jamb?" >> No, sir.

"You mean you can't tell whether it was the front door or not?" >> Not in that picture.

"Well, let's compare it and look at it along with this photo. Does that help you to tell us?" >> There's a jamb on here, on this picture, but I can't tell if it's a screen door or the front door from that.

"And you know that that is a picture taken while you were standing at the front porch, looking into the hallway, isn't it?" >> Yes, sir.

"And you're telling us that you can't identify for us whether that is a hinge upon which the front door hung?" >> No, sir.

"Well, then we'll ask the jury to consider it. Let me ask you this question: Do you recognize the fact that the hinge is swung open?" >> It's open. Yes, sir.

"Mr. Vasquez, you told us earlier, did you not, that a flashover could be mistaken as an explosion by witnesses?" >> The sound of it.

"Did you know that the witnesses said that they never saw any flames on the front of the house until they heard the explosion? Did you know that?" >> I don't remember, sir.

"That's a fact. They've testified to that here in court." >> Okay.

"And when the witnesses are viewing the house and there's no flames along the front of the house, and then they hear what sounds like an explosion and suddenly the house is engulfed in flames. Is that what you identify as a flashover?" >> Inside the bedroom, yes, sir.

"They talked about the front of the house, that they didn't see any flames on the front of the house until they heard the explosion. Did you know that?" >> No, sir.

"All right. Pass the witness."

FURTHER EXAMINATION OF MANUEL VASQUEZ
Wednesday, August 19, 1992

Alan Bristol has some redirect for Manuel Vasquez.

"Mr. Vasquez, when you were doing your initial investigation, did you eliminate the potential accidental causes of fire?" >> Yes, sir.

"What causes did you eliminate?" >> The causes that I eliminated were the accidental causes, which was the electrical or the gas cause. And I also eliminated the possibility that the little girl might have set the fire.

"And how did you eliminate the little girl, Amber?" >> First of all, the heaters were turned off. And I did not find any remnant of paper around the heater or anywhere. And the other fact is that the burn patterns on her body were not consistent with the burn patterns in that bedroom.

Interesting.

"In your opinion, Mr. Vasquez, could Cameron Todd Willingham have been in the bedroom where Amber was found when the fire started?" >> No.

"Why do you reach that conclusion?" >> The burn patterns and the heat patterns in that room, he would have been a victim of the fire.

"In your opinion, could Cameron Todd Willingham have gotten out of the house from the bedroom that Amber was found in, after the fire started, without sustaining injury?" >> No, sir.

"Without sustaining smoke inhalation?" >> No.

"Based upon your investigation and your examination of the scene and your conclusions, can you tell what the arsonist intended to do by setting this fire?" >> Yes.

"What is that?" >> The intent was to kill the little girls.

"Pass the witness."

<<>>

David Martin has some further cross-examination.

"Mr. Vasquez, the patterns that you believe you detected in the bedroom could have been caused just as easily by lamp fluid as by charcoal lighter fluid, couldn't it?" >> Any combustible fluid.

"Would have caused the same marks?" >> Yes, sir.

"Now, Mr. Vasquez, I'm going to ask you a hypothetical question, all right?" >> Yes, sir.

"You agreed, did you not, that this could have been the combustible liquid that was on the floor, lamp oil." >> Hypothetically speaking, yes.

"I mean, you don't know what it was, do you?" >> No, sir.

"And on a shelf in the hallway could have been a gas oil lantern like this one, couldn't there?" >> Yes.

"And a child could have gotten ahold of it and splashed the combustible liquid out of here, couldn't they, onto the floor?" >> Yes, sir.

"It would have burned the same way as you found, wouldn't it? >> Yes, sir.

"And a child's gate between the bedroom and the hallway could have been there. You don't know whether it was or not, do you?" >> No, sir. I don't.

"But we know that there was no door there, don't we?" >> Not when I was there.

"And we know the door pins were in the hinges, weren't they?" >> Very high.

"Excuse me?" >> They were very high, the hinges.

"What difference does it make? Weren't there door hinges there, with the pin still in them?" >> There was a hinge on the door, yes.

"With the door pin in the hinge, right?" >> Yes, sir.

"And a child could have gotten this or a similar lantern off of the shelves in the hall and spilled a combustible liquid, like that lantern oil, on the floor in the hall, couldn't they?" >> Just in the hall?

"If you'll just play along with me and answer the questions I ask." >> Yes, sir.

"I'm trying to develop here, Mr. Vasquez, a scenario that could have occurred, and demonstrate for the jury that your findings were not inconsistent with such a scenario. Do you see where I'm headed?" >> Yes, sir.

"And the same splashing of a combustible liquid out of this lantern in the hall would account for what you say is puddles and floor patterns, wouldn't it?" >> Yes, sir.

"And then the child could have held it and climbed over the child's gate into the bedroom. You didn't find any connecting puddles, did you?" >> No, sir.

"And then, once in the bedroom, for whatever reason, child's play, we don't know, spills some of this same liquid in the bedroom. Could she not have done that?" >> Yes, sir.

"And then that flame could have been ignited with a cigarette lighter." >> Open flame?

"Cigarette lighter, a match?" >> Yes, sir.

"And you didn't find anything that would rule that out, did you?" >> No, sir.

"It could have happened just the way I've described." >> Yes, sir.

"Did you know that both parents in the home were smokers?" >> Yes, sir.

"And that there were numerous cigarette lighters in the house?" >> Now that, I don't know.

"You examined one that was found in there, didn't you?" >> No, sir.

"You didn't see any of them?" >> No, sir.

"Well, the police have them, we'll ask them about that." >> Okay.

"And then the fire, you believe, started in the bedroom. You told us that." >> Yes, sir.

"And then you acknowledged that there was some period of time during which the bedroom was burning and the hallway was not." >> That's correct.

"And you didn't examine the debris in the hall?" >> No, sir.

"Pass the witness."

<<>>

Alan Bristol has some more redirect.

"Mr. Vasquez, Mr. Martin just asked you a hypothetical question. He just went through a scenario or theory with you, is that right?" >> Yes, sir.

"He just asked you: Would it be possible for a two-year old child, Amber, to have taken a lantern, poured it in the hall, climbed over that a gate, poured it in the bedroom, started the bedroom with a match or a lighter, then climbed back over, then went back into the bedroom on the west side of the house? He asked you if that was a possibility." >> When you speak hypothetically, anything is possible.

"From your investigation and examination of the actual scene, is that scenario or hypothetical a possibility, in your opinion?" >> Hypothetically speaking, yes. In reality, it is not.

"And why do you say that?" >> A child, in my experience, does not go pouring combustible liquid in the hallway and in the bedrooms and then lighting it up, or in the porch. She doesn't have the maturity to do that, sir.

"You heard Mr. Martin's scenario involving the lamp, his hypothetical question to you about the child climbing over the gate, pouring it, climbing back over it, pouring it in the bedroom, lighting it: and, I assume, went outside at some point and poured it along the porch. Do you agree with that scenario?" >> In reality?

"In reality." >> No, sir.

"Is there anything that Mr. Martin has asked you, or shown you, or asked you hypothetically that would change your opinions that you previously testified about?" >> No, sir.

"Pass the witness."

<<>>

We're not through. David Martin has some further cross-examination.

"You mean it takes a child of some degree of maturity to accidentally spill something on the floor?" >> No, sir.

"Mr. Vasquez, you cannot tell who spilled or poured the liquid you believe was on the floor, can you?" >> Yes, sir. I can.

"So, for example, when you find a piece of material on a floor and it has something poured or spilled on it, you can take a look at the spill or the pour and you can tell who did it?" >> No, sir. I can't. That I cannot. It has to burn first, and there are other indicators and evidence that I have to use.

"If you'd just first answer the question that I asked." >> Yes, sir.

"You can't tell who poured it or spilled it on the floor, from the pour or the spill or the burn pattern, can you?" >> No, sir.

"It could have been accidentally spilled." >> Yes, sir.

"Pass the witness."

<<>>

Not done yet. Bristol has some more redirect. There's always more redirect.

"Mr. Vasquez, in your opinion, did anything other than an accelerant cause the burn patterns, the floor patterns, the puddling effects that you found?" >> No, sir.

"Pass the witness."

<<>>

Still not done. Martin has some more cross. There's always more cross. I'm starting to feel like a spectator at Wimbledon.

"And you've never been wrong?" >> To my knowledge, everything that I have said is corroborated by evidence.

"I mean, in fifteen years, or twenty, or twenty-five, you've never been wrong, have you?" >> If I have, sir, I don't know. It's never been pointed out.

"Pass the witness."

And finally, blessedly, Bristol has no further questions.

FURTHER DELIBERATION OF MANUEL VASQUEZ
Thursday, August 20, 1992

When Jorge points out that Vasquez had declared the fire a homicide three days before he examined the scene, Lee looks as if he's been backed over by a dump truck. He won't be recovering anytime soon. It's Edie who responds.

"I believe Dr. Zamora testified only that he spoke with unidentified personnel from the State Fire Marshal's Office. I'm confident he never testified that it was Manuel Vasquez specifically that he spoke with."

Jorge: "Perhaps. Perhaps some other person who had not visited the scene, some other person who had not seen the evidence, perhaps that person informed Dr. Zamora that the twins were victims of homicide."

I believe Edie should cut her loses on this one.

Edie: "You're only assuming that the person Dr. Zamora spoke with hadn't visited the scene."

Uh, oh.

Jorge: "No, I am quite certain that no one from the State Fire Marshal's Office visited the scene before Dr. Zamora identified the cause of death as homicide."

Edie's smart enough to realize Jorge is not bluffing. She staked everything on the Vasquez testimony, everything including her sense of self-righteousness. And now this strange, seemingly simple man has made her look bad. She knows better than to pursue her case further, but she can't help herself.

"I suspect you couldn't name more than one person from that office. How can you be so certain none of them, not one of them, visited the site before the autopsy?"

Jorge: "Do you not remember? Fire Chief Fogg, the gentleman with the wonderful name, he told us."

Edie looks puzzled, thinks for a moment, then is struck by the same force that silenced Lee.

Sports Fan Ward: "What am I missing here?"

Bitter Ted: "He said no such thing. The only guy Fogg talked about was this Vasquez guy."

Jorge: "So you agree that Mr. Vasquez was not honest with us when he said he made no judgements before examining all the evidence?"

Uh, oh.

Ted: "You're twisting everything around. I was just agreeing with her when she --"

Edie: "Please, don't help me."

Jorge: "You remember of course that Chief Fogg testified, while under oath, that he was the person who requested assistance from the State Fire Marshal's Office. He thought about doing so on Christmas day, and he placed the call the next day. That would be the twenty-sixth. So I cannot understand how anyone from the state office could inform the medical examiner two days earlier that the twin girls died of the homicide. In fact, now that I explain it out loud, I fear I must wonder as well about the testimony of Chief Fogg."

Edie: "I'll concede that there are problems with their testimony about when they were contacted, but --"

Jorge: "Pardon me. My point was not that they were contacted early or late. That was not my point. My point was that Deputy Vasquez must have made up his mind before he conducted his examination. My point was that maybe the fire didn't speak to him as much as he spoke to the fire."

Timid John: "You know what I didn't like about that guy? He would never admit he was wrong, and never admit the other side might be right, even on a tiny little point. He claimed he had never been wrong in any of his investigations, and then wouldn't even agree with the defense attorney that it is colder in December than in August."

Young Jack: "That's right. I noticed that too. And he claimed the front door had to be closed and when they showed him a picture of the hinges in the door jamb, he said he couldn't be sure if that was the right door jamb, even though he took the picture."

Harriet: "Remember when the defense counsel asked him if he knew that the neighbors testified the door was open when they first saw the house, and that no fire was coming out then? Did you see the look on his face?"

Jack: "And if the front porch was set on fire like he said, why didn't any of the neighbors see it. They kept saying there was only smoke until the explosion."

John: "And he said he didn't even notice the oil lamp in the hallway, and never saw a lighter. I don't understand how you can rule out all accidental causes of a fire and not even notice an oil lamp or find any lighters in a house of two smokers."

Jack: "And he didn't know about the cigarette lighters either. How can someone investigate a fire and not know about all the cigarette lighters that were found?

Ad Agency Robert: "My favorite was when he said the burned-up shelf was a ladder. You'd have to have some pretty long legs to climb that ladder."

Edie: "The evidence is still there regardless of what you may think of Deputy Vasquez --"

Jorge: "And Chief Fogg, I now fear."

Edie: "And Chief Fogg. Fine. My point is that the evidence is still there: the pour patterns, the V-patterns, the multiple origins, the melted aluminum, the threshold soaked with lighter fluid. I'm unwilling to accept that he would invent that evidence."

Harriet: "No one is suggesting that anyone fabricated evidence, except for that invented by Johnny Webb of course."

I give her a little thank you smile for the mention.

Harriet: "What some of us are suggesting is that the evidence is subject to multiple interpretations, and that Deputy Vasquez is predisposed to select the interpretation most harmful to the defense. Perhaps that's why he so seldom concludes a fire isn't arson."

Edie: "Then give me another explanation for the burn patterns on the floor."

Harriet: "Manuel Vasquez already gave you an alternative explanation, one that would free Willingham."

Uh, oh.

Edie: "I know. I know. He conceded that the patterns could hypothetically, and he said hypothetically, be caused by debris that fell from the ceiling, but he said he was very careful about that."

Harriet: "But he didn't explain how he was careful. He didn't explain what he did to rule out the possibility the patterns were caused by falling debris. He just said he was careful. What does that mean? Now I ask you, what do you think he meant by that?"

Edie: "I don't know. I presume he compared to the fallen debris with the patterns on the floor and they didn't match."

Young Jack: "He couldn't have. He had them remove the debris before he got there."

Edie: "That's simply not correct, sir. You saw the pictures of the hallway. The debris was all over the ground. He took those pictures."

Jack: "Oh, the hallway, you're right."

Jorge: "See how easy it is to admit when you are wrong."

Good one.

Jack: "But even there he couldn't have done that, because he said other people cleaned things up while he was looking somewhere else. When I said he told them to clean things up before he got there, I was talking about the bedroom. That picture shows the floor had been scraped clean.

"In fact, I remember that when he talked to Fogg on the phone, he told him to go ahead and mark the location of the bodies. Someone scraped the floor, and someone marked the location with spray paint, and that's the way he found it when he arrived. That was his picture."

Harriet: "Maybe that's why he didn't say it wasn't important to secure the fire scene. He ordered people to change it before he even got there. He didn't even want to see it as it was right after the fire. Now that's no way to conduct an investigation."

Jack: "That's right! When I was talking about securing the crime scene, assuming it even is a crime scene, I was talking about outsiders getting in and messing up the evidence. I didn't think it would be the firemen who messed it up."

Jorge: "Forgive me, but I fear it is worse than that. Deputy Vasquez did not even bother to look through the debris, either before or after they removed it at his instruction. He said the little girl Amber could not have started the fire by playing with the space heater because he found no burned paper near the heater. Perhaps there was not burned paper nearby because he told them to remove everything."

Jack: "That's right!"

Jorge: "I think if he had not told them to remove the debris, he might have found paper there, or something nearby that might have burned in the heater. I think also he might have found Amber's missing sock. If the sock had been found in her bedroom, it would tell me than she went from her bedroom to her father's bedroom just as he said she did. Now we will never know."

Jack: "I told you they should have guarded the house."

Ward: "Well, I don't know about the rest of 'em, but I'm getting a little tired of this yakkity yakking back and forth. It's getting us nowhere. So I'll have to break it up. I'm changing my vote to not guilty."

Lee: "You're what?"

Ward: "You heard me. I've had enough."

Lee: "What do you mean you've had enough? That's no answer."

Ward: "Hey listen, you just take care of yourself, huh?"

Jorge jumps to his feet. He's clearly agitated at Ward.

Jorge: "What kind of a man are you? You have sat here and voted guilty because there are some baseball tickets burning a hole in your pocket. Now you have changed your vote because you say you are sick of all the talking?"

Ward: "Now listen, buddy."

Jorge: "Who tells you that you have a right to play like this with a man's life? This is an ugly and terrible thing to do."

Ward: "Now wait a minute. You can't talk like that to me."

Jorge: "If you want to vote not guilty, then do it because you are convinced the man is not guilty, not because you've had enough. If you believe he is guilty, then vote that way. Or don't you have the courage to do what you think is right?"

Ward: "Now listen --"

Jorge: "Guilty or not guilty?"

Ward: "I told you: not guilty."

Jorge: "Why?"

Ward: "Look, I don't have to --"

Jorge: "You do have to! Say it! Why?"

Ward: "Cause I don't think he's guilty. Okay? I said it."

Jorge is still agitated, but he resumes his seat.

Marti: "That's six guilty, five not guilty, one abstention."

I think it's time.

Me: "I have a proposal."

Marti: "Does it have anything to do with Johnny Webb?"

Me: "No."

Marti: "Because you don't seem to care for jailhouse informants."

Me: "No, I don't care for them."

Marti: "And you seem to get somewhat worked up when you speak of them."

Me: "I've been known to do that. I've been practicing my restraint, though."

Marti: "How's that working out?"

Me: "I still have room for improvement."

Marti: "Okay. Let's hear your proposal."

Me: "Initially Harriet was the only person to vote not guilty, and everyone tried to talk her out of her vote. Since then, the sentiment has moved quite a bit in her direction. Edie, on the other hand, has made the most cogent case for Willingham's guilt. A number of people are now trying to get her to change her vote."

Marti: "Continue."

"I propose we lay out a diagram of the house on the floor and have Edie walk through that diagram as she recreates how she believes Willingham set this fire. Of course we can't use a full-scale layout, but if we move this table all the way to the wall, each room in the diagram could be big enough to step into."

Edie: "I'll agree to that if you'll agree to recreating how you think Willingham escaped without getting hurt?"

"Agreed."

Marti: "Gentlemen, ladies, if you would all please stand, we have a table to push aside."

For the next ten minutes, the jury room is in a state controlled chaos. Chairs are moved about, the table is pushed aside, and the outline of the floor plan appears at our feet.

There are no more paper cups in the water cooler dispenser. All but one of them have been magically transported to the jury room floor, outlining the rooms of the Willingham house. We didn't have enough cups for the entire house, so we outlined just the front and center bedrooms, the hallway, and the front porch. Because the cups tend to get kicked over when we moved from room to room during testing, several of us engaged in a stompfest during which we flattened the makeshift walls of the alleged crime scene.

When we're finished, the result is not pretty, but it's surprisingly large and it's definitely functional. Everyone stands around the perimeter and stares down at it. Reactions vary from pride to disgust.

Young Jack: "I think we did a hell of a job."

Bitter Ted: "Of course you would. You just wanna see this guy get off."

Boisterous Lee: "Whadda ya gonna prove with this thing anyway?"

Marti: "We'll find out soon enough."

Edie: "You first."

"Okay. Let me see. I'm Willingham, so I'm sleeping in this room here in this center bedroom."

I step into the small space defined by flattened cups as the center bedroom.

"The twins are sleeping on the floor in their bedroom, there and there."

I point to the spots where in the picture someone had spray painted the locations of the bodies .

"Amber is the only one who's awake. She's wearing just underpants and a pair of socks. She's over here by the space heater, where it's warm."

I step from the center bedroom to the corner of the children's bedroom.

"She's playing too close to the heater, maybe even putting something inside it."

Edie: "But Vasquez said all the space heaters were off. He didn't say the gas valve was in the off position, as Chief Fogg said. I recall distinctly that Vasquez said the space heater was off. In fact, he said all the space heaters were off."

"That's the problem with not securing the scene. He can't testify to the condition of the heaters when the fire crew first arrived. The most-timely report was that of Chief Fogg, and he said the gas valve was turned off, not the heater. And even Fogg's report was after the fire had been put down and the house had been made safe. It doesn't make any sense that someone would control a space heater with the gas valve rather than the heater control, so right now I'm assuming the heater was on."

Edie: "Given that you state it as an assumption, I'll accept that."

"Thank you. Okay. Something catches on fire and drops onto the carpet. Amber moves away and watches the carpet start to burn."

I inch backwards towards the imaginary doorway.

"She's afraid of the fire, but at this point she's more afraid to tell me. Remember I'm Willingham now. She's more afraid to tell me she's been playing with the space heater again, so she hesitates and the fire begins to grow."

Lee: "Who would leave their own kids alone in a room with a space heater going like that?"

I ignore him.

"Before long, she's more afraid of the fire than she is of me getting mad, so she tries to leave the room. But there's a childproof gate blocking the doorway. She can climb over it when she puts her mind to it, she's large enough, and she's done it before, but it takes her awhile. Meanwhile, the fire is billowing smoke out of the room and into the hallway, along the ceiling, just like Vasquez said it would.

"On her way over the gate, Amber snags one sock and leaves it behind. The sock is the last thing on her mind though. She's no longer afraid that I'll get mad at her. Now she wants me to fix things, to make it all okay. I won't be able to do that.

"The smoke is getting thicker, darker and hotter. It's dropping lower and lower, and now it's just terrifying.

"She runs into my bedroom screaming for me. 'Daddy, Daddy.'"

I step back into the bedroom outlined on the floor.

"I wake up and the room is filled with smoke. Amber's screaming but I can't see her, I can't see anything. I tell her to run to the front door, that we'll go out the front door.

"My pants are right beside the bed. I feel around for them, find them without any trouble, and pull 'em on. There's no time for anything else. I can't hear Amber anymore, and I can't see anything. I hunt for her again but I still can't find her. I tell her again to run for the front door, but it's really scary in the hallway now, and I don't know where she is or where she went.

"I get on my hands and knees and I crawl to the hallway."

I step into the hallway outlined on the floor.

"I look to my right. It's filled with smoke but it doesn't seem like the fire is that way. There's no escape that way because we taped the back door shut to keep the house warm. We even put a refrigerator in front of the door because we never use if any more.

"I can't go right in any case. My children are to the left. I look to the left and I know the fire is that way. I can hear it. I can see the glow from their bedroom. I have to go left.

"I stay low. The hallway isn't on fire yet, but still it's getting harder to breathe. I crawl to the doorway of my children's bedroom and I look inside. All I see is dark smoke that seems to glow red hot. I can't see my children.

"The childproof gate is in the way so I stand up because I'm going to step over it, but my hair catches fire and my face feels like it's going to as well. I can't stand it and drop back to the floor. Flames are now crawling along the ceiling, coming out of the bedroom, into the hallway, crawling along the ceiling of the hall, and no matter how low I stay, it's hot and terrifying and so hard to breathe.

"I know the twins were sleeping on the floor not too far from the gate, and I know they're close to the ground and I think maybe I can still save them. So I grab the gate and I try to open it, but its so hot and I can't see, and before I can open the gate, something from the ceiling falls on me. Suddenly I'm on fire. My shoulder is burning like someone stuck me with a red hot poker.

"I panic and try to beat the burning stuff from my shoulder. And then, to my eternal shame and self-loathing, I save myself. I leave my daughters and save myself.

"I crawl to the door in panic and open it. I crawl onto the porch and collapse. I lie there sucking in the outside air. It's so fresh and so cold that I just drink it in and for a moment, and I'm relieved that I'm safe.

"And that's when the real horror strikes me. My children are still inside. Even Amber is inside. She must have run away from the flames, to the kitchen maybe. I've got to save her. I've got to go back inside and save them all.

"I try to go back. I really do, but it's so hot now, I can't tell you how hot it is, I hope you'll never feel anything that hot, I hope no one ever feels anything like that again. It's so hot it's like hell.

"I can't do it. I can't save my own children. They're burning up in there, and I can't save them. I remember falling to my knees and screaming, but I don't remember anything after that. I only remember that I saved myself and let my children die."

And the room falls silent once again.

I let the time pass. I can hear the clock tick.

And tick.

And tick.

Then I step off the scale-model porch and turn it over to Edie.

"Okay. Now you can show us how you think he killed his children."

Tick.

Tick.

Tick.

Tick.

She stares at me.

Tick.

Tick.

Tick.

Edie: "Alright."

She won't give up easily.

Edie: "I'm Willingham. I start here on the porch and I pour lighter fluid beneath the windows. I don't realize that it will leave brown stains later to give me away.

"Then I go to the front door. I soak it in lighter fluid, inside and out, and I put so much fluid on the door that it runs down onto the threshold."

Timid John: "How can the lighter fluid run down onto the threshold if the door is open. The door must be open if you coat it inside and outside with lighter fluid."

I intervene.

"She gave me the courtesy of speaking without interruption. We owe her the same courtesy."

John: "Sorry."

He disappears back into the crowd.

Edie. "Okay. I soak only one side of the door, the outside, and I soak it so thoroughly that the excess runs down to the threshold. I know that if the door is on fire, no one will be able to get in and save the children. I don't realize that I used so much fluid that the door will completely burn up and the threshold will test positive for lighter fluid."

She steps into the hallway.

"I pour fluid onto the hallway floor. Not the whole floor, mind you, just that portion of the floor up to the children's door. If the firefighters get through the front door they'll have to fight their way through this portion of the hallway.

"Then I step over the childproof gate and step into the bedroom. The twins are sleeping where they were found, on the floor, just like you said. Amber is sleeping in her bed. I pour fluid all over the floor, from this corner to this corner, and from this one to this one. I even pour lighter fluid under Amber's bed. I want to insure that this works.

"Then I step out into the hallway, just beyond doorway. I light a match. I've got plenty of matches because if you remember, we both smoke. I can light the match without fear of explosion because I've used lighter fluid, not gasoline. If I'd used gasoline, I'd be dead at this point. We would all be dead. The whole house would explode.

"But I didn't use gasoline. I used lighter fluid, and it just lies there soaking into the carpet waiting for someone to set it on fire, waiting for me to throw the match. So I throw the match into the bedroom and in a whoosh the carpet catches fire. It doesn't explode, it just quickly spreads over the carpet in the same pattern I poured the fluid. It begins sending flames to the ceiling. The fire is burning hottest on the floor, just like Vasquez said it would in an arson fire, and the floor is getting hot, just like Fogg said it was he was trying to put out the fire I started.

"And then I walk down the hallway and out the door. I turn around and stand at the threshold. I light a second match, and I throw it into the hallway. With another whoosh, the hallway carpet catches fire. As it reaches the wall, it climbs in a V-pattern. I didn't realize at that time the V-pattern would be another clue to give me away."

"I shut the door --"

Edie hesitates for a second. She's trying to decide whether it's better to describe the door as being open or closed. Vasquez said it was closed, and she's trying to defend Vasquez' testimony. The Barbees, on the other hand, were clear in her testimony that they only saw smoke when they first arrived. The front porch wasn't on fire and the front door certainly wasn't closed and burning. Edie strikes a compromise. She closes the front door but she doesn't light it on fire.

"Finally, with a few more matches, I set the porch on fire in several locations under the window. I didn't realize that someone would be able to tell from the burning and charring of the outside wall beneath the window that I set the house on fire. But I had to set that area on fire. I had to keep the firefighters from entering the window and saving the children.

"Then I crouched down outside the door and waited for the neighbors to arrive. As soon as they did, I started screaming that my children were in the house and needed to be saved."

Edie steps off the make believe porch and stands with the rest of the crowd looking at the makeshift diagram on the floor. Some of my fellow jurors appear quizzical as they try to make sense of if all.

Edie, on the other had, is looking uncomfortable. She realizes her story is full of flaws. I'm not sure if she yet recognizes its fatal weakness.

Jorge: "Pardon me. How did the young girl Amber get into the center bedroom? The State's first witness said you carried her in there. Did you carry her in there?"

Edie: "Uh, no. She was awakened by the fire and she ran in there hoping I would save her, but I was on the porch trying to kill her."

Jorge: "Then she climbed over the childproof gate and ran through the fire in the hallway without burning her foot or her sock?"

Edie: "No, I guess not. I carried her in there, just as I told Johnny Webb."

Uh, oh.

Jorge: "Did you then strangle her or suffocate her so she would stay in the bed?"

Edie: "Uh, yes, I did. I strangled her."

Jorge: "And did you then wad up a piece of paper, set it on fire, and touch that paper to your daughter's forehead and arm?"

Edie is cringing now, but she's not ready to quit. In fact, she seems to find a new resolve, almost as if she thinks she's figured something out."

Edie: "Yes, I did. I wanted the police to find her there and conclude that she had been playing with the space heater and had accidentally started the fire."

Jorge: "I understand."

Edie has sullied herself to maintain her theory, but she may have bought herself a brief reprieve. At least she hopes she has.

Jorge: "But now I am confused. If you wanted them to believe she had been playing with the space heater, why did you turn off all the space heaters, as Deputy Vasquez said you did?"

Edie looks as if she has just swallowed a bee. Still, she won't give up.

Edie: "I didn't. One of the firefighters must have turned the gas valves off when securing the house after the fire."

She realizes she slipped when she talked about securing the house.

Edie: "I mean when they were making sure the fire wouldn't start up again."

Jorge: "Or to prevent an explosion if the fire has damaged the gas lines. Because as we all learned from Mr. Vasquez and his explanation of the bed that fire doesn't melt metal but it does react with it."

Edie: "Correct."

Jorge: "Why did you start the fire under her bed if you intended to carry her to your bedroom and strangle her there?"

Edie: "I'm not sure. I changed my mind at the last moment."

Harriet: "You said you closed the front door, and your story is consistent with Deputy Vasquez' testimony. Can you tell us why you closed the door?"

Edie: "I was trying to make it more difficult for firefighters to rescue anyone."

Harriet: "But you didn't light it on fire. You took the trouble to soak it with lighter fluid to light it on fire."

Edie: "Now that I think about it, I remember that I soaked the inside of the door with lighter fluid, not the outside. That way the door would burn on the inside. Together the door and hallway would delay any rescue attempt.

Harriet: "But you closed the door, you're certain of that."

Edie: "I think I closed the door, yes."

Harriet: "Because one of the Barbee daughters looked and said the front door was open before the house seemed to explode."

Edie: "She was mistaken. People make mistakes sometimes."

Harriet: "But not deputy state fire marshals?"

Edie: "He only said he wasn't aware of any mistakes he might have made. He never said he didn't make any. And with respect to this case, he said he was very careful and confident of his conclusions."

Harriet: "But it's up to us to decide if his conclusions are correct or not correct."

Edie: "That's what we're trying to do."

Harriet: "But it's not what we were trying to do when we all voted without first deliberating, was it?"

It's the first time I've seen any hint of anger from Harriet. Edie doesn't quite know what to say.

Edie: "I guess not."

She seems contrite. She's almost broken. It's going to take some finesse, however, to bring her the rest of the way. It's obvious, however, that Jack won't be the one to finesse her.

Jack: "What about his injuries? I mean your injuries. How'd your hair get all burned and your eyelashes get singed? How'd you get that burn on your shoulder? When did you breathe all that smoke into your throat? How about that? Vasquez says they were self-inflicted. Tell us how you self-inflicted those wounds."

Jorge and Harriet parried with a foil. Jack now comes slashing with a battle axe.

Edie simply steps aside.

Edie: "Once again, Deputy Marshal Vasquez was wrong on a minor point. My injuries are not self-inflicted. They are the natural and expected consequences of my being so close to so much fire. Remember, I set three different fires, in three different locations, and I was close to each of them. And while they didn't explode, they weren't exactly tame either. Is there anything else I can explain to anyone?"

Finally it's time.

"Yes. I have just one issue I'd like to discuss, if that's okay."

Edie: "Certainly."

"I would like to talk about that burned plastic lighter fluid bottle they found on the front porch. Do you remember that?"

Edie: "Yes."

She's wary. She smells a trap. I need to misdirect for a bit.

"There was a lot of argument about how full or empty it was when it burned. The defense suggested it was pretty full because he wanted a lot of fluid in there to flow across the porch and explain the marks on the porch that way. The prosecution wanted it to be empty. Now I have the opportunity to ask you directly. Was that bottle full or empty when you were done?"

Edie: "It was empty, naturally."

"Of course it was. I thought it was pretty silly of David Martin to suggest otherwise."

Edie just looks at me.

"But it was full, or pretty full when you started, correct."

Edie: "Yes."

"Well it would have to have been, wouldn't it?"

She sees where I'm going. She doesn't answer.

"How big was that bottle anyway? A pint maybe?"

Edie: "Maybe. Maybe a bit larger. I don't know. I think it was larger."

I take the single cup I withheld from the floor diagram. I examine it with feigned attention.

"These cups hold five ounces, I believe. Water cooler cups like these are usually the real small ones at three ounces or slightly larger ones such as this at five ounces. Marti, does that look like five ounces to you?"

Marti is smiling and not trying to hide it.

Marti: "Indeed it does."

"And how many ounces are there in a pint?"

Marti: "Sixteen, I believe."

"That seems right to me. So four of these cups would be twenty ounces. Ward, did I do that math correctly?"

Ward: "What?"

"Yes. So it seems to me as if four of these cups could hold as much lighter fluid as that one burned bottle. That seem right to you, Edie?"

She knows it's over.

Edie: "Yes. That seems about right."

I walk over to the water cooler and I fill the cup. I return to the layout on the floor.

"You said you poured lighter fluid on the bedroom floor."

Edie doesn't answer. I empty the cup onto the floor, within the boundaries of the front bedroom. The water quickly soaks into the carpet.

Lee: "Good luck setting that on fire."

I go to the water cooler and return with a second cupful of water.

"And you said you then poured lighter fluid on the hallway floor."

Edie doesn't answer. She's become a blank slate. She's neither defensive nor agreeable. She stands there with her arms folded across her chest. She's accepting defeat. Harriet and Jorge are smiling.

I empty the cup onto the floor, within the boundaries of the hallway. The water quickly soaks into the carpet.

Lee: "Are you planning on burning your kids or drowning them?"

I make another trip to the cooler and return with my third cupful.

"And then, as I recall, you soaked one side of the front door."

I empty the cup in the approximate location of the front door, make one more trip to the cooler and return with my fourth and final cupful.

"And finally you soaked the porch."

I empty the final cup onto the floor, within the confines of the porch. The water soaks into the carpet.

I look at Edie. She looks at me. We understand one another because we're both the same. We're each too clever by half.

Me: "Convinced?"

Edie: "I'm convinced."

Me: "Madam Foreperson, I call for a final vote."

Lee: "What the hell you talkin' about? What the hell is going on here?"

Edie: "I was wrong, Lee. I didn't think it through. It didn't occur to me that no one could create a puddle across an entire, full-size bedroom with a small amount of lighter fluid, much less the carpet, the hallway, a porch, and a door as well. It didn't occur to very many people, it seems. I'll give the prosecutor the benefit of the doubt and assume he's simply dense, as I am. I don't know what to say about a defense attorney that fails to see such a fatal flaw in the State's case. And I guess most people in this room were in too big of a hurry to vote guilty to give the issue much thought. That's no excuse for me, though. It simply didn't occur to me, and that's what I have to live with. I was willing to send someone to their death on bad evidence. I wasn't just willing, I was insistent."

Marti: "All of those voting not guilty, please raise your hand."

<<>>

Harriet raises her hand of course. She was the only one to do so on the first ballot, and she does so again on this one.

Jorge raises his hand. As he does so, he turns to Harriet and whispers to her.

"I want to thank you for voting not guilty on that first ballot. You saved me from making a terrible mistake. You taught me how wonderful this country can be."

Harriet gives him a beautiful smile. I'm afraid there's not much to smile about.

John and Jack each raise their hand. They were among the first to change their minds, among the first understand the meaning of reasonable doubt.

John will never lose his timid demeanor, but that demeanor has always been a façade. He has always had what it takes inside to stand up and be counted when it really matters.

Jack will be on another jury some day, and he will simply nod when someone young and fresh claims to know nothing about jury duty.

Ward raises his hand. I wonder if he really believes Willingham is innocent. Maybe he simply has a reasonable doubt about Willingham's guilt. That would be a sufficient and noble justification for changing his vote. Maybe, though, the baseball tickets really are burning holes in his pockets.

Nondescript Ed raises his hand, and so does Ad Agency Robert. We never heard much from them. They seemed content to sit in the background and go with the flow.

Marti raises her hand. She has been the best foreperson I've ever seen. She never took sides, at least not after that first vote, a vote I'm sure she now regrets. After that, she let both sides make their points and make them passionately, but she never let matters get seriously out of hand. She gave not the slightest hint of how she was leaning. Having learned quickly from her initial mistake, she made sure this jury would actually deliberate the evidence before reaching a final verdict. I respect her for that.

I raise my hand for the first time. I had doubts about the State's case from the moment the prosecution had the gall to put Johnny Webb up there and take an oath to tell the truth, the whole truth, and nothing but the truth. And I should let it be at that, lest I fail to restrain myself.

As I feared though, neither Boisterous Lee nor Bitter Ted raise their hands. They will never admit they might be wrong. For them, December will always be as warm as August.

Lee: "Brother! I've seen all kinds of dishonesty in my day but this little display takes the cake. You come in here with your heart bleeding all over the floor about some poor schlup trying to heroically save his kids and suddenly all these others are voting like sheep. Well, you're not getting through to me. I've had enough. What's the matter with you people? You all know he's guilty. He's got to burn. You're letting him slip through our fingers."

Ted: "He's right and I'm not going to let it happen. You can talk at me until my ears fall off, but I'm going to hang this jury sure as you're standing there. This guy isn't going to get away with it. He won't stand a chance next time. They'll put him down like the mad dog he is. It'll just take a little longer that's all. And there's nothing you can do about it. Nothing."

And Harriet utters the last words I'll ever hear her from her regarding the trial of Cameron Todd Willingham.

"Perhaps you're right."

THE VERDICT

The actual jury in the trial of Texas v. Cameron Todd Willingham left the courtroom at 10:25 AM to begin its deliberation. It returned at 11:42 AM. It required only 77 minutes to reach its verdict.

"Okay, members of the jury panel, have you reached a verdict?" >> Yes, sir, we have.

"Would you pass it to the bailiff, please?"

"We, the jury, find the defendant guilty of the offense of capital murder."

"Members of the jury panel, we're going to be in recess until 1:15, and we will start the punishment phase of this case. I want everyone to remain in the courtroom until such time as the jury panel is outside the courtroom. Excuse me just a minute. Did you want the panel polled?"

"May we, Your Honor?"

"Yes, sir. Members of the jury panel, the question that I ask you is: Is this your verdict? And just answer 'Yes' or 'No,' and I'm going to call just last name only."

"Harris?" >> For it.

"Just 'yes' or 'no.'" >> Yes.

"Okay. Dunbar?" >> Yes.

"Holmes?" >> Yes.

"Formby?" >> Yes.

"Watson?" >> Yes.

"Cook?" >> Yes.

"Martin?" >> Yes.

"Roper?" >> Yes.

"Dechaume?" >> Yes.

"Holloway?" >> Yes.

"Horse?" >> Yes.

"And Ponder?" >> Yes.

"Okay. Now you all may leave at this time."

<<>>

The jury returned after their lunch to hear the punishment phase of the trial. Based on evidence presented at the punishment phase, they were to decide whether Cameron Todd Willingham would be sentenced to death or life imprisonment without the possibility of parole.

As his first witness, John Jackson called Stacy Willingham, and declared her to be a hostile witness. Stacy believed in Todd's innocence. It's a mystery why David Martin didn't call her as a defense witness during the guilt-innocence phase of the trial.

"State your name for the record, please, ma'am." >> Stacy June Willingham.

"Who is your husband?" >> Cameron Todd Willingham.

"Is that the same person who's present in this courtroom, the defendant in this capital murder case?" >> Yes.

"How long have you been married to Cameron Todd Willingham?" >>Since October the 1st of 1991.

"So you were married some two months before the children were killed; is that right?" >> Yes.

"Todd Willingham has been violent and abusive to you from the first time you met; is that correct?" >> No.

"Isn't it a fact, Mrs. Willingham, that Todd Willingham tried to kill your babies, even before they were born?" >> No.

"Isn't it a fact, Mrs. Willingham, that he beat you on a regular basis at your house on 11th Avenue, on a regular basis." >> No, he did not.

"Is it not a fact that you sought help at neighbors' houses, and particularly the house of John Bailey, saying that Mr. Willingham had threatened you and the children and you wanted to call the police from his house?" >> No. I went to John Bailey's one time because Todd was in the yard, arguing, and I wanted him to leave and he wouldn't leave, and so I went to John Bailey's to call the cops, because --"

"On that same occasion, were you present when Todd Willingham, your husband, threatened to kill several people?" >> That day there?

"At any time, ma'am." >> No; I wasn't.

"That never happened?" >> Todd has never threatened to kill anybody, in front of me.

"Well, who'd he threatened to kill, not in front of you, then?" >> No one. He's never said anything like that.

"Isn't it a fact that the children, Amber in particular, were afraid of your husband, Cameron Todd Willingham?" >> No.

"You're aware that your husband has tried to blame these events on your children, do you understand that?" >> I understand that, but I heard the statement the guy wrote.

"You understand your husband is guilty of killing your children; do you not, Mrs. Willingham?" >> I understand that's what everyone thinks.

"But you don't think that, do you?" >> No, I don't.

"Can you tell us why you have suffered these years of abuse at his hands and not protected yourself or the children?" >> I have not suffered abuse from him. There was nothing with my kids, either. He's never hurt those kids.

"Well, are you the one who hurt the kids?" >> No, I am not.

"Pass the witness."

<<>>

After the examination of Stacy Willingham, the proceedings only got worse.

Karen King testified that Todd once beat Stacy when she was pregnant with the twins and did so in an effort cause a miscarriage.

Kimberly Lynn King testified that Todd thought a VCR was a good trade for Amber. "Well, it was right after her and Todd got in a fight, and she called us at my mom's house to go over and get her and Amber; and when we got there, Todd was gone and she said that Todd took the VCR and that he said it was an even trade for Amber; that he would take the VCR and she could have Amber and it was an even trade."

Randy Petty testified that Todd once told him he had been cruel to animals. "He said him and Davie stole a dog off a guy and took it out and killed it. He said he beat it in the head with a stick and then run over it with a car." During cross-examination, Petty conceded he raised pit bulls, but denied he raised them as fighting dogs.

Detective Jimmy Hensley of the Corsicana Police department testified that Todd had a bad reputation. He did not further clarify.

Detective Ted Montgomery of the Ardmore, Oklahoma police department testified he had arrested Todd three or four times for delinquency of a minor, residential burglary, and auto theft.

Cooke County Sheriff's Deputy Larry Dennison testified Todd had a bad reputation. He did not further clarify.

Gainesville Police Captain Richard Schlaudroff testified Todd had a bad reputation. He did not further clarify.

Carter County Assistant District Attorney Maria Malowney testified that she had prosecuted Todd a number of times, primarily for misdemeanor offenses related to paint sniffing. She also testified that Todd was charged with feloniously pointing a weapon at two eighteen year olds. "When we ultimately recovered the weapon, it turned out that it was a BB gun."

John Bailey lived across the street from Todd Willingham. He testified that Stacy once came to his house seeking his help because Todd had yelled obscenities and threatened her. He testified further that he once heard Stacy and Todd arguing and during that argument heard Todd say, "Get up bitch, and I'll hit you again."

Navarro County Sheriff's Detective Don Sullivan testified that he was a fingerprint expert. He testified further that he matched fingerprints found on something called a Penitentiary Packet (bearing the name Todd Willingham) with the fingerprints of Todd Willingham.

Licensed Professional Counselor Tim Gregory testified that a hypothetical person perfectly matching the description of Cameron Todd Willingham would be a sociopath. "In my opinion, there is not much chance of any type of rehabilitation at all." He also testified that the hypothetical Todd would "absolutely" be a continuing threat to society. Under cross examination, Gregory testified he had never interviewed Todd, Todd's family members, or anyone associated with Todd. He had, however, gone geese hunting with John Jackson.

Navarro County Criminal District Attorney Patrick Batchelor testified that Todd had once been placed on probation for stealing a car. He also testified that Todd had a bad reputation.

<<>>

For his last witness, John Jackson then pulled out his big gun, figuratively put it to the head of Cameron Todd Willingham, and fired.

Dr. James Grigson is rightfully known as Doctor Death. Dr. Grigson would eventually testify against one-hundred and sixty-seven defendants facing the death sentence. Only a few escaped with their lives. Former Texas Criminal Court of Appeals Judge Marvin Teague summarized Dr. Grigson's effectiveness.

> [W]hen Dr. Grigson testifies at the punishment stage of a capital murder trial ... the defendant should stop what he is then doing and commence writing out his last will and testament because he will in all probability soon be ordered by the trial judge to suffer a premature death.

In other cases, based on little or no examination of the defendant, Dr. Grigson swore under oath that he was able to predict, frequently with 100% certainty and on several occasions with 1000% certainty, that the defendant would pose a future danger to society if allowed to live.

The juries loved him. Not only was he a doctor, he somehow seemed to be one of them. He didn't speak in technical terms, he spoke in terms jurors could understand. He used his stature to reinforce what they already believed they knew.

In one case, Grigson sensed reluctance on the part of a one juror to put a man to death. Knowing that juror was the mother of a fourteen-year-old daughter, he testified that the defendant was the type of man who, if ever released, would rape and kill a fourteen-year-old girl. The jury voted unanimously for death.

Grigson, however, has been proven wrong in each of those few cases where his predictions have been put to the test. In one trial, a savvy defense attorney presented to Dr. Grigson a hypothetical case of a deprived black youth with a record of arrests prior to being imprisoned at age nineteen for a violent offense. "What would be your prognosis?" Dr. Grigson testified that he saw only more of the same ahead for this young man.

It turned out that young man was Ron LeFlore who went on to a distinguished career with the Chicago White Sox. The jury nonetheless voted eleven-to-one for the death penalty.

In the case of Randall Dale Adams, Grigson described Adams as an incurable and extreme sociopath with no regard for the life or property of others, a continuing danger to society. Adams however was exonerated before he was executed, based largely on the documentary *The Thin Blue Line*. Not once during his twelve years of wrongful imprisonment, nor in all the years since, has Adams committed a known act of violence.

In 1995, Grigson was expelled from both the American Psychiatric Association and the Texas Society for Psychiatric Physicians. Those organizations determined that he violated his code of ethics when he diagnosed defendants without having interviewed them, and when he testified with 100% certainty about the future dangerousness of the defendants.

Texas prosecutors nonetheless continued to rely on Dr. Grigson's persuasive powers. In the case of Cameron Todd Willingham, John Jackson used Dr. Grigson as his final witness during his case in chief.

<<>>

"Would you state your name for the record, please, sir?" >> James P. Grigson.

"And, Dr. Grigson, can you tell us what you do?" >> I'm a medical doctor. I specialize in psychiatry. I'm self-employed.

"Can you give us an idea of your experience and education and background insofar as your specialty is concerned?"

At this point, Dr. Grigson provided a long and impressive list of credentials.

"What does your practice basically consist of at this time?" >> I'm ninety-eight to ninety-nine percent in doing forensic or legal psychiatry.

"Do you do this on a regular basis,?" >> Five days a week and sometimes over the weekends, so it's very regular.

"In the course of your practice, do you have occasion to come in contact with persons of abnormal psychology on a regular basis?" >> Every day. Yes, sir.

"We've heard the term in this courtroom 'sociopath' and also 'sociopathic behavior.' Can you describe what that means?" >> Yes, sir. A sociopath is a slang term for antisocial personality disorder. It has previously been called a psychopath, a sociopath. But it means an individual that does not have a conscience. Their only interest is in their own self-gratification and pleasure. They're repeatedly breaking the rules. They con, manipulate, use people. They have disregard for other people's property. And then the more severe form are those individuals that have disregard for other human beings.

"Is that type of behavior often manifested by persons repeatedly committing crime?" >> Yes, sir, it is. That's typical, classical.

"With regard to persons who fit into this category, have you found that there is any substantial hope of rehabilitation of this type of individual?" >> After that individual has gotten past their late adolescence or into young adulthood, if they have been involved in any type of violent behavior, there's nothing that's going to change that. If they have not been involved in violent-type behavior, then maybe ninety-five percent of them at age thirty will go ahead and start conforming to the law. But if there is violence involved in their antisocial behavior, then there is no form of medication or no form of rehabilitation that's going to change or modify their behavior.

"Dr. Grigson, let me pose a hypothetical situation for you; and I'll ask you to listen to this and at the end I'll ask you a question about whether a person who exhibits these characteristics would fall into the category you've described.

"Assume with me a situation where we have an individual who has exhibited antisocial behavior as a juvenile, through paint sniffing and property crimes. He's a person who's manipulated younger children to assist him in criminal activities. As an adult, he's continued to participate in criminal activity, such as theft, substance abuse and assaultive conduct. His relationship with women is marked with violence and abuse. Assume with me that he assaulted his wife or girlfriend when he found out she was pregnant, in an attempt to cause or create a miscarriage of the child. He has made threats of death to others and, continued to engage in antisocial behavior through his young adulthood. He has engaged in violent acts against animals, including beating a dog to death and running over the dog with a car. He has not attempted to rehabilitate himself, although he's been given numerous opportunities. And he, apparently, has an obsession with death and destruction.

"Doctor, do you have an opinion as to what type of individual this hypothetical describes?" >> Well, you're describing the typical extremely severe sociopath.

"Do you have an opinion as to whether an individual who fits this hypothetical could be rehabilitated to any marked extent?" >> No. An individual that's been involved in the type of behavior that you're describing, I mean, we don't have any type of medical treatment. There's no pill; there's nothing that I know of, in the way of rehabilitation, that works with that type of individual.

"The person such as I've described in the hypothetical, in your opinion, would such a person be a continuing threat to society?" >> Oh, absolutely; certainly.

"Pass the witness."

<<>>

David Martin called many friends and family members to testify on Todd's behalf. As his last witnesses, he recalled Stacy Willingham, this time to testify for the defense.

"Stacy, the accusation has been made by a witness that you told them that Todd beat you up when he found out you were pregnant and he tried to make you abort. Is that true?" >> No. Todd went to the doctor with me just about every time I was pregnant with them twins.

"And did the doctor ever tell you that he found some indication of you having been beaten?" >> No.

"How did Todd act when you had the sonogram done?" >> He was excited. He thought one of them was a boy. They were both girls, and he just said, you know, "Well, they'll be just like Amber."

"Was he happy about it?" >> Yes.

"Was he happy when you became pregnant with Amber?" >> Yes.

"And how did he act when the children were born?" >> He was excited. He wasn't there when Amber was born, but he was when the twins were born.

"And was he excited when you brought the babies home?" >> Yes. We both brought the twins home.

"Did he ever give you any indication that he didn't want the children or didn't like them or didn't want them?"" >> No. No.

"Did he ever trade you Amber for a VCR?" >> Do what?

"Kimberly King testified that you told her that Todd, more or less, traded Amber for a VCR and that he said he got the better end of the deal. Do you remember anything like that?" >> No.

"Do you remember ever telling anybody that he had beat you up in an attempt to make you miscarry?" >> No. I didn't.

"And did he have a close relationship with his daughters?" >> Yes, he did.

"And when you worked, did he take care of them?" >> Yes .

"Did he teach Amber how to talk?" >> Yes.

"Did he bathe the children, change their diapers and feed them?" >> Yes. And he also potty-trained Amber, too, for me.

"Were you ever aware of any mistreatment by him toward the children?" >> No.

"And did he name the children?" >> Yes; he named all three of them.

"Witnesses have said that you have told them on numerous occasions that he's beat you. Are you telling us that is not true?" >> Todd had -- no -- I mean, they know we've fought, but I have never said Todd's beat me numerous times. I've never said that.

"John Bailey testified that he heard a fight at your house one night, where he heard someone get hit and Todd say, "Get up, bitch." Do you remember anything like that? Ever happen, to your recollection?" >> No, it -- no, it -- no, it didn't.

"Pass the witness."

<<>>

After the punishment phase testimony, the jury was dismissed until the next morning. They arrived at 9 AM the next day to receive their instructions from the judge and hear the closing arguments of the attorneys.

For reasons I find indefensible, the State is always allowed to speak both first and last during closing arguments. John Jackson chose to use all of his time to have the final words with the jury.

"The state waives its right to open, and we reserve the right to close, Your Honor."

Robert Dunn closed for the defense and did a poor job of it.

"I want you to understand that we have brought this man's family, and we had a host of relatives and families, and they are not the most educated, the most articulate, or the most knowing, but they are the man's family. And if a man's family won't come and stand up for him at a trial, and if a man's family won't speak good for him, who will?"

John Jackson absolved the jurors should they decide to put the defendant to death.

"Cameron Todd Willingham wrote his own sentence when he committed each crime. He wrote his own sentence when he abused his wife, when he tortured a dog, when he tried to kill his children before they were ever born, when he refused every attempt at rehabilitation. He refused -- he refused every single piece of help that was ever proffered to him. And, members of the jury, he wrote his own sentence when he poured that lighter fluid on the floor of the babies' room here in Corsicana, Texas, and he set it ablaze and he killed those children."

Jackson then reminded the jurors of the legal standards for sentencing the defendant to death.

"Members of the jury, the evidence requires that you answer the first question: Do you find from the evidence beyond a reasonable doubt there is a probability that the defendant would commit criminal acts of violence that would constitute a continuing threat to society? The evidence requires, members of the jury, that you answer that question 'yes.'

"The second issue: Do you find, taking into consideration all of the evidence, including the circumstances of the offense, the defendant's character and background and the personal moral culpability of the defendant, there is sufficient mitigating circumstance or circumstances to warrant the sentence of life imprisonment, rather than death be imposed? Members of the jury, there is only one appropriate answer to that question according to the evidence in this case, and that answer is 'no.'"

Jackson then quoted from *Beowulf*, though he identified the text only as being from a bit of ancient verse. He asked that the lessons of *Beowulf* be applied to the defendant.

"As I was preparing for this case, I ran across a bit of ancient verse that describes the anomaly, the aberration of Cameron Todd Willingham. It talks about demons; it talks about monsters. That ancient hand wrote, '*The Almighty hand drove those demons out and they're exiled; they're shut away from men, they're split into a thousand forms of evil. Spirits and themes, monsters, a brood forever opposing the Lord's will and again and again defeated.*'

"I'm asking you to defeat the evil of Cameron Todd Willingham now and forever by your answers to these questions.

"Thank you."

<<>>

The jury retired at 10:15 AM. They returned one-hundred and five minutes later, at 12:05 PM, just five minutes late for lunch.

"Members of the jury panel, have you reached a verdict?" >> Yes, sir.

"Would you pass it to the bailiff?"

"At the time that I read the verdict, I don't want any uproar out of the audience, regardless of what the verdict might be.

"The answer to Special Issue No. 1 is 'yes.' And the answer to Special Issue No.2 is 'no.'

"Mr. Martin and Mr. Dunn, do you all want the panel polled?"

"Yes, sir."

"Members of the jury panel, my question to you is this: Is this your verdict? And I'm going to use last name only."

"Harris?" >> Yes.

"Dunbar?" >> Yes.

"Holmes?" >> Yes.

"Formby?" >> Yes.

"Watson?" >> Yes.

"Cook?" >> Yes.

"Martin?" >> Yes.

"Roper?" >> Yes, sir.

"Dechaume?" >> Yes.

"Holloway?" >> Yes.

"Morse?" >> Yes.

"And Ponder?" >> Yes.

"Members of the jury panel, we appreciate very much you being here with us these few days. I'm going to let you leave at this time. Let me say this to you: The previous instructions given to you with reference to conversation amongst yourselves or with anyone else is no longer of any force or effect. You can talk to anyone you want to or not talk to them. It's your choice.

"And I want everyone to remain in the courtroom until the jury panel is outside. You all may leave at this time.

"Cameron Todd Willingham, you're hereby sentenced to -- to the -- to -- given the death penalty. And you're hereby remanded into the custody of the Navarro County Sheriff, who will deliver you to the Texas Department of Corrections. No date for the sentence to be carried out at this time because it requires an automatic appeal to the Court of Criminal Appeals. And that concludes this hearing.

"And you're remanded into the custody of the Sheriff."

INTERLUDE

A few jurors went on record regarding their reasons for finding Cameron Todd Willingham guilty of murdering his three children. They commented soon after the trial and they commented again in 2009 after the Willingham case came to national attention.

The most frequently recorded of those jurors, Dorenda Dechaume (later Brokofsky) explained that they paid little attention to Johnny Webb. Manuel Vasquez, on the other hand, "was very important." He was not, however, the only factor in their decision. Dechaume explained the jurors were bothered that Willingham simply stood outside and watched the fire burn. "He didn't do anything."

Juror Henry Ponder agreed.

> There was evidence of a fire that was deliberate. Not getting the children out of the house. Getting the car out of the way. It was all there.

Another juror said she would have found him guilty solely because he did not try to save his children.

The jurors noted that Willingham did not take the stand and offered no declarations of innocence. They were unimpressed with the defense theory that Amber spread an accelerant throughout the house then set it on fire. According to juror Dechaume, "none of us could see how that would work."

Dechaume became the most interesting, most frequently quoted of the jurors. She would reveal in one interview that her entire family was "good friends" with Chief Doug Fogg. She said she explained that to both the prosecution and defense prior to her selection as juror, but neither side seemed to care.

She explained that most jurors wanted to give substantially fewer than the seventy-seven minutes they did grant to Willingham.

> A lot of them wanted to vote right away. Me and two other people wanted to go over the facts of the case. It was unfair to go straight in there and decide. We went through everything we could have.

When she was informed that more recent understanding of fire may disprove the conclusions of Douglas Fogg and Manuel Vasquez, she began to doubt her vote.

> Did anybody know about this prior to his execution? Now I will have to live with this for the rest of my life. Maybe this man was innocent.

But she would oscillate between doubt and certainty.

> All you can go on when you are on a jury is what is put before you. I stand by my vote -- guilty.

I don't sleep at night because of a lot of this. I have gone back and forth in my mind trying to think of anything that we missed. I don't like the fact that years later someone is saying maybe we made a mistake. That the facts aren't what they could've been.

They're wanting me to say I can't sleep at night. They want me to say I did wrong. I can't say that.

When you're sitting there with all those facts, there was nothing else we could see. Now I don't know. I can't tell you he's innocent, I can't say 100 percent he's guilty.

All I can go by is what I had seen then.

I've got to stand in front of my God one day and explain what I did.

<<>>

The appellate courts found no legal flaws in the trial of Cameron Todd Willingham. They made no effort to determine whether he may have actually been innocent. It was not their job to do so. That awesome responsibility belonged to the jury.

Regarding Willingham, the Texas Criminal Court of Appeals summarized the evidence against him in a fashion most favorable to the State, as they are legally obliged to do.

> The evidence adduced at trial was that on December 23, 1991, appellant poured a combustible liquid on the floor throughout his home and intentionally set the house on fire, resulting in the death of his three children. Amber, age two, and twins Karmon and Kameron, age one, died of acute carbon monoxide poisoning as a result of smoke inhalation, according to autopsy reports. Neighbors of appellant testified that as the house began smoldering, appellant was "crouched down" in the front yard, and despite the neighbors' pleas, refused to go into the house in any attempt to rescue the children. An expert witness for the State testified that the floors, front threshold, and front concrete porch were burned, which only occurs when an accelerant has been used to purposely burn these areas. This witness further testified that this igniting of the floors and thresholds is typically employed to impede firemen in their rescue attempts.
>
> The testimony at trial demonstrates that appellant neither showed remorse for his actions nor grieved the loss of his three children. Appellant's neighbors testified that when the fire "blew out" the windows, appellant "hollered about his car" and ran to move it away from the fire to avoid its being damaged. A fire fighter also testified that appellant was upset that his dartboard was burned. One of appellant's neighbors testified that the morning following the house fire, Christmas Eve, appellant and his wife were at the burned house going through the debris while playing music and laughing.
>
> At the punishment phase of trial, testimony was presented that appellant has a history of violence. He has been convicted of numerous felonies and misdemeanors, both as an adult and as a juvenile, and attempts at various forms of rehabilitation have proven unsuccessful.

The jury also heard evidence of appellant's character. Witnesses testified that appellant was verbally and physically abusive toward his family, and that at one time he beat his pregnant wife in an effort to cause a miscarriage. A friend of appellant's testified that appellant once bragged about brutally killing a dog. In fact, appellant openly admitted to a fellow inmate that he purposely started this fire to conceal evidence that the children had recently been abused.

Dr. James Grigson testified for the State at punishment. According to his testimony, appellant fits the profile of an extremely severe sociopath whose conduct becomes more violent over time, and who lacks a conscience as to his behavior. Grigson explained that a person with this degree of sociopathy commonly has no regard for other people's property or for other human beings. He expressed his opinion that an individual demonstrating this type of behavior cannot be rehabilitated in any manner, and that such a person certainly poses a continuing threat to society.

<<>>

Unlike the jurors and the appellate courts, David Martin did not wait for the outcome of the trial to decide his client was guilty. He knew from the beginning. Since the case came to national attention in 2009, Martin has not been shy about sharing his belief with print and television audiences. He seems eager to do so.

We hired [a defense expert] and he said 'Yep. It's arson.' It was really very, very clear what happened in the house. Everybody who saw it, of course, reached the same conclusion.

I was in the house. I talked to the cops. I talked to the firemen who were there very first on the scene. I looked at the pictures. When you walk through that house, the children's bedroom was set aflame, obviously, by an accelerant.

God forbid that somebody was executed who was innocent. Nobody wants that to happen. But for somebody so obviously guilty like Willingham, it's a travesty to make it seem like it was something other than what it was.

When asked about juror Dechaume being good friends with prosecution witness Douglas Fogg, David Martin failed to see any potential conflict.

In a small town like Corsicana, lots of people knew Doug Fogg.

Regarding Manuel Vasquez, who died in 1994, David Martin has been considerably more charitable.

Vasquez was one of the most competent experts I ever cross-examined. He was a straight shooter and an honest guy.

Martin turned to lurid prose to describe the loathing he felt for his client.

I never think about [Willingham], but I do think about those year-old babies crawling around in an inferno with their flesh melting off their bodies. I think that he was guilty, that he deserved death and that he got death.

AFTERMATH

LIME STREET

Thursday, March 7, 1991

Firefighters intentionally set fire to the house on Lime Street in Jacksonville, Florida. The house had just been refurbished with carpeting, curtains, and furniture. Nonetheless, one of the firefighters walked into the living room, put a flame to the sofa, and walked out.

The house was soon repaired and the furniture replaced.

Firefighters once again set fire to the house, but not before they spread gasoline around the living room. Twenty thousand dollars went up in flames.

<<>>

Five months earlier, the house next door had burned. The circumstances of that fire at 527 Lime Street were eerily similar to those of the fire that would later take place at 1213 11th Avenue in Corsicana, Texas.

In Jacksonville, a sheriff's officer saw the smoke while he was driving nearby. He rushed to the scene and found Gerald Lewis standing in his yard, screaming that people were still inside. Smoke and flames were pouring from the windows and front door.

Minutes later the fire trucks arrived. One firefighter knocked down the flames on the front porch and entered through the front door. Another entered through the rear door. He saw flames overhead and on the stairway.

Outside Gerald Lewis was screaming. "They're all dead. They're all dead."

Firefighters found one of the dead, a small child, near the top of the stairs. They found two other children nearby. They then found a pregnant woman, then a fourth child in the bedroom, kneeling against a bed burned to its box springs. They located a second adult female victim elsewhere. All were burned beyond recognition.

The dead included Gerald Lewis' wife and her 12-year-old daughter. The other victims included the pregnant sister of Gerald's wife and her three children aged 5, 4, and 2. There were two survivors. Gerald Lewis had managed to save himself and his own three-year-old son.

One witness described Lewis as agitated. Another claimed Lewis was simply standing in front of the house, watching it burn. One noted that Lewis had neither called 911 nor asked anyone else to do so. Instead, they claimed, he simply banged on the door of the long-abandoned house next door.

Lewis told an investigator that he had a few beers and his wife didn't want him in the house when he'd been drinking. She had a restraining order against him for domestic violence, but the order allowed him inside the house with her permission. He was unemployed and she let him sleep in the car. They were scheduled for divorce in three days.

The night of the fire, after having been told to leave the house, he climbed into the car, drank a beer, and went to sleep. He awoke twenty minutes later and saw smoke coming from the living room window.

His wife was trying to retrieve a garden hose to fight the fire. He ran inside. His sister-in-law handed him a pot full of water and he poured it on the sofa. It was the only thing that was burning. His wife and sister went upstairs to get the children.

He tried to follow them upstairs, but the smoke became too intense. The room was getting hotter. His own son was following him up the stairs. He grabbed his son and ran outside.

As he stepped off the porch, he heard a loud whoosh. The entire house erupted in flames. He estimated that it all happened in just three to five minutes.

The investigators suspected arson. Sofas smolder, they don't combust that rapidly. Also, the fire had been aggressive. The broken window glass wasn't coated with smoke as it would have been had the fire burned slowly. The blistering of the wooden floorboards indicated the fire was most intense near the floor.

Most significantly, there were pour patterns in the hallway, evidence of a liquid accelerant. They found a bleach bottle in the car, partially filled with gasoline.

All the evidence pointed to an accelerant enhanced fire.

The investigators concluded that Lewis had taken his son from the house and, while the others were still inside, poured gasoline in the living room and hallway. Then, while standing safely on the porch, he lit the fire.

Gerald Lewis was arrested and charged with one count of arson, one count of manslaughter for the seven-month old fetus, and six counts of first-degree murder. The State planned to seek the death penalty. Lewis was still in the interview room when they informed of the charges. He said simply "I think I need a lawyer." He then laid down across two chairs and went to sleep.

It was not the behavior expected of someone who had just lost people he claimed to care for.

<<>>

Had Gerald Lewis been defended by David Martin and Robert Dunn, it is beyond reasonable doubt he would have been convicted of capital murder and executed. Lewis, however, had the astoundingly good fortune of being defended by Public Defender Pat McGinnis. McGinnis knew a few things about fire.

One thing McGinnis knew was that the fire scene had to be investigated as quickly as possible, that the evidence had to be preserved. It was a weekend and McGinnis' supervisors were out of town. He put the Public Defender's office "on the hook for a few thousand dollars," as he described it, and hired two fire investigators from Tampa to examine the scene.

The investigators found melted pots and pans in the hallway. The kitchen faucet was in the "on" position. Pieces of a melted garden hose were on the porch.

The wood samples taken from inside the house tested negative for accelerants.

The gasoline in the bleach bottle, Lewis explained, was for mowing the yard. There was a pile of freshly cut lawn clippings in the back yard. Comparisons of the gasoline from the bleach bottle and from the lawn mower matched.

Furthermore, claims that Lewis didn't seek help failed to pan out. Lewis said he had jumped in front of a moving car and pleaded with the driver for help. The driver said she was late to work and wouldn't have time to make the call.

The Public Defender's Office, not the police or prosecutor, found that woman. She confirmed that Lewis had jumped in front of her car and she almost hit him. She confirmed that he pleaded with her to call 911.

<<>>

Lucky as Gerald Lewis was to have Pat McGinnis as his attorney, he was even luckier to have Frank Ashton as his prosecutor. Though Ashton still believed Lewis was guilty, he hired fire investigator John Lentini to further examine the evidence.

Lentini agreed that the fire seemed to result from arson. There were, after all, the classic pour patterns in the living room and hallway. And the fire had been so aggressive that the victims had died from smoke inhalation rather than heat and flames. Said Lentini later, "I thought I was going to send Gerald Lewis to get a shot of electricity."

The prosecution team was further bolstered by the addition of arson expert John DeHaan. DeHaan worked for the California Department of Justice, but they were happy to lend DeHaan's expertise.

It was DeHaan that noticed the house right next door was almost identical. It had the same floor plan as the Lewis house. It was apparently built at the same time by the same builder. Better yet, it was scheduled for demolition. DeHaan proposed the prosecution team burn the house to prove the prosecution theory and disprove the defense theory.

Chief Assistant State Attorney John Delaney not only agreed to the test, he authorized $20,000 for its conduct. Given the cost of pursuing a capital murder case to its intended conclusion, the cost was small.

The intentional burning of the house on Lime Street would be one of the first full-scale fire reenactments in history.

<<>>

Everything had to be right. Inmates from the Duval County jail installed new 3/8" sheetrock drywall just like that in the Lewis house. They carpeted with the same type of carpeting, replaced broken windows and covered them with the same type of curtains. They even added the same type of wallpaper.

The prosecution team found a family that had purchased the same model sofa as the one that had burned in the Lewis house. They purchased it from the surprised family. They located a similar coffee table and similar television, and they placed those just as they had been in the Lewis house. They placed bags of clothes in the hallway, because bags of clothes had been in the hallway next door.

While a crew was trying mightily to make the condemned house identical to the one next door, Lentini and DeHaan were working to make sure it was different in critical detail. They installed temperature sensors, carbon monitors, and video cameras to record the critical parameters and behavior of the historic fire soon to be set.

<<>>

Everyone expected the fire to smolder, develop slowly, then possibly reach flashover in fifteen to twenty minutes. Everyone knew that was the way non-accelerated fires behaved. They knew that not because anyone had tested burning sofas. They knew because they had learned from their predecessors, who had learned from their predecessors, who had ...

Rather than smolder, the first of three cushions began to burn quickly when lit. More specifically, the oil-based polyurethane in the cushions began to burn quickly. A wall of black, toxic smoke rose from the sofa. Soon a second cushion caught fire.

A plume of smoke rose and hit the ceiling. It spread outward in a layer of thick, incredibly hot gases. Within three minutes, the gases at the perimeter were being forced down the walls by those still rising to the center of the room from the sofa. As the gas cloud crawled down the wall and approached the floor, its temperature rose to more than eleven hundred degrees Fahrenheit. The black cloud, now glowing red, radiated its energy to every corner of the room.

Suddenly, the entire room exploded.

Flashover.

Every piece of furniture, every curtain, the carpeting, the bags of clothing, anything combustible burst into flames. The windows shattered. The flames raced up the stairs and into the hallway. The fireball caused the hallway to flashover. Fire exploded out the front door and onto the porch.

It happened in just four and a half minutes.

No one had ever before recorded an event such as the one that had just occurred on Lime Street on the 7th of March, 1991.

<<>>

Firefighters raced into the room and extinguished the fire. One of them was overheard to say, "We may have just proved the defendant's case."

Prosecutor Frank Ashton was duly impressed. "There was enormous heat, unbelievable amounts of heat. Everything caught on fire. You saw flames coursing out of that room and up the stairs. Nobody knows whether those folks upstairs had any chance to get out. You just don't know."

Fire experts Lentini and DeHaan were equally impressed. When they examined the room, they found the classic signs of an accelerated fire. There on the floor were what appeared to be pour patterns. There on the walls were multiple V-patterns. Burn trailers connected the rooms. Crazed glass lay on the porch.

The flashover confused everything. It was so hot that the floors ignited, though not a bit of accelerant had been added. Burning bits of material fell to the floor, and those that fell near the walls created the distinctive V-patterns. The explosive nature of the event caused gas and flame to burst through the windows and the door.

And it all happened in under five minutes.

When Lentini and DeHaan examined the temperature and carbon monoxide measurements, they were in for another surprise. The carbon monoxide levels did not increase more rapidly than the temperature, as they had expected. People who were not in the room where flashover occurred would not have necessarily been exposed to high levels of carbon monoxide.

With the first fire, they had tested the defense theory in the case. The results were absolutely consistent with the story Gerald Lewis had told. The characteristics the prosecution team had interpreted as evidence of arson were instead the natural expression of a flashover. The fire experts had been wrong.

<<>>

The second fire was designed to be just like the first, with one exception. This time the firefighters would pour gasoline on the floors. They would use the same amount of gasoline as was missing from the bleach bottle found in the car. For that simple and utterly rational decision, they should apparently be credited with great insight. Sometime later, similar insight would escape their counterparts in Corsicana, Texas.

After the structure was repaired and the furniture was replaced, the house was once again set on fire. This time, though, the firefighter lit the gasoline from the porch. This time, they would test the prosecution theory.

This time, flashover occurred after five minutes. The accelerated fire took a slightly longer to develop than the non-accelerated fire. Other than the time and the gasoline residue, the two fires were essentially identical.

Many long-held beliefs went up in flames.

<<>>

After the Lime Street fire, neither the fire experts nor the prosecutors believed they could in good conscious argue that Gerald Lewis was guilty of arson. Frank Ashton summed it up.

"This was a horrific situation. Six people were dead. And if somebody set a fire intentionally to kill those people, it is a horrible, horrible crime. But on the other hand, if the fire were accidentally set by a child in the house, or somebody else in the house, it is equally horrible to take somebody who is totally innocent and to try them for a crime because there is some circumstantial evidence that they might be guilty, and convict them of it and send them to Death Row."

Frank Aston took substantial heat for his decision, so to speak. The die-hards wanted Lewis tried regardless of the test results. Aston explained to them why he refused to put Lewis before a jury of his peers.

"Most jurors tend to believe [the prosecutor's] case. The defendant has two strikes against him. The police have arrested him and the State Attorney's Office is prosecuting him. So you run a great risk of having an innocent man convicted."

<<>>

Though Deputy State Fire Marshal Manuel Vasquez testified he had never been wrong in any of his fifteen hundred investigations, the Lime Street fire proved otherwise. It did so seventeen months before Manuel Vasquez sealed the fate of Cameron Todd Willingham.

> "The first incendiary indicator is the auto-ventilation. The inconsistency of the fire going out of window and the fire going out of the door. That's inconsistent with fire behavior. That's an indicator that it's a possible incendiary fire."

In the unaccelerated Lime Street fire, several firemen were standing in the hallway breathing fresh air until just fifteen seconds before flashover. They were lucky to survive. The flashover in the living room sent fire upstairs and into the hallway. The fireball in the hallway caused flashover there. The flashovers caused the fire to explode out the front door and windows. In the words of Manuel Vasquez, it auto-ventilated.

> "Also puddle configurations, pour patterns, --"

In the unaccelerated Lime Street fire, the flashover in both the living room and hallway created burn patterns that were visually indistinguishable from pour patterns and puddle configurations. Only by testing for accelerants could the patterns be distinguished as pour patterns rather than flashover patterns.

"-- low char burning, charred floor, --"

In the unaccelerated Lime Street fire, the radiated heat from the flashover was sufficiently intense to cause low burns along the walls and floors, and to char the base of the walls and doorways.

"-- the fire right underneath the bed, --"

In the unaccelerated Lime Street fire, the radiated heat from the flashover was sufficient to ignite the carpet under the sofa. Follow-on laboratory testing prompted by the Lime Street fire showed that burning under beds and furniture is a common effect of flashover.

"Heat rises. So when I found that the floor is hotter than the ceiling, that's backwards, upside down. It shouldn't be like that. The only reason that the floor is hotter is because there was an accelerant".

In the unaccelerated Lime Street fire, the radiated heat from the flashover was sufficient to ignite the floor along with almost every other area and item in the room. To an improperly trained, unskeptical eye, the room might look as if it had burned hotter on the floor than the ceiling.

"The whole bedroom is a point of fire origin. Also the hallway is another area of fire origin. ... And then the examination of the porch, the front of the door is another area of origin. So there were three areas of origin ... Multiple areas of origin indicate that they were intentionally set by human hands.

The unaccelerated Lime Street fire demonstrated that a flashover in one room can trigger a flashover in an adjacent room. Each flashover can leave burn patterns on the floor that are visually indistinguishable from pour patterns and puddle configurations. A fire started at a single source, should it flashover, may exhibit evidence that can be misinterpreted as multiple areas of origin.

"Burn trailers are a burnt path. ... All this area has burn trailers and pour patterns. These are indications that somebody poured something there."

In the unaccelerated Lime Street fire, the flashover created marks on the floor that were visually indistinguishable from trailer marks and pour patterns.

"I noticed right here a burn pattern from the floor in a 45 degree angle going up. That is one of the indicators of the origin of a fire. It's a V-pattern."

In the unaccelerated Lime Street fire, the flashover left multiple V-patterns. V-patterns indicate only that something on the ground caught fire and spread upward along the wall. They do not indicate at what point that area caught fire. The flashover caused multiple areas near the floor to ignite and create V-patterns.

"Because, like I said, the fire leaves the burn patterns. You can't alter the burn patterns. You cannot pollute the fire scene. You can try, but you can't."

The unaccelerated Lime Street fire proved that flashover irrevocably alters the evidence a fire leaves in its wake, making it hard to distinguish arson from an accident. Use of an accelerant can be definitively established only by testing for accelerant residue.

"All I'm doing is looking at the facts, at the evidence. That's all I'm using."

John Lentini now teaches that the rules of thumb used by fire investigators before the Lime Street fire were assumptions, and bad assumptions at that. "It was witchcraft, really."

"It's a set fire. It's an incendiary fire, and consequently is a crime of arson."

John Lentini willingly accepted that he had been wrong. "This was my epiphany. I almost sent a man to die based on theories that were a load of crap."

"The intent was to kill the little girls."

"Cameron Todd Willingham, you're hereby given the death penalty."

"And the fire does not lie. It tells me the truth."

OAKLAND

The Great Basin Desert consists of the high, arid expanse between the Sierra Nevada and Rocky Mountain Ranges. In autumn, air rises from the desert, reaching elevations higher than the surrounding peaks. On occasion, high altitude winds push this mass of dry air westward over the Sierras. There gravity takes over; the air mass plummets down the mountainside and races towards the California coast.

During its descent, the air pressurizes, increases in temperature, and decreases in relative humidity. By the time it reaches the population centers, it is sometimes twenty degrees hotter, uniquely dry, and utterly irritating.

In the south, they are known as the Santa Ana winds. In the north, they are Diablo winds. Raymond Chandler wrote of them in his detective story *Red Wind*.

> It was one of those hot dry Santa Anas that come down through the mountain passes and curl your hair and make your nerves jump and your skin itch. On nights like that every booze party ends in a fight. Meek little wives feel the edge of the carving knife and study their husbands' necks. Anything can happen.

Early in the morning of October 20, 1991, the Diablo winds curled over the top of the Sierras and began their race towards the coast.

<<>>

Unaware what awaited them, twenty-five firefighters were tending to hotspots remaining from a small brushfire in the Oakland-Berkeley hills. Surrounding them, the hills were covered with five years of drought-dry brush and freeze-damaged trees. California is a place of extremes.

Temperatures had been running well into the nineties. Fire conditions were high, but at least the winds had been calm. The firefighters had no particular trouble putting down the most recent brushfire.

The Diablo winds arrived from the northeast. Just a breeze at first, they grew rapidly. Before long, they would swirl and gust to sixty-five miles per hours.

Air that just yesterday had been gently rising from the Great Basin Desert now picked up a single ember from a single hot spot and carried it to a tree nearby. That tree exploded into fire and the Diablo winds spread the seeds of flame far and wide. The resulting firestorm would be the worst in the nation since a fire razed San Francisco after the earthquake in 1906.

Twenty-five people would die. One hundred and fifty would be injured. Nearly 3500 houses and apartments would be destroyed. One and a half billion dollars in property value would go up in smoke.

The fire scene would be one of house after house burned to the ground. Fire investigators have a name for homes so consumed. They call them black holes.

<<>>

It had been only seven months since John Lentini and a few others intentionally set fire to the house on Lime Street. Though Lentini was transformed by the experience, most of his colleagues were not. Some demeaned him for not pursuing the case against Gerald Lewis based on the "pour patterns" alone. Proponents of traditional fire-cause determination complained he would deprive them of their most valuable tools. Since then, Lentini has responded by quoting Max Planck, German physicist and founder of quantum theory.

> "A new scientific truth does not triumph by convincing its opponents and making them see the light, but rather because its opponents eventually die, and a new generation grows up that is familiar with it."

Lentini and others paraphrase the concept more succinctly. "Science advances one funeral at a time."

It wasn't John Lentini's idea to set the Lime Street house ablaze. John DeHaan deserves that credit. Lentini however seems able to recognize a good idea when he hears one. When his wife, Judy, suggested he might want to investigate the Oakland fire scene, he rounded up a small team of like-minded colleagues and set off for the ruins still smoldering in the hills.

During the next four days, John Lentini, David Smith, and Richard Henderson examined fifty of the burned out homes. What they learned might have saved Cameron Todd Willingham.

<<>>

Manuel Vasquez concluded that Cameron Todd Willingham intentionally killed his children.

> "The intent was to kill the little girls."

He based his lethal conclusion on fire scene characteristics he interpreted as evidence of arson.

> "It's a set fire. It's an incendiary fire, and consequently is a crime of arson."

Despite his obligation to remain informed of the latest developments in fire investigation, he was either unaware of or ignored the lessons of the Lime Street fire set intentionally by open-minded prosecutors seventeen months earlier.

> "To my knowledge, everything that I have said is corroborated by evidence."

Manual Vasquez would also be unaware of or would ignore the lessons of the fires that destroyed so many homes and lives in Oakland ten months before his testimony in Corsicana.

"This is the aluminum threshold. Aluminum melts at 1200 degrees normal. Wood fire does not exceed 800 degrees. So to me, when aluminum melts, it shows me that it has had a lot of intense heat. The only thing that can cause that is an accelerant. You know, it makes the fire hotter. It's not normal fire."

Most of the houses destroyed by the Oakland fire became black holes. They were burned to the ground. Some houses, however, died still standing, as had the house on 11th Avenue. The lessons from Oakland are most directly applicable to black hole fires. Much can be learned, however, applicable to partially burned homes, particularly partially burned homes that survived flashover.

The Oakland fires, for example, were unaccelerated fires. No one went from house to house setting matches to accelerants poured in bedrooms and hallways. Yet the fires burned far hotter than the 880 degrees Manuel Vasquez attributed to an unaccelerated fire.

Consider the glass. Some glass softens at temperatures as low as 1,200 $^{\circ}$F. Most glass melts around 1,500 $^{\circ}$F. John Lentini wrote of the glass they found at Oakland. "Glass of all descriptions was found throughout the Oakland fire. Some was crazed, some was melted, some was smoked, some was clear. Some ... even flowed down the hillside."

Manuel Vasquez argued that only an accelerant could create a fire hot enough to melt aluminum, noting correctly that aluminum melts around 1200 $^{\circ}$F. Copper, by comparison, melts near to 2000 $^{\circ}$F. At Oakland, the investigators found melted copper in 84% of the homes they examined.

<<>>

"The significant part about this bed is ... the metal frame ... This indicates that the white part was subjected to intense heat. Metal reacts to heat. You don't burn metal, but it leaves the mark there. That's intense heat right there. And there was more intense heat on this side than on this side of the bed."

Manuel Vasquez argued that the oxidized metal bed frame was evidence of intense heat. With respect to that specific point, he was correct. Lentini wrote of the oxidized metal they found at Oakland. "What we learned was that, while [steel] may give the appearance of melting, it may be only heavily oxidized."

However, when Manuel Vasquez extended his argument to suggest that oxidized metal is evidence of an accelerated fire, he was wrong. John Lentini wrote of the frequency they found fire damaged metal in the unaccelerated fires they investigated. 'To our surprise, [apparently] melted steel was identified in 98% of the structures examined."

<<>>

The springs were on the floor, just completely burned. This one right here had a spring in it, and we turned the spring over and what did I find? The springs were burned from underneath. This indicates there was a fire under this bed because of the burn underneath that bed.

From the Oakland fire, John Lentini and the others learned that an investigator should be careful about drawing conclusions based on the location of burn patterns on bedsprings. "We noted during our inspection that the apparent melting of bedsprings occurred randomly, in lines, circles, on corners, and in the middle of the springs. Thus, a 'pattern' of apparent melting was found to have no particular significance."

<<>>

Multiple areas of origin indicate that they were intentionally set by human hands.

One the most powerful arguments made by Manuel Vasquez was that he found multiple indicators of arson. So compelling was this argument, the defense never proposed an alternate scenario involving a single point of origin. The defense never argued that an innocent child playing with a match, a cigarette lighter, or a space heater could unintentionally burn down a house. Instead the defense posited an alternate scenario absurd on its face, that a two-year-old girl wandered from room to room, spreading lamp oil in three separate locations, and then lit the three locations on fire.

In this regard, the lesson from the Oakland fire is unambiguous. "In the Oakland fires, we found multiple 'indicators' in the majority of the scenes."

<<>>

The Lime Street and Oakland fires did not simply prove Manuel Vasquez to be wrong. They proved him to be spectacularly and lethally wrong. Most distressingly, they provided the proof well before he testified. Had Manuel Vasquez kept current with the most recent developments in fire science, and had Manuel Vasquez been willing to admit error, Cameron Todd Willingham would never have been brought to trial.

HURST

"I started looking, and what I found is that there are, for all practical purposes, an infinite number of bad arson cases. A whole lot of people are in prison using the same kind of baloney as in the Willingham case." -
- Gerald Hurst

At first glance, Gerald Hurst doesn't look like our country's most distinguished fire investigator. He long ago grew tired of his clothes being stained black from his fire experiments and investigations. With his unique flair for problem solving, he began wearing all black. His shoes and socks are black, naturally. His shirt is black. Even the suspenders that hold up his black sweat pants are black.

His beyond-shoulder-length hair is black, at least it used to be. Now it's closer to the gray of his beard. It's combed back in a no-muss, no-fuss style.

When coupled with his substantial height, his dark and wild presence is hard to ignore.

He works pro bono. Few could afford to pay him what he's worth. He's not in need of the money in any case. He is a gifted man who has benefited handsomely from some clever ideas. He invented a safe-to-transport explosive more powerful than dynamite, and fireworks that won't explode during manufacturing. He holds the patent for the modern formulation of Liquid Paper. He even invented the Mylar balloon.

For those of you frustrated that Mylar balloons deflate too quickly, Hurst has an explanation.

"If you're careful in the manufacturing, a balloon could stay inflated essentially forever. Manufacturers today don't want that much longevity, if you know what I mean. A month is good for them so people will buy another balloon."

He keeps a Minnie Mouse balloon in his basement office to prove his point. Minnie has remained well-inflated there for more than twenty-five years.

<<>>

"He's a genius and an angel. I thought I'd be in prison for the rest of my life." -- Sonia Cacy

According to The People of Texas, Sonia Cacy moved in with her seventy-six-year-old Uncle Bill Richardson to torment him and eventually kill him. She intended to inherit his oil lease royalties and his property in Carlsbad, New Mexico.

Prior to her arrival, Uncle Bill's life had been trouble free. Afterwards, small fires mysteriously sprang up. On three occasions since her arrival, the fire department responded to put out the fires. These fires, Texas explained, were test fires set by Sonia to determine the fire department's response time.

On November 10, 1991, Cacy put her plan into action. After dressing herself in a short nightgown to distract those who might attempt to save her uncle, and after fortifying herself with drink, she tip-toed to her sleeping victim, poured gasoline on him, and set him ablaze. She didn't anticipate the fireball would race to the ceiling, bounce off, singe her hair and cover her with soot.

Having previously measured the firefighters' response time, she arranged to be climbing out the window just as they arrived. She was not satisfied, however, with the passive (but not inconsequential) distraction of her skimpy night clothes. She actively impeded efforts to fight the fire. She was verbally abusive and one of the firefighters was forced to restrain her.

Sonia Cacy did not, however, anticipate the capability and professionalism of the Bexar County labs. The technicians there would find gasoline in Uncle Bill's clothes. That direct evidence of arson would make sense of the more extensive, more bizarre evidence.

The state's case was compelling. The defense case was not. Cacy's court appointed attorney called no expert witnesses to challenge the State's medical and forensic findings, and he would flounder when he cross-examined the State's witnesses. Nonetheless, he would bill the court $15,000 for services rendered. As is frequently they case, the court would pay him less than half. The court paid him $6,900.

After a five-day trial, the jury returned with a guilty verdict. They deliberated for only two hours. According to one of them: "One of Cacy's biggest handicaps was not being able to bring experts to her defense. The state presented more people who could explain what happened. Their expert witnesses were very persuasive, particularly in interpreting the forensic evidence."

Sonia Cacy was sentenced to 55 years.

In 1995, things were looking somewhat brighter. She had been granted a new sentencing hearing, and Gerald Hurst had became involved at the request of her new attorney. "I've never seen such bad work," he would later say of the state's forensic work. "It was primitive."

Despite his testimony at the new sentencing trial, the jurors increased rather than decreased Cacy's sentence. Instead of 55 years, Sonia Cacy was to spend 99 years in prison.

Over the next three years, Hurst would round up a team of two dozen fire and medical experts, all of whom worked for free. He would visit the still-boarded fire scene. Most significantly, he would examine the lab tests himself.

Hurst is well qualified to review lab results such as those used to imprison Sonia Cacy. He holds a doctorate in chemistry from Cambridge University.

Before his advocacy for the wrongfully accused and convicted, he worked as a chief scientist for an explosives company.

When he was done with his review, he prepared a 34 page summary for the Texas Board of Pardons and Paroles. Regarding the forensic test results from the Cacy trial, he wrote:

> I personally reviewed the prosecution's gas chromatograms ... and noted that they showed only the numerous hydrocarbon compounds that are produced by the thermal decomposition (pyrolysis) of synthetic materials common to fire scenes in general and the Richardson house in particular. In order to verify my conclusions I later forwarded copies of these chromatograms to numerous leading specialists in fire debris analysis.

> The original data print-outs have been reinterpreted by a large number of the most reputable analysts in the United States, Canada and Australia. The experts are unanimous in their opinion that the chromatograms relied on for the analysis do not show the presence of gasoline or any other class II accelerant. Included among these experts are Dr. Richard Henderson of Southeastern Research Labs, who teaches arson debris analysis at the FBI, Dr. Wolfgang Bertsch, who teaches the subject at the University of Alabama, John Lynch of Atomus, Brian Dixon of the Canadian Forensic Science Center in Toronto, Tony Cafe of T.C. Forensic, an arson debris laboratory in Australia and Andy Armstrong of Annstrong Forensic Labs in Dallas.

> In addition, the opinion of the preceding experts has been confirmed independently by numerous experts chosen by the Wall Street Journal and separately by ABC News. I know of no case in the history of arson debris analysis which has undergone the extensive scrutiny of evidence applied to this single sample.

If accepted as correct, that one segment of Hurst's report by itself would destroy the State's case. If Sonia Cacy did not douse her Uncle Bill with gasoline, then she is innocent. Hurst, however, did not stop with the cause of the fire. He challenged the cause of death as well.

He noted that, according to the autopsy, Uncle Bill's airways were not filled with soot. He noted also a carbon monoxide level of only 11 percent. That is consistent with a heavy smoker, and Uncle Bill was certainly a heavy smoker. By comparison, the two dogs that died in the fire had carbon monoxide levels of 40 and 60 percent.

Hurst noted finally that the autopsy revealed narrowing and hardening of the arteries. The left descending artery was eighty percent blocked. Of that he wrote:

Three respected forensic medical examiners. Dr. R. K. Wright of the University of Miami Medical School, Dr. Scott Denton, Deputy Medical examiner of Cook County, Illinois and Dr. Ed Friedlander of the American Health University in Kansas City, have studied the work of Dr. Bux and they all concur that the autopsy evidence indicates that the decedent died of a heart attack, probably while fighting the accidental fire he had started, and his body was burned after death. This scenario is completely incompatible with the prosecution theory that the death occurred as a result of being ignited while asleep. The three medical examiner reports speak for themselves. However, even a layman can understand that the absence of soot in the lungs and trachea of the decedent is a strong indicator that he was not breathing while being burned.

Uncle Bill, as it turned out, had a penchant for starting fires. Coupled with his heaving smoking, his seventy-six years and resulting dementia, Uncle Bill's firebug behavior was a probable cause of the fire that killed him. It was also the probable cause for the three previous fires that prompted responses from the fire department, and at least six others that occurred before Cacy ever arrived to care for him. Even before Cacy arrived, Uncle Bill had been hospitalized as a result of heating a spray paint can over an open flame burner. He had intentionally burned an old house on his oil lease. He had set fire to the seat of his pickup. He had cigarette burns on nearly all his bedding, clothing, and furniture.

Hurst spent pages blasting the State of Texas for its pathetic and inexcusable misunderstanding of fire behavior. He described the state's theory that a fireball erupted and covered Sonia with soot to be no more scientific than a scene from a Saturday morning cartoon:

This allegation is based on junk science or Saturday morning cartoon scenes. Freshly poured gasoline in cool weather does not produce a fireball. Furthermore, the flames of a gasoline fire will not cover one in soot. Experimental verification of this principle is a simple task. Waving the hands over a gasoline fire, without severely burning them, does not deposit visible soot. Except in cases of prolonged exposure to smoke, soot on a person's body comes from contact with walls or floors at a fire scene or through contact with someone who has touched, sooty surfaces.

Regarding the bouncing fireball, he wrote:

Fireballs do not bounce or 'come back down.' The flames from gasoline in a room form a thin jet which spreads across the ceiling in a layer which slowly increases in thickness with time. Sonia's singed hair was a result of her attempt to go over Officer Kurtis when he was entering the house on hands and knees. Kurtis observed flames coming out of the upper area of the doorway. It is a common occurrence for people to singe their hair on attempting to enter a room in which fire is present. Hair singeing under the same circumstances of trying to enter a flaming room also occurred in my most recent case and similar scenarios are well-documented in numerous other cases.

It turns out that Sonia was attempting to re-enter the house when the fire department arrived. She was not exiting in a timely effort to distract them. And while she did struggle with the firefighters, it was because they refused to enter the house to save her uncle, and she wanted to go back in. They physically restrained her.

> The allegation is true. Sonia did try to save her uncle and she did curse the police for restraining her. However, Sonia's actions were not improper under the circumstances. The police and firemen made no attempt to rescue Uncle Bill, although they only surmised that he was dead. Instead of bringing the old man out, they treated the fire area as a crime scene from the moment of arrival and concentrated on preserving evidence rather than saving a life.

Hurst also addressed the common claim that a fire burns hot and fast only as a result of an accelerant:

> The prosecution's heavy emphasis on the supposed fast, hot, smoky nature of the fire was based on the report of Steve Kenley, a part-time fire investigator [and] rancher. ... Kenley's analysis is incorrect. It is based on what fire investigators refer to as "old wives tales." These myths are a form of junk science principles which have been thoroughly disproved by more recent research. A mattress or piece of padded furniture in a room can, on ignition, create such rapid flaming that the room will come to flashover conditions within three minutes. That is, the room can become so hot without any accelerant that every surface therein will burst into flame simultaneously. There was no flashover in the Richardson house because of the high level of ventilation.

In the conclusion to his 34-page take down of the state's case, Hurst wrote:

> I conclude that Sonia Cacy was convicted as a result of unrebutted junk science. Had she been provided with reasonably competent counsel and a bare minimum of competent expert help in the areas of fire investigation, fire debris analysis and pathology, all of the supposed scientific evidence used against her could have been exposed as worthless to the jury. This was a case based mainly on esoteric but misapplied science which was beyond the ability of the attorneys and jury to understand without guidance from suitable defense experts.

<<>>

The Texas Board of Paroles and Pardons is not noted for being soft on crime. There is little evidence they take kindly to people they believe to be ruthless, scheming, cold-blooded murderers.

The Texas Board of Paroles and Pardons, however, pardoned Sonia Cacy after she had served just 5 years of her 99 year sentence. According to Cacy's appellate attorney: "While technically, the parole board did not consider her guilt or innocence, I've got to believe they were swayed by the fact 20 experts came forward to offer their services pro bono."

According to Gerald Hurst: "They kept telling us, 'We don't listen to that kind of stuff.' But they did listen."

<<>>

Patricia Ann Cox is Cameron Todd Willingham's cousin. She learned of Gerald Hurst from television, as had so many of the people he helped. After an unexplained delay of nearly a year and a half, she finally reached him by phone not long before the scheduled execution. Gerald Hurst spent more than three years working to free Sonia Cacy. He would have two weeks to save the life of Cameron Todd Willingham.

His report was five pages long. The first page described the fire scene. The last page included little more than the date and his signature. The substance of the report was three pages long, less than a tenth that of his successful Cacy summary.

With respect to Manuel Vasquez' reliance on so-called trailers, pour patterns, and puddle configurations, Hurst did not fault Vasquez. Instead he acknowledged that Vasquez' interpretation of the patterns, while wrong, was consistent with the standards at that time.

> A decade ago, fire investigators would often look at a flash-over fire scene and note various burn patterns of varying degree which appeared to be shaped like irregular pours of liquid. It was fairly common practice for the investigator to cite these patterns as proof of the use of an accelerant. With the advent of NFPA 921, it became more and more widely realized that post-flashover burning in a room or hallway produces floor burn patterns which cannot be differentiated from burns imagined to be caused by liquid accelerants. Full scale testing ... showed that post-flashover burning, even of relatively short duration, makes it impossible to identify accelerant burns visually. Thus it becomes impossible to visually identify accelerant patterns under these conditions. The subject fire included post-flashover burning of considerable duration as evidence by the hallmark of flashover, flames pouring from windows and doors.

With respect to Vasquez' claims that he had discovered multiple points of origin, Hurst was less charitable:

> The Fire Marshall reported multiple fire origins. Actual multiple fire origins create a powerful case for arson. However, multiple origins can only be demonstrated when two or more areas of fire are completely isolated from one another. In this post-flashover fire, all the burn areas were clearly contiguous in the sense that they were at least joined by obvious radiation and/or conduction mechanisms. The finding of multiple origins was inappropriate even in the context of the state of the art in 1991.

Hurst was unimpressed regarding Vasquez' interpretation of V-patterns:

> Contrary to the Fire Marshal's report, V-patterns are only sometimes indicators of the point of origin of a fire and only rarely indicators of the use of a liquid accelerant. If a fire is snuffed out before flashover, a V-pattern ... may suggest that the object below the V started the fire. However, once a fire passes the flashover stage, original patterns often become overwhelmed and new V-patterns will form from the burning of such common items as wooden door frames, combustible objects on the floor, etc.

Hurst was particularly dismissive of Vasquez' interpretation of the front door threshold.

The fire Marshal alleged that the charring of wood under the aluminum threshold was caused by liquid accelerant burning under the threshold. The phenomenon is clearly impossible. Liquid accelerants can no more burn under an aluminum threshold than can grease burn in a skillet even with a loose-fitting lid. The charring of wood under a threshold is a common occurrence in post-flashover fires. The thermal radiation at doorways is extremely high because of the turbulent mixing of hot, fuel-rich gases with incoming fresh air. This radiation is often high enough to melt the threshold (660 degrees C).

Regarding the brown rings on porch, he wrote:

The identification of the presence of an accelerant based on brown rings on a cement floor is baseless speculation. A great deal of brown rust and soluble iron salts is created at fire scenes. When the puddles of fire hose water evaporate they often leave brown material trapped in the surface pores of the cement. The presence of an accelerant can only be established by chromatographic analysis in the laboratory.

Rather than conclude his report with a conclusion or a recommendation, Hurst finished his report abruptly after discussing the reason why lighter fluid was found in the wood portion of the front door threshold:

The fire Marshal reported that kerosence was found in a single sample of wood taken from bottom the doorway adjacent to the cement porch. ... A burned can of charcoal lighter was also found on the same concrete floor. ... Therefore, the presence of this material is an expected occurrence in the wake of the fire. Fire from the can would be dispersed an [sic] floated across the concrete by the action of the concrete [sic] by the action of the immiscible water from the fire hoses.

With that jumbled last sentence, Hurst completed the body of his report. Obviously rushed for time, he would add no conclusion. He dated his report "the 13 day of February 2004." There were only four days left. He signed it and turned it over to Willingham's appellate attorney, who then faxed it to Governor Perry.

PERRY

James Richard "Rick" Perry became Governor of Texas on December 21, 2000 when George Bush resigned to become President of the United States. From that date through mid-October 2010, Rick Perry watched over 224 executions.

The first of those executions took place within three weeks of Perry's inauguration. Jack Wade Clark was executed on January 9, 2001 for rape and murder. Clark used his final words to apologize for his crime.

> First, I would like to say to the family that I am sorry, and I do ask for forgiveness. There will be also a funeral mass at St. Thomas and I would like to invite all of those from the State and the family to be there if they would like to come. My last words will be: And He was the light that shineth in the hearts of all man from the foundations of the world. If we confess our sins He is just and true to forgive us of our sins and cleanse us from all unrighteousness. Peace and goodness.

Clark was pronounced dead at 6:27 PM. He became #240, the 240th person executed by Texas since the death penalty was reinstated in 1976.

Approximately one-third of the 224 people executed so far during Rick Perry's watch, 83 by my count, would do as Jack Clark. They would admit their sin, apologize for their crime, or beg forgiveness.

The second person executed under Perry's watch was Alvin Uriah Goodwin III. Goodwin killed an acquaintance during a chump-change robbery. Goodwin merely said "Goodbye" in Irish.

Half of the 224 people executed so far during Rick Perry's watch, 113 by my count, would do as Alvin Goodwin. They would neither confess their crime nor declare their innocence. Some would say nothing, some would avoid speaking of the crime, and some would be intentionally ambiguous.

The first person executed who might be problematic for Perry is #250, Mack Oran Hill. Hill was executed for murdering a business associate. He used his final words to declare his innocence.

> First, I would like to tell my family that I love them. I will be waiting on them. I am fine. I hope that everyone gets some closure from this. I am innocent. Lubbock County officials believe I am guilty. I am not. Travis Ware has the burden on him to prove that he did not commit felonies. He needs to be stopped or he is going to do it time and time again. The power is invested in you as a public official to do your job. That's all Warden. I love y'all.

The State of Texas had no physical or forensic evidence to tie Mack Hill to the murder. They relied instead on the testimony of multiple witnesses facing their own legal problems. At least three of those witnesses later claimed they had been offered sweet deals by the prosecutor for testifying against Hill and keeping quiet about it.

Whether Rick Perry recognized it or not, the three rogue witnesses posed him a serious conundrum. If their trial testimony was truthful beyond a reasonable doubt, why should their post-conviction claims not be accepted with equal certainty? Alternatively, if all three witnesses lied post-conviction about the illicit deal making, why should they be believed regarding their pre-conviction testimony about Mack Hill's guilt?

Perry's problem was compounded by the historic responsibility assigned to governors to insure that anyone executed is in fact guilty. The U.S. Supreme Court reinforced the importance of that executive duty when it refused to adopt it as its own. In *Herrera v. Collins*, Chief Justice Rehnquist wrote:

> Clemency is deeply rooted in our Anglo American tradition of law, and is the historic remedy for preventing miscarriages of justice where judicial process has been exhausted...

> Executive clemency has provided the "fail safe" in our criminal justice system. It is an unalterable fact that our judicial system, like the human beings who administer it, is fallible. But history is replete with examples of wrongfully convicted persons who have been pardoned in the wake of after discovered evidence establishing their innocence ... Recent authority confirms that over the past century clemency has been exercised frequently in capital cases in which demonstrations of "actual innocence" have been made...

> History shows that the traditional remedy for claims of innocence based on new evidence, discovered too late in the day to file a new trial motion, has been executive clemency.

So uncertain was Ohio Governor George Ryan of his ability to fulfill his "fail safe" responsibility, he put a moratorium on all executions until he could be confident that innocent people would not be executed. Governor Ryan did so more than a year before Governor Perry did nothing to stop the execution of Mack Oran Hill.

Perry, as had his predecessor, managed his conundrum via willful ignorance. That willful ignorance is epitomized by the summary prepared by his attorney general before each execution. The summary for Mack Hill begins:

> Texas Attorney General John Cornyn offers the following information on Mack Oran Hill, who is scheduled to be executed after 6 p.m. on Wednesday, June 6, 2001. Hill was convicted of the capital murder of Donald Johnson on July 7, 1989, in Lubbock, Texas. A summary of the evidence presented at trial follows.

After this introduction, the two-page summary consisted of three sections. The first section summarized the crime as presented by the State. Almost no eyewitness evidence was mentioned to bolster the State's case. No physical or forensic evidence was mentioned whatsoever. No exculpatory evidence is to be found anywhere within the document.

The second section listed Hill's appellate history. Obviously, all appeals had failed. The list, however, provided comfort that other people had considered the case already. The list would be invaluable to anyone wishing only to rubber-stamp the decisions that had brought Mack Hill to within six days of his death. Nowhere in the appellate history, however, was it mentioned that the appeals were based in large measure on prosecutors purchasing testimony.

The third section discussed Hill's prior criminal history, typically as brought forth during the penalty phase of the trial. The history is not limited to crimes proven by the state. Any negative assertion, if made under oath, is included. No mitigating claims are mentioned. Nowhere did John Cornyn mention that Texas once again relied on James Grigson, Dr. Death, to convince the jury that Mack Hill would be an ever-present threat to society he was unless executed.

The summary was apparently sufficient for Rick Perry. He ordered no stay of execution. He did not appeal to his appointees on the Texas Board of Pardons and Paroles to consider the case carefully. He did not ask his Attorney General to investigate the witness tampering allegations. He did not apparently ask even for a more balanced summary to fulfill his "fail safe" duty.

<<>>

Vincent Edward Cooks was #256. Rick Perry had been Governor slightly less than one year and it was time to perform his "fail safe" duty for the seventeenth time. Cooks was convicted of killing an off-duty police officer during a substantial money transfer operation. There were many witnesses to the crime. The police took twenty of them to the station.

Only one witness identified Cooks from a photo lineup, but that witness then failed to identify Cooks during the live lineup. Only one witness managed to identify Cooks at the live lineup, but that witness had already failed to identify Cooks from the photo lineup. Cooks was the only person who appeared in both the photo and live lineups. That's a known source of error. The witness had initially described the shooter as being 5'10" tall and weighing between 210 and 220 pounds. Cooks was 6'3" tall and weighed 260.

The person who got the best look at the shooter, who actually wrestled with the shooter for the money bag, initially described the shooter as being 5'7" tall and weighing 180 pounds.

Though Cooks was 5 to 8 inches taller and 40 to 80 pounds heavier than the shooter, these two witnesses and an admitted accomplice formed the core of the State's case. Rather than face a capital murder charge, the admitted accomplice struck a deal for twenty years in exchange for his cooperation.

Though the shooter did not reportedly wear gloves, his fingerprints were not found on the murder weapon, the money, the money bag, or the getaway car. Cooks' fingerprints, however, were found on a second car not far from the crime scene.

Shortly before his execution, Cooks' attorney requested DNA testing of a baseball cap preserved as evidence. The witnesses positively identified the cap as having been worn by the shooter. Recent improvements in DNA testing could provide substantial insight into Cooks guilt or innocence. The court failed to rule on the request before Cooks was executed.

The summary prepared by Rick Perry's Attorney General, John Cornyn, failed to mention even one piece of physical, forensic, or witness testimonial evidence tying Cooks to the crime. Cornyn certainly did not mention the failure of most witnesses to identify Cooks, the questionable reliability of the few who did, or the lack of fingerprints. When listing the appellate history, Cornyn did not mention the potentially probative DNA.

Vincent Edward Cooks was executed on schedule on December 12, 2001. He used his final words to proclaim his innocence for one last time, as would 27 others executed so far under Rick Perry's watch.

> Tell my family I love y'all. Watch out for Momma. Don't want to talk too much, I will cry. I'll just cry everywhere. I'm sorry, Teach, for not being a better son and not doing better things. It wasn't your fault. You raised me the way you should. At least I won't be there no more. I miss you, too. I see you there, you doing alright? I sent you a letter. Neckbone, there's a sheet, I got your name on it. Keep on writing, now. ... Charles, keep the right, now. You people over there. You know what these people are doing. By them executing me ain't doing nothing right. I don't weigh 180 pounds and 5'7". Take care, love y'all. Did Roger come up here yet? Tell Pat and them I love them. I'm gonna go ahead and let them do what they're gonna do. Help your sister, see ya later Pat, love ya Becca. Do what you do, Warden.

<<>>

Kia Levoy Johnson would become #305 at 6:18 PM on June 11, 2003. He was the 65th person executed during Rick Perry's 903 days in office. Under Perry's watch, Texas was putting them down at the rate of one every other week. The sheer number of executions would pose a challenge to any governor taking his "fail safe" obligation seriously.

Perry's new Attorney General, Greg Abbott, provided the following description of the crime and the evidence against Johnson.

> In the early morning hours of Oct. 29, 1993, Kia Levoy Johnson entered a Stop 'N Go convenience store and approached the counter. When store clerk William Matthew Rains came to the counter, Johnson pulled a gun from his waistband and fired one shot. Rains fell on the floor. Johnson then demanded that Rains give him the register key. Rains threw a key to Johnson who attempted to use it to open the cash register. When the key broke, Johnson took the contents portion of the register and exited the store. For approximately 45 minutes after the robbery Rains attempted

to reach a phone but was unable to do so because he had lost his motor skills. Rains' body was discovered in the early morning hours of Oct. 29, 1993, when another customer entered the Stop 'N Go.

The details of the offense were captured on a store security camera. When the local news broadcast the video, a longtime friend identified Johnson and called Crime Stoppers. An officer of the San Antonio Police Department and another of Johnson's acquaintances also recognized Johnson from the videotape. The videotape was admitted into evidence and played for the jury.

Abbott's summary of the three people who recognized Johnson on the video is at odds with most other reports. The witnesses are more frequently described as the uncle of Johnson's common law wife (who admitted his loathing for Johnson while on the stand), a drug addict who had not seen Johnson in fifteen years, and a jailhouse snitch who had previously testified for Texas for reduced sentences.

Apparently, the uncle must have been a San Antonio Police officer, though not involved in the case in any official capacity. Apparently Abbott chose to describe a drug addict that Johnson had not seen for fifteen years as "a longtime friend." And apparently Abbott chose to describe a serial jailhouse snitch as an "acquaintance."

Abbott's summary does not mention that the FBI was unable to match Johnson's photo with the person on the videotape. Nor does the summary mention that the video showed the shooter placing his hands on the counter. None of the prints from that counter matched Johnson's.

Kia Levoy Johnson went to his death quietly, saying only: "Tell Mama I love her and tell the kids I love them, too. I'll see you all."

<<>>

The United States Supreme Court imposed a de facto moratorium on capital punishment in 1973, and effectively lifted that moratorium in 1976. This marked the beginning of the "modern day" death penalty in the United States.

From 1976 to mid-October 2010, 1230 people were executed in the United States. Nearly 40% of those, 463 to be precise, were injected with lethal chemicals while strapped to a gurney in Texas.

From 1976 to mid-October 2010, seventeen people who had been on death row were exonerated by DNA evidence. All but one of those exonerations were in states other than Texas.

Texas vigorously resists post-conviction DNA testing, as they did in the case of Vincent Edwards Cooks and as they are doing now in the case of Henry "Hank" Watkins Skinner. As a result, only one person has ever been freed from Texas' death row by DNA test results. That person is Michael Blair, now serving a life sentence for vile crimes he actually did commit.

DNA cases, however, are relatively infrequent. Typically no DNA is left behind at a crime scene to tell a tale. DNA statistics, therefore, seriously understate the magnitude of the wrongful conviction problem.

From 1976 to November 3, 2009, all states other than Texas executed 733 people. They also exonerated from death row 122 others. Those 122 exonerees represent 14% of all those who exited death row either on a gurney or walking free.

Since the death penalty was re-instituted in 1976, Texas has executed 463 people and exonerated only 11. That's slightly greater than 2%.

Assuming Texas juries are equally likely to wrongfully convict an innocent person of capital murder as are juries spread across the rest of the county, Texas should have exonerated 66 people. Instead, Texas exonerated only 11. If the jury-accuracy assumption is correct and the math is sound, Texas has wrongfully executed 55 people.

Under Rick Perry's watch, Texas has executed 224 people and exonerated just 4. That's slightly less than 2%.

Assuming Texas juries are equally likely to wrongfully convict an innocent person of capital murder as are juries spread across the rest of the country, Texas should have exonerated 32 people under Perry's watch. Texas has exonerated only 4. If the jury-accuracy assumption is correct and the math is sound, 28 innocent people have been wrongfully executed under Perry's watch.

Perhaps it is simply an amazing coincidence that of all 224 people executed under Perry's watch, 28 used their final words to proclaim their innocence.

<<>>

Ernest Willis was the first of the four people exonerated under Rick Perry's watch. His alleged crime took place in 1986 in the small town of Iraan, named after Ira and Ann Yates. According to Willis, he awoke near four in the morning to find his house on fire. Fully clothed except for his boots, he ran to the rear bedroom to awaken the woman who had passed out there just a few hours earlier. The flames drove him back.

He ran to the front bedroom to alert his cousin and the woman he was with, but the flames drove him back. After saving himself, he ran around the outside of the house banging on windows and yelling "Fire!" His cousin dove naked through a bedroom window. The two women, recent acquaintances, died inside.

The police quickly grew suspicious of Willis. He didn't act right. He wasn't coughing. He seemed unconcerned about the victims. His hair and clothes weren't burned. His feet weren't burned even though he claimed to have run through a burning house. Investigators found pour patterns in the house, though no trace of gasoline or other accelerant were found. He failed a polygraph test. It was a slam dunk case of capital murder.

While the appellate courts found no flaws with the Willingham trial, they did find one with the Willis trial. It seems the State had pumped Willis full of two anti-psychotic medicines, Haldol and Perphenazine, though Willis was "always quiet", "never any problem", and definitely not psychotic. According to one doctor who testified at a hearing to reopen the Willis case, the standard dosage of Haldol for a person "barking at the moon" is fifteen milligrams per day. They gave Willis forty milligrams per day, in addition to an undetermined amount of Perphenazine.

The prosecutors claimed they knew nothing of the doping, though they used Willis' dopey demeanor against him. The called him "vicious", an "animal" and a "satanic being." They spoke of his "deadpan, insensitive, expressionless face" and his "cold fish eyes," those "weird eyes," that would "pop open like in some science-fiction horror film."

After Willis experienced the normal disappointments in the appellate system, one court finally felt that drugging a defendant out of his skull went beyond the bounds even for Texas. Willis was granted a new trial.

Rather than retry Willis immediately, the new prosecutor contacted two fire science experts to review the evidence. One of those experts was Gerald Hurst. In summary of his investigation, Hurst wrote: "There is not a single item of physical evidence in this case which supports a finding of arson."

On October 6, 2004, Ernest Willis became the first of the four people to be exonerated from death row under Rick Perry's watch.

<<>>

Exonerations result not because of our judicial system, but in spite of it. Ernest Willis would clearly have been executed if he had not eventually been represented by the international law firm of Latham and Watkins. That law firm worked on the Willis case pro bono for nine years, through multiple appeals, before winning a new trial. During that nine-year stretch, they used five lawyers, a private investigator, a professor of psychology, a neuropharmacologist, and several fire experts.

The cost of a defense such as Willis received is measured in millions, and is not funded by any State. No prisoner on death row can afford such representation. A select few are fortunate enough to have it fall in their laps, typically after public awareness has been raised by family, friends, journalists, death penalty opponents, or advocates for the wrongfully convicted.

Cameron Todd Willingham was not one of those select few. He was represented by a competent, sincere, and dedicated appellate attorney, Walter M. Reaves, Jr. Working pretty much by himself, Reaves was no match for the legal phalanx that is the Texas judicial system. On February 17, the same day Gerald Hurst signed his five page report, Reaves faxed a desperate plea for clemency to Governor Perry.

<<>>

February 13, 2004

Governor Rick Perry
State Capitol
1400 Congress Ave
P.O. Box 12428
Austin, Texas 78711

Sent by facsimile transmission to: 1-(512)-463-1849

Re: Cameron Todd Willingham

Dear Governor Perry,

I am writing this letter to you on behalf of Cameron Todd Willingham. This letter is a request for a reprieve. Currently, Mr. Willingham is scheduled for execution on February 17, 2004.

I have represented Mr. Willingham since his direct appeals were exhausted. As with many capital cases, the defense he received was far from perfect. This is especially so for his representation on appeal, which was a main focus of the post conviction proceedings. Mr. Willingham's lawyer on appeal neglected to raise a number of important issues. Had those issues been raised, I do not think we would be in this position. However, we are, and that has been through the courts. Even Mr. Willingham recognized the lack of quality of the briefs filed for him, but was not able to obtain any assistance, even though he asked for permission to represent himself.

I realize these issues have been through the courts, and are not something that you wish to review again. However, there are some things that have not been through the courts, that I think should be considered. Ever since I started reviewing the case, I have had serious questions about Mr. Willingham's guilt. There are a number of circumstances which pointed in another direction. The evidence tying him to the crime was almost entirely circumstantial. The evidence could have led as easily elsewhere, mainly to his wife.

One of the most critical pieces of evidence at trial came from an inmate witness. I know you are fully aware of the problems with that type of witness. I think there were even more problems with this witness than normal. Everyone I have talked with agrees that he is not someone that was credible or worthy of belief. Nevertheless, he got on the witness stand and testified to admissions made by Mr. Willingham. We have been able to do little with that. I think that is an issue that raises serious questions about the criminal justice system in death penalty cases, I do not believe it is enough to merely present evidence to a jury, and leave the decision to them. Instead I believe prosecutors have an obligation, if not ethically, at least morally, to ensure that there are no doubts about any of the evidence they present. I do not think you can say the evidence from Mr. Webb was of that type. Nevertheless, as with many cases, the evidence was put before the jury, and presumably, they gave it some weight.

The other evidence that did not come before the jury, was the fact that there was an insurance policy on the children. However, Mr. Willingham was not the beneficiary. Instead, it was his wife. He was not even aware of the policy; he first became aware after he had been arrested for this offense. Almost immediately after his arrest, she cashed in on the policy and went out and purchased a new truck. Needless to say, her actions were not that of a grieving mother. There is also additional evidence leading to her. After the trial, a witness came forward, and indicated she saw Mrs. Willingham, as well as three other individuals at the house that morning. The information was extremely exculpatory, and led to the filing of a motion for new trial. The witness subsequently recanted, and claimed that she did not see what she claimed, and had fabricated the story. However, it is curious that at least one of the persons she names was connected to Mrs. Willingham. There were messages left on the answering machine by that person, and I do not believe this person had any way of knowing that.

Only recently I have discovered that the fire was probably not set by anyone. Dr. Gerald Hurst has offered his assistance in this case, and is submitting an affidavit which will be filed with the Courts. Dr. Hurst's opinion is that the fire was not intentionally set. He has rebutted almost all of the claims made by the fire marshal. Most are either not supported by the science, or are no longer generally accepted principles. Dr. Hurst has been involved in several other cases, and successfully obtained the release of persons who were convicted of crimes almost identical to this one. This is something we have just come across, and I think it clearly deserves further inquiry.

There is nothing more I would like than to be able to present you with evidence of actual innocence. I think we are close with Dr. Hurst, but he needs more time to conduct a complete investigation: I think this is something that merits serious consideration. The death penalty, whether you agree with it or not, should be reserved for the most serious crimes. More importantly, it should be reserved for those crimes about which there is no doubt about the guilt of the person. This is not an area where we should have to guess, or entertain concerns or doubts. If there are any doubts, I think we have an obligation as a society to prevent the execution. We are all aware of the numerous cases over the last few years where persons have been exonerated years after the crime. Many times it takes years for such evidence to develop. An execution destroys any chance that person may ever have at establishing their innocence. We already know that a number of people who have been exonerated were on death row. We have no idea whether there were any persons who have been executed, and who could have established their innocence. Obviously, once the execution occurs, there is no motivation to pursue an investigation.

We are currently still working on attempting to obtain evidence of innocence, and I believe have come extremely close. I feel that we are closer than ever, which is the reason for asking for this reprieve; I believe there are still serious questions left on this case, that should be pursued. For that reason. I am requesting a reprieve to allow us the opportunity to do that. We do have an investigator who has volunteered and agreed to do that, and has started working on the case. We also have obtained the assistance of Dr. Hurst, and there is no telling how many others may offer assistance when they learn about the case.

I trust that you will give this matter your full and thoughtful consideration. If there is any additional information I can provide, I would be more that happy to do so.

Thank you for your time given in this matter.

> Very truly yours,
>
> Walter M. Reaves, Jr.

<<>>

The fax cover sheet reads:

> Number of Pages (including this page): 4

Reaves letter was three pages long. It seems Reaves had not yet received Hurst's report, signed that same day. Indeed, it seems Reaves did not fully appreciate the value of Hurst's work. He mentioned Hurst only after flailing at the testimony of Johnny Webb, and only after suggesting Stacy may have set the fire. He sounded desperate because he was.

In introducing Hurst, he destroyed his own suggestion that Stacy may have set the fire:

> Only recently I have discovered that the fire was probably not set by anyone.

Then he underplayed the significance of Hurst's findings:

> He has rebutted *almost all* of the claims made by the fire marshal.

<<>>

There would be a delay before Perry would have an opportunity to see the Hurst report. Reaves' clemency plea was hand delivered to the office of Perry's Attorney General, Greg Abbott.

Sometime on or before the 17th, the day of Willingham's scheduled execution, Greg Abbott's office came into possession of a copy of the Hurst report. Someone slapped a cover page on the report and faxed it Governor Perry without comment.

> To: Mike Schofield, Governor's Office
>
> Subject: Willingham
>
> Date Sent: February 17, 2004
>
> Time Sent: 4:25 PM

The execution was scheduled for 6:00.

Willingham was pronounced dead at 6:20 PM.

The case of Cameron Todd Willingham was over.

POSTLUDE

December 23, 1991

Corsicana started its day under a full moon and clear skies. Clouds would begin rolling in eight hours later. By 10 AM, they would blanket the sky.

The temperature had a mind of its own. At midnight, it was a chilly 53 °F. It would never get any warmer. By 9 AM, the temperature had dropped to 48. By the beginning of Christmas Eve, it would be 46.

The small, wood-frame, rental house at 1213 West 11th Avenue was poorly equipped to resist even those modestly cold temperatures. Constructed forty years earlier, the house was poorly insulated and poorly maintained. The tape around the back door was a sorrowful admission to the house's inability to keep precious warmth from escaping.

The small house had no central heating system. Instead, it relied on three gas-fired, internal-flame space heaters to replace the warmth that escaped with little resistance through walls, windows, ceiling, gaps and crevices.

One such space heater was in the front bedroom, the bedroom where the three young girls slept and played. Two-year-old Amber would occasionally play with the heater. More than once, her mother would catch her "putting things too close to it." More than once, her father would give her "whuppings" for doing so.

On that particular morning in Corsicana, Amber's mother left the house when the clock struck 9 and the thermometer hit 48. She didn't turn off the space heater, as she might have done had the day been warmer. She just turned it down.

"I remember turning it down. ... I always thought, Gosh, could Amber have put something in there?"

DEDICATION

I dedicate this book to Michael Ledford, John Maloney,
and the hundreds of others wrongfully convicted on bad fire science.

A NOTE ON *TWELVE ANGRY MEN*

In each of the books I write for *The Skeptical Juror* series, I am obliged to create eleven characters and a story line for the jury deliberations. In *The Trial of Byron* Case, I was inspired by characters directly from my own sojourns in a jury room. In *The Trial of Cory Maye*, I was inspired by a British mini-series called *The Jury*. It's available on Netflix. If you watch that two-disc series, you will recognize Angela, my force-of-nature foreperson, and Kyle, my timid accountant-type who finally found the nerve to speak his mind.

The characters and deliberation in this book were inspired by the 1957 movie *Twelve Angry Men*. In his introduction to the *Turner Classic Movies* presentation, Robert Osborne described the movie succinctly, as he always does.

"We're going to start with what may be the most compelling courtroom drama of them all. It's a film which incorporates suspense, drama, and intensity like no other, and does so without ever leaving one solitary room, and that's amazing. The title is Twelve Angry Men, *co-produced by and starring Henry Fonda, who considered it one of his three favorites of all the films he's made, the others being* The Grapes of Wrath *and* The Ox Bow Incident.*

"This time Fonda's a member of a jury sequestered for a murder case, one involving a Puerto Rican teenager, one who's accused of knifing his father. It looks pretty much like an open-and-shut case to eleven of those jurors, but one man has a reasonable doubt, and that causes the fireworks."

<<>>

Anyone who has watched and remembers *Twelve Angry Men* will have no doubt that my fictional jury deliberations were inspired by that movie.

I modeled eleven of my jurors on its actors. In my book, for example, Sports Fan Ward plays a similar role to that played by Jack Warden. Timid John sits in the same seat as did John Fiedler, and John Fiedler did indeed play therapy patient Mr. Peterson in *The Bob Newhart Show*. Timid John, however, is not that much different than juror Kyle from *Cory Maye*. Boisterous Lee is clearly similar to Lee J. Cobb. Marti is a variant of Martin Balsam, different both in gender and competence.

I dared not assume the skeptical juror role portrayed by Henry Fonda, for he was more subtle and persuasive than I can hope to be. Instead I assigned that role to Harriet. I placed myself in the next chair, and I frequently reminded myself I needed to be more like her.

At various points throughout the jury deliberation, I adapted dialogue from the movie. Sometimes I elected not even to rephrase. How could I, for example, deign to change Henry Fonda's refusal to vote guilty without first deliberating the evidence?

Lee: "Then what do you want?"
Harriet: "I just want to talk."

Why would I bother update the means of execution in Lee J. Cobb's dying argument?

Lee: "He's got to burn. You're letting him slip through our fingers."

<<>>

I borrowed from *Twelve Angry Men* not because it made my job easier, for it certainly did not, but because I wanted to pay homage to the movie. It has special meaning for me. One prosecutor, angry that I had thwarted his conviction and wanting a retrial, compared me to Henry Fonda in the movie. He did not intend it as a compliment to me; he merely wanted to convince the judge that the State would prevail if the defendant were retried. I nonetheless accepted it as a compliment, though the parallel had never occurred to me as I struggled to save a stranger, someone who turned out to be a fine and decent man.

The movie, of course, portrays jury deliberation to be more dramatic than it really is. I've yet to see a juror threaten another with a knife, or witness one break into tears while ripping apart a photo of his own son.

On the other hand, *Twelve Angry Men* expresses many of the concerns I have about jury behavior. Jurors tend to be insufficiently skeptical of the prosecution, too willing to convict without a thorough deliberation of the evidence. Jurors are too eager to relieve the State of its burden of proof, too willing to deprive the defendant of his presumption of innocence. Too many jurors base their votes on convenience or intimidation rather than conviction. These are not lessons I learned from the movie. They are lessons I learned behind a closed jury room door.

<<>>

Because the movie impressed me as realistic in critical regards, I long wondered about it as an academic and potentially-educational challenge. Could the characters in *Twelve Angry Men* be applied to a real-world case? Was their behavior portrayed in the movie applicable only to a fictional case constructed merely to that end?

When the transcripts of the Willingham trial became available online, I decided to test my hypothesis that the lessons and jury depictions from *Twelve Angry Men* are applicable to real-world juries. The cases, both fictional and factual, dealt with a charge of capital murder. In each trial, the prosecution built a seemingly overwhelming case of guilt beyond a reasonable doubt. In each deliberation, many among the jury attempted a quick vote for guilty.

In each case, however, there was room for reasonable doubt. The doubt was there, buried beneath an onslaught of prosecution testimony, uncovered by a defense attorney who believed his own client to be guilty, waiting silently to be discovered by at least one juror willing to deliberate before casting a verdict.

<<>>

I was not surprised to find that real life is more difficult and less romantic than the movies. Henry Fonda asked for one hour, just one hour, to deliberate his case. In the real world, one hour is woefully inadequate.

In the movie, the deliberations took two hours. In my world, I spent eight days trying to save a man I believed to be factually innocent.

In the movie, Henry Fonda was able to convince even his most stubborn colleagues, Lee J. Cobb and Ed Begley, to acknowledge reasonable doubt of guilt. In the movie, the jury acquitted the defendant.

In this book, Harriet was unable to convince her most stubborn colleagues, Lee and Ted, to change their vote. In this book, the deliberations resulted in a hung jury.

In my world, I failed to convince two of my fellow jurors.

In the movie, Henry Fonda walked out of the courthouse comfortable that he had done his job. Imagine, however, that Henry Fonda had been unable to convince those last two jurors to change their vote, knowing the defendant would be retried and certainly convicted.

Would he be as comfortable during that closing walk down the courthouse steps? Would he be able to sleep that night or the next? Would he ever free himself of the thought that an innocent man was severely sentenced because of he failed to convince two angry men?

GENERAL NOTES

Modifications to the Trial Transcripts

I have taken editorial license with the trial transcripts to make the testimony more readable.

I have excluded the opening and closing statements.

I have excluded the judge's reading of the jury instructions.

I have excluded most of the lengthy qualifications cited by some witnesses.

I have removed speaking crutches such as "All Right", "And", "Now", and "Okay" from the beginning of many attorney questions.

I have eliminated incomplete thoughts.

I have joined multiple answers into a single answer, with concurrent deletion of the intermediate questions.

I have eliminated redundant and irrelevant questions and answers.

I have rearranged some testimony, particularly in the case of Manuel Vasquez, make the testimony seem less disjointed.

I have omitted the testimony of several minor witnesses.

Because of the editorial changes made to the transcripts, the transcripts as presented in this book should not be cited as official or strictly accurate.

Prelude

The fire investigator quoted was Manuel Vasquez, now deceased. The quotes are inexact. The exact questions and answers, taken from several locations in the transcript, follow:

> Let me say this: The fire is telling me this. The fire tells a story. I am just the interpreter. I am looking at the fire, and I am interpreting the fire. That is what I know. That is what I do best. And the fire does not lie. It tells me the truth.
>
> The intent was to kill the little girls.
>
> Question: And have you ever been wrong in a conclusion that you make?
>
> Answer: Not to my knowledge.
>
> Question: I mean, in fifteen years, or twenty, or twenty-five, you've never been wrong, have you?
>
> Answer: If I have, sir, I don't know. It's never been pointed out.

<<>>

I presume, but do not know with certainty that Willingham's "I love you" comment was directed at Elizabeth Gilbert. Gilbert spent five years visiting, writing, and attempting to exonerate Willingham. Shortly before his execution, she was in a car accident and paralyzed from the neck down. Doctors told her she would never walk again.

In his September 7, 2009 *New Yorker* article "Trial by Fire", David Grann offered the following quote from her:

> *All that time, I thought I was saving Willingham, and I realized then that he was saving me, giving me the strength to get through this. I know I will one day walk again, and I know it is because Willingham showed me the kind of courage it takes to survive.*

Early in 2010, Elizabeth Gilbert walked 80 yards with a walker.

<<>>

I presume, but do not know with certainty, that Willingham's "I hope you rot in hell" comment was directed at his ex-wife Stacy.

In his *New Yorker* article "Trial by Fire", David Grann ended his article suggesting Willingham's last words were:

> *The only statement I want to make is that I am an innocent man convicted of a crime I did not commit. I have been persecuted for twelve years for something I did not do. From God's dust I came and to dust I will return, so the Earth shall become my throne.*

Grann did not include Willingham's "I love you" and "I hope you rot in hell" comments.

The Texas Department of Criminal Justice web site excludes only the "I hope you rot in hell" statement. They replace it with:

> *[Remaining portion of statement omitted due to profanity.]*

Their unwillingness to print profanity provides a charming contrast with their willingness to execute so many of their own.

According to Indiana's Office of the Clark Country Prosecuting Attorney, Willingham's extemporaneous statements were as follows:

> He expressed love to someone named Gabby and then addressed his ex-wife, Stacy Kuykendall, who was watching about 8 feet away through a window and said several times, "I hope you rot in Hell, bitch." He then attempted to maneuver his hand, strapped at the wrist, into an obscene gesture. His former wife showed no reaction to the outburst.

See http://www.clarkprosecutor.org/html/death/US/willingham899.htm

According to David Bry and the blog *The Awl*, Willingham's final words were:

> "I hope you rot in hell, bitch. I hope you fucking rot in hell, bitch. You bitch. I hope you fucking rot, cunt. That is it."

Grann reports that Stacy turned against Todd after finally reviewing the case documents. I wonder if she turned against him once Willingham's appellate attorney Walter Reaves begin suggesting that she, rather than Todd, may have started the fire.

Grann reports that Stacy refused Todd's request to have his tombstone placed near their children's graves. I read elsewhere that Stacy taunted Todd, telling him she was going to have more children with another man. I wonder if she tried to hurt him also by taking away the only thing he had left: his proclamation of innocence.

In October 2009, after the Willingham case came to increased public attention, due in large measure to David Grann's *New Yorker* article, Stacy issued a statement claiming Todd had confessed just before his execution.

> He said the night before the fire we got into an argument and you had said it again that you were going to divorce me. I told him yes I did say that. He told me that he believed I was going to but he couldn't let that happen. Todd told me that it was stupid but it was like an obsession. He said if I didn't have my girls I couldn't leave him and that I could never have Amber or the twins with anyone else but him. He told me he was sorry and that he hoped that I could forgive him one day.

David Grann published an update to his article challenging her statement, noting that it was inconsistent with her other testimony and statements to reporters.

In October 2010, Stacy was offered an opportunity to testify under oath at a Court of Inquiry being held by District Judge Charlie Baird. That Court of Inquiry was considering whether Willingham may have been wrongfully executed. Stacy declined to testify under oath. Instead she repeated her claim to reporters.

Introduction

All exterior and interior photographs of the Willingham house were taken by Manuel Vasquez as part of his investigation. They are part of the public record of the case.

I obtained the exterior photograph of the Navarro County Courthouse from the Wikimedia Commons.

Jury Room: Texas v. Willingham

The literary jurors in this book are pure fiction. I modeled eleven of them on the actors from the 1957 movie *Twelve Angry Men*.

Marti's counterpart is Martin Balsam. In his script, Reginald Rose described this juror as:

> A small, petty man who is impressed with the authority he has and handles himself quite formally. Not overly bright, but dogged.

Marti is clearly different than the person described by Reginald Rose or portrayed by Martin Balsam.

Timid John's counterpart is John Fiedler. In his script, Reginald Rose described this juror as:

> A meek, hesitant man who finds it difficult to maintain any opinions of his own. Easily swayed and usually adopts the opinion of the last person to whom he has spoken.

In both the movie and my book, the juror I call Timid John found the courage to stand up for his convictions. My character John in *Willingham* is little different than my character Kyle in *Maye*, though Kyle dressed more meticulously.

Boisterous Lee's counterpart is Lee J. Cobb. In his script, Reginald Rose described this juror as:

> A very strong, very forceful, extremely opinionated man within whom can be detected a streak of sadism. He is a humorless man who is intolerant of opinions other than his own and accustomed to forcing his wishes and views upon others.

The personality described by Rose was preserved in both the movie and my book. I fear I see some of myself in Lee. Lee's stubbornness, but not his demeanor, reminded me of the two hold-out jurors from the case that that transformed me.

High Society Edie's counterpart is E. G. Marshall. Reginald Rose described this juror as:

> Seems to be a man of wealth and position. He is a practiced speaker who presents himself well at all times. He seems to feel a little bit above the rest of the jurors. His only concern is with the facts in this case, and he is appalled at the behavior of the others.

E. G. Marshall portrayed Rose's description accurately in the movie. For a while, I toyed with the idea of placing myself in his seat. I fear also that I see some of myself in Edie.

Young Jack's counterpart is Jack Klugman. Reginald Rose described this juror as.

> A naive, very frightened young man who takes his obligations in this case very seriously but, who finds it difficult to speak up when his elders have the floor.

The movie and my book stayed true to the character described by Reginald Rose.

Nondescript Ed's counterpart is the relatively unknown Edward Binns. Reginald Rose described this juror as:

> An honest but dull-witted man who comes upon his decisions slowly and carefully. A man who finds it difficult to create positive opinions, but who must listen to and digest and accept those opinions offered by others which appeal to him most.

I found myself unable to develop this character in my book. I worked around the problem by describing him as nondescript and by generally excluding him from the deliberations.

Sports Fan Ward's counterpart was Jack Warden. Reginald Rose described this juror as:

> A loud, flashy-handed salesman type who has more important things to do than to sit on a jury. He is quick to show temper, quick to form opinions on things about which he knows nothing. Is a bully and, of course, a coward.

Rather than focus on his vocation, I focused on his avocation. In the movie, this juror wanted to finish the deliberations quickly so that he could attend a ball game. I did not perceive this juror to be a coward. I did not intentionally portray him as such in this book.

Harriet's counterpart is Henry Fonda. Reginald Rose described this juror as

> A quiet, thoughtful, gentle man. A man who sees all sides of every question and constantly seeks the truth. A man of strength tempered with compassion. Above all, he is a man who wants justice to be done and will fight to see that it is.

I considered placing myself in the seat of Henry Fonda. I realize, however, that I'm in danger of too much preaching and too little listening. I decided to sit in the seat of the next juror. In the movie, that seat was occupied by Joseph Sweeny. That juror is described by Reginald Rose as:

> A mild gentle old man long since defeated by life and now merely waiting to die. A man who recognizes himself for what he is and mourns the days when it would have been possible to be courageous without shielding himself behind his many years.

I acknowledge that I am older than most. I hope no other part of that description applies.

I switched the seats of the next two jurors. I wanted to place Bitter Ted directly across from Boisterous Lee. The juror sitting to my right was therefore Jorge. Jorge's counterpart in the movie was George Voskovec. Reginald Rose described that juror as:

> A refugee from Europe who has come to this country in 1941. A man who speaks with an accent and who is ashamed, humble, almost subservient to the people around him, but who will honestly seek justice because he has suffered through so much injustice.

I'm aware from my research into the case of Johnny Frank Garrett that refugees from the Mariel boatlift were relocated around the county and to western Texas specifically. I decided to modify my juror accordingly.

As the book developed, I realized I had made Jorge the most perceptive of the jurors, more perceptive than even Harriet. I continued with that pattern even after I recognized it.

Bitter Ted's counterpart was Ed Begley, Sr. Reginald Rose described that juror as:

> An angry, bitter man. He is a man who antagonizes almost at sight. A bigot who places no value on any human life save his own, a man who has been nowhere and is going nowhere and knows it deep within him.

I perceived Boisterous Lee and Bitter Ted to be the same character, separated only by a degree that was certain to come with age. I placed them across the table from one another hoping they could see themselves in a jury room mirror.

I did not portray Ted as a bigot, as described by Rose and portrayed by Begley. My personal experience is that there is little racial, ethnic, or gender bigotry in the jury deliberation room. I qualify that statement by noting that I have served on juries only in Southern California. I have reason to believe my observations are not universal in this regard.

The bigotry that I have observed in the jury room is directed towards the defendant.

Ad Agency Robert's counterpart was Robert Webber. Reginald Rose described that juror as:

> A slick, bright advertising man who thinks of human beings in terms of percentages, graphs, and polls and has no real understanding of people. He is a superficial snob, but trying to be a good fellow.

I didn't perceive this juror as either slick, bright, or a snob. Other than Nondescript Ed, I found him to be the least interesting character. I provided him few lines. I left him with the now tired line about running something up a flagpole and the strange line about the stoop. "I have a thought. So why don't I just throw it out on the stoop and see if the cat licks it up."

Reginald Rose's original script is online. Search using keywords: twelve angry men script.

To learn of the actors that played in the movie, see the online site International Movie Database (IMDB). Search there for the twelve angry men 1957.

<<>>

The following dialog segment was adapted from the movie.

> Lee: "You really think he's innocent?"
>
> Harriet: "I don't know."
>
> Lee: "You sat in court with the rest of us. You heard what we heard. The man's a child killer. You could see it. They proved it a dozen different ways. Do you want me to list 'em?"
>
> Harriet: "No, thank you. Not right yet."
>
> Lee: "Then what do you want?"
>
> Harriet: "I just want to talk."

The following dialog segment was adapted from the movie.

> Harriet: "I guess I just think it shouldn't be this easy to send someone to death row."
>
> Ward: "Who says it's easy for me? Just because I voted fast? I honestly think the guy's guilty."

The following dialog segment was adapted from the movie.

> Timid John: Oh. ... Well ... Lemme see. I guess I just think he's guilty. I mean nobody proved otherwise."
>
> Harriet: "The defense doesn't have to prove anything. The burden of proof is on the prosecution. They have to prove he's guilty."
>
> Marti: "And they must do so beyond a reasonable doubt."
>
> John: "Sure, I know that. What I meant was -- well, anyway, I think he's guilty."

The following dialog segment was adapted from the movie.

> Harriet: "They could be wrong."
>
> Ward: "Whadda you trying to say? Those people testified under oath."
>
> Harriet: They're only people. People make mistakes. Don't you think they could they have been wrong?"
>
> Ward: "Well, no, I don't think so".
>
> Harriet: "Do you know for certain?"
>
> Ward: "Come on, no one can know for certain, but they can't all be wrong."
>
> Harriet: "That's one of the things we could talk about."
>
> Boisterous Lee: "We are talking, aren't we? Aren't we? What about the confession?"

Timid John: "Excuse me. There's some people haven't talked. Shouldn't we go in order?"

Lee: "They'll get a chance to talk. Be quiet a second will ya? What about the confession? Let's talk about that."

Testimony of Johnny Webb

In the movie, there was no snitch. During the trial of Cameron Todd Willingham, the snitch was the lead witness for the prosecution. The jurors in that trial explained they paid little attention to Johnny Webb. That is unfortunate. Johnny Webb's testimony provided evidence that Willingham's prosecutors were willing to fabricate evidence against him to win their case.

Less than five years after the jury voted to put Cameron Todd Willingham to death, the Texas Board of Pardons and Paroles released Johnny Webb early. He had served only five years of his fifteen year sentence. His criminal history suggested he would likely return to a life of crime. At one time or another, he had been convicted of robbery, burglary, forgery, auto-theft, and distribution of drugs. He claimed his criminal behavior stemmed from drugs and alcohol. There was no real reason to believe he would be better able to control his addictions if released early than he had been prior to his most recent arrest.

Prosecutor John Jackson, however, spoke in favor of Johnny Webb's early release. Though Jackson considered Webb to be "an unreliable kind of guy," Jackson nevertheless troubled himself to argue in favor of Webb's early release. "I asked them to cut him loose early."

According to Jackson, his endorsement had nothing to do with the assistance Johnny Webb had provided him during the Willingham trial. Of course not. Jackson explained that he was merely concerned about Webb's safety and well being. He claimed that Johnny Webb had been targeted by the Aryan Brotherhood.

A few months after his early release, Johnny Webb was caught with cocaine and returned to prison.

In March of 2000, eight years to the month after his conviction for robbing a woman of her purse, Johnny Webb sent John Jackson a Motion to Recant Testimony. It read in part: "Mr. Willingham is innocent of all charges."

John Jackson apparently failed to inform Cameron Todd Willingham's defense team of this surprising turn of events. Instead, John Jackson may have explained the consequences of perjury to Johnny Webb. If the recantation were true, Jackson may have pointed out, Webb's testimony during the trial of Cameron Todd Willingham would have been false.

Soon thereafter and without explanation, Johnny Webb recanted his recantation.

During an interview after his release, Johnny Webb effectively recanted the recantation of his recantation. Speaking of Willingham, he said:

> It's very possible I misunderstood what he said. ... My memory is in bits and pieces. I was on a lot of medication at the time.

He then added:

> The statute of limitations has run out on perjury, hasn't it?

I obtained the post-conviction information regarding Johnny Webb from David Grann's *New Yorker* article "Trial By Fire." That article, published in September of 2009, substantially heightened public interest in Willingham's case. "Trial by Fire" is available online. Search using keywords: Trial by Fire Grann.

According to the trial transcripts, Johnny Webb testified he suffered from "post dramatic stress syndrome." I have no way of knowing whether that humorous error came from the mouth of Johnny Webb or the keyboard of the court reporter. I elected to treat the transcript as accurate.

Testimony of the Barbee Family

The transcripts spell the family name as either Barbe or Barber. I believe the correct spelling is Barbee, and have used that spelling throughout the book.

Deliberation of the Barbee Testimony

The following dialog segment was adapted from the movie.

> Ted: "What do you think you're gonna accomplish? If you want to be stubborn and hang this jury, he'll be tried again and found guilty, sure as he's born."
>
> Harriet: "You're probably right."
>
> I'll let Harriet handle it. She's doing fine. I'm back to subtlety and restraint.
>
> Sports Fan Ward: "So what are you gonna do about it? We can be here all night."
>
> Harriet: "It's only one night. A man might die."
>
> Boisterous Lee: "Well, whose fault is that? Did anyone force him to kill his kids?"

The following dialog segment was adapted from the movie.

> Jorge: "I have always thought that a man was entitled to have unpopular opinions in this country. This is the reason I came here. I wanted to have the right to disagree. In my own country, I am ashamed to say I do not.
>
> Ted: "Whadda we got to listen to now? The history of your country?"
>
> Ward: "Yeah, let's stick to the subject."

Testimony of John Henry Bailey

I did not include the testimony of John Henry Bailey. Bailey testified after the three Barbee witnesses. The heart of his testimony follows:

> "Let me ask you: Were you at home the next day after the fire took place?" >> Yes, I was after lunch.

> "Did you observe anything across the street that seemed unusual to you?" >> Well, I seen Todd and his wife. They came home, well, they came back to the burned out house. They were going through a lot of the debris. I called the police department because I was pretty sure there was an ongoing investigation.

> "Did you have an opportunity to observe their demeanor while they were going in and out of the house?" >> Yes, sir, I did. It was not the attitude of people that just lost their children should have had. It was more of a laughing, cutting-up type attitude.

> "Did the police arrive at that premises?" >> Yes, sir, they did.

> "Did you notice anything unusual insofar as change of demeanor at that time?" >> Yes, sir. Everything got certainly somber, more the attitude they should have had the whole time.

Testimony of Jerry Long

I did not include the testimony of Jerry Long. Long testified after John Henry Bailey. The prosecution used him to suggest Willingham tried to place the blame for the fire on an electrical problem, and did so while the fire was still raging. The substantive portion of his direct examination follows:

> "Did he ever try to explain to you what had happened with the house or anything like that?" >> Well, he just told me he pointed up to the meter where the wires come from, the utility pole, up to the house. He pointed up to those, told me that he had been having trouble with those, that they had been having trouble with the electricity in the house.

> "So, he was trying to tell you about problems with wiring at this time." >> He just pointed where the wires met the house and told me that he had been having electrical trouble with the electricity in the house."

During cross examination, David Martin exposed the hypocrisy of John Jackson's questioning, should any of the jurors have been listening:

> "There were sparks when you got there? Sparks from the electric wires?" >> Yes, sir.

> "You asked him where the sparks were coming from? Take a moment to recall, if you will." >> I may have. I don't remember asking him that.

> "But when you got there, the electricity was popping and there was sparks?" >> Yes, sir. It would pop and then it would stop. It wasn't continuously sparking.

> "You asked him where the sparks were coming from?" >> I may have. I don't remember.

Testimony of Steven Vandiver

The trial transcripts spell the last name as Vandavor. I believe the correct spelling is Vandiver. I have used that spelling through the book.

Testimony of Jason Grant

I did not include the testimony of Jason Grant. Grant was apparently a member of the Corsicana Police department and in uniform when he testified. He testified that he witnessed Willingham's behavior during a television interview, and it was not as expected from someone who had just lost his children.

> "All right. Did you have an opportunity to observe him while the camera crew was filming?" >> Yes.

> "Did his attitude or demeanor continue during that filming?" >> I believe towards the end of the filming, he was crying. His wife was also there with him. She was crying.

> "Then at a later time after the cameras stopped, did you have an opportunity to view him or see him?" >> Yes.

> "What was his demeanor at that point?" >> Well, he was -- he calmed down again. And as a matter of fact, I believe we went over to his -- I guess his in-law's house maybe. The camera crew also went over there.

> "You had an opportunity, I'm sure, to hear Mr. Willingham talk to the camera crew on that occasion. Would that be fair statement?" >> Yes.

> "Was there any particular thing he was most concerned about in the course before that interview?" >> He was -- he kept asking the news people if they had a station in Oklahoma. He wanted -- he had a lot of family and friends up there in that part of the state. He wanted to make sure they were going the see this, and he asked them several different times would his friends be able to see this on television in Oklahoma.

Testimony of Andrew Armstrong

I did not include the testimony of Andrew Armstrong. Armstrong testified that people working at his lab found traces of kerosene on the wood threshold sample, but found not other traces of accelerant on any other sample. That conclusion was obvious from the testimony of the other witnesses.

Deliberation of the Firefighters' Testimony

The following dialog segment was adapted from the movie.

> Lee: "He was just trying to bait me."

> Edie: "He did a pretty good job."

Testimony of Ethel Baptist

During the trial, Ethel Baptist testified before the firefighters testified. I moved her testimony to place it as the first of the medical witness testimony.

Testimony of Grady Shaw and Juan Zamora

During the trial, Grady Shaw testified after Juan Zamora. In the book, I placed Shaw's testimony before that of Juan Zamora. By doing so, I ordered the medical testimony as receiving nurse, emergency doctor, medical examiner. I hoped to help the reader by presenting the testimony according to the chronology.

Testimony of Charles Odom

I eliminated the testimony of Charles Odom. He performed the autopsy on Amber. His testimony was quite similar to Dr. Zamora's testimony regarding the autopsy of a body recovered from a fire. I used Zamora's testimony rather than Odom's testimony because Zamora was the only one of the two asked about the cause of death on the autopsy report. The date of that report belies the testimony of Douglas Fogg and Manuel Vasquez regarding their ability to withhold judgement until after a careful survey of the fire scene.

Deliberation of the Medical Witness Testimony

The following dialog segment was adapted from the movie.

> Jorge: "Pardon me. I have made some notes here."
>
> He rises and begins referring to a sheet of paper he holds in his hand.
>
> Jorge: "I would like to say something please."

The following dialog segment was adapted from the movie..

> Ad Agency Robert: "I have a thought. So why don't I just throw it out on the stoop and see if the cat licks it up."
>
> That causes smirks and laughter among most the jurors. I give it a smile. Even Jorge smiles. Harriet finds no humor in it.
>
> Marti: "See if the cat licks it up?"

The following dialog segment was adapted from the movie.

> Jorge: "Maybe you don't fully understand the term reasonable doubt?"
>
> Ward: "Whadda ya mean I don't understand it? How do you like this guy? I'm telling ya they're all alike. They come over here running for their life, and before he can even take a deep breath they're telling us how to run the show. Boy, the arrogance of this guy!"
>
> Marti: "Enough! Who's got something constructive to say?"

The following dialog segment was adapted from the movie.

> Ward: "And we go into extra innings."

The following dialog segment was adapted from the movie.

> Ted: "I'll tell you what I think. We're going nowhere here. I'm ready to walk into court right now and declare a hung jury. There's no point in this going on any more."

Direct Examination of Manuel Vasquez

Vasquez testified that "with the exception of a few, most all of" the fires he investigated resulted from arson. That claim was challenged by the Innocence Project's Arson Review Committee chaired by John Lentini. In their "Report on the Peer Review of the Expert Testimony in the Cases of State of Texas v. Cameron Todd Willingham and State of Texas v. Ernest Ray Willis", they note that in the period from 1980 to 2005, the Texas State Fire Marshals Office determined 50% of the fires they investigate resulted from arson.

Vasquez testified that "Unfortunately, fires injure a lot of people -- kill a lot of people. It's about 50%."

According the Arson Review Committee, data from the U.S. Fire Administration reveal that, between 1995 and 2005, the nationwide average annual percentage of fires that resulted in death was 0.2%, and the average annual percentage of injuries was 1.2%.

<<>>

According to the transcript, Vasquez described the picture in the utility room as depicting "the grim ripper." I have no way of knowing whether he actually said that or the court report mis-reported his testimony. For this book, I presumed the transcript was correct.

According to the transcript, Vasquez claimed that blood has an "infinity" rather than an "affinity" for carbon monoxide. I have no way of knowing whether he actually said that or the court reporter mis-reported his testimony. For this book, I presumed the transcript was correct.

I merged the redirect examination of Manuel Vasquez with the direct examination of Manuel Vasquez.

<<>>

I suspect the authorities were conflicted by the possibility that Amber started the fire and what they believed was indisputable evidence of arson. I infer this from the Vasquez testimony: "I examined this space heater because if it was an accidental fire, the space heater caused the fire."

Though he discussed the other space heaters and the electrical system, he specifically said that if the fire was an accident, it started at the space heater in the children's bedroom.

Consider also this Vasquez testimony: "First of all, the heaters were turned off. And I did not find any remnant of paper around the heater or anywhere."

He first speaks of all the heaters. He then focuses once again on only the heater in the children's bedroom. He did not say he found no paper around any of the heaters. He said he found no paper around the heater, as if he had only one in mind.

On a side note, it is natural he found no paper around the heater. Assuming it hadn't burned up (an unlikely assumption), the room was cleared of debris before Vasquez arrived.

I suspect the authorities were concerned about the space heater being the source of an accidental fire because Stacy told them during interviews that Amber had a history of playing with the space heater.

Cross Examination of Manuel Vasquez

I merged the re-cross examination of Manuel Vasquez with the cross examination of Manuel Vasquez.

Further Deliberation of Manuel Vasquez

The following dialog segment was adapted from the movie.

> Ward: "Well, I don't know about the rest of 'em, but I'm getting a little tired of this yakkity yakking back and forth. It's getting us nowhere. So I'll have to break it up. I'm changing my vote to not guilty."
>
> Lee: "You're what?"
>
> Ward: "You heard me. I've had enough."
>
> Lee: "What do you mean you've had enough? That's no answer."
>
> Ward: "Hey listen, you just take care of yourself, huh?"
>
> Jorge jumps to his feet. He's clearly agitated at Ward.
>
> Jorge: "What kind of a man are you? You have sat here and voted guilty because there are some baseball tickets burning a hole in your pocket. Now you have changed your vote because you say you are sick of all the talking?"
>
> Ward: "Now listen, buddy."
>
> Jorge: "Who tells you that you have a right to play like this with a man's life? This is an ugly and terrible thing to do."
>
> Ward: "Now wait a minute. You can't talk like that to me."
>
> Jorge: "If you want to vote not guilty, then do it because you are convinced the man is not guilty, not because you've had enough. If you believe he is guilty, then vote that way. Or don't you have the courage to do what you think is right?"
>
> Ward: "Now listen --"

Jorge: "Guilty or not guilty?"

Ward: "I told you: not guilty."

Jorge: "Why?"

Ward: "Look, I don't have to --"

Jorge: "You do have to! Say it! Why?"

Ward: "Cause I don't think he's guilty. Okay? I said it."

Further Deliberation of Manuel Vasquez

Surprisingly, in my opinion, no one in the trial addressed the issue of whether there was sufficient accelerant to create puddles over as much area as indicted in the diagram. No one even mentioned the size of the lighter fluid bottle.

I was also surprised to hear the lighter fluid container described as a bottle. I found only one photograph of a lighter fluid container from the fire scene, and that was a small can.

For my demonstration, I presumed the bottle was slightly larger than a pint. It wouldn't make much difference if the bottle were a quart. It would take gallons of fluid to create puddles the size indicated in the diagram, to soak that much carpet, to soak both sides of the door, and to soak the front porch near the house along its entire length.

The following dialog segment was adapted from the movie.

> Lee: "Brother! I've seen all kinds of dishonesty in my day but this little display takes the cake. You come in here with your heart bleeding all over the floor about some poor schlup trying to heroically save his kids and suddenly all these others are voting like sheep. Well, you're not getting through to me. I've had enough. What's the matter with you people? You all know he's guilty. He's got to burn. You're letting him slip through our fingers."

Testimony of Amy O'Shea

Though the defense only presented two witnesses, I included neither of them. I alluded to the testimony of Amy O'Shea. She was a babysitter for the Willingham children. She testified that she could not imagine that Cameron Todd Willingham would kill his children.

Testimony of James McNalley

I did not include the testimony of James McNalley. McNalley was an inmate and knew Johnny Webb. I repeat the critical portion of McNalley's transcript below. Most of it was given outside the presence of the jury to see if it would be allowed in by the court. It was not due to a hearsay objection by John Jackson.

McNalley refers to someone named Joe Jackson. Recall that Joe Jackson was an inmate assigned a cell not far from that of Cameron Todd Willingham.

The following portion of the testimony was heard in front of the jury.

> "Did you hear Johnny Webb talking to Joe Jackson about this case?" >> Yeah; there was me and Kevin Franklin.

> "And during that conversation did Joe Jackson suggest or give information to Johnny Webb?" >> Well, they were talking about something else and then Joe told me and Kevin to come up, that he wanted us to hear this.

> "And about when was this?" >> The first week in May.

> "All right. And Johnny Webb was there talking outside your door?" >> Right; he was cleaning up then; and this is in the evening time.

At this point, John Jackson objected, the jury was excused, and the testimony continued in their absence.

> "Well, Mr. McNally, when did you hear this conversation between Joe Jackson and Johnny Webb?" >> That would be around the first week in May, after I got there.

> "And tell us what the conversation was about." >> Well, like I said, I was sitting on my bed, because I was doing some legal work for another guy; and Kevin and Joe said, "Well, come here; I want you to hear this;" or Joe did. Me and Kevin come up then. I says, "What do you want?" He said, "Well, Webster, listen to this." I say, "Okay;" so I'm sitting there listening and then Joe is telling this Webb guy, he says, "Why, I heard that" -- they

said that "Todd put a wag on an ex or something like that," whatever. Anyway, and that his wife is supposed to have shook the kid to death or something like that.

"And this was Joe Jackson telling this to Timothy Webb?" >> Yeah; telling to a guy by the name of Webb that cleans floors on our floor.

"Johnny Webb; not Timothy; I mean Johnny Webb." >> Johnny Webb; I don't -- I don't even know the guy's name.

"Okay. Do you know the guy's name is Webb?" >> Yeah; that's what I thought his name was.

"And you heard Joe Jackson give this information to him?" >> Yeah; he told that -- well, he said, "This is jailhouse talk; what we've been hearing and stuff." And he told that to this Webb guy.

"And did you have a conversation with Webb about his allegations that he was being threatened or abused by the --" >> Yeah.

"--deputies?" >> Right. I had to take notes. (Exhibited some notes.) He came back a couple of days later and said back in April some deputies threatened his life or something like that. And I said, "What about" -- because he wanted Kevin Franklin, who was doing appeal work for another inmate there, to help him out. And Kevin said that he wouldn't do it because he knew the guy was lying. Then when he approached me, I said, "There's no way because, No.1, I don't believe a deputy would threaten you there."

"And what did Webb say to you about that?" >> Well, he said some deputies, you know, just threatened him; and I says, "Well, if they threatened you, then call the FBI;" I says, "they've got a number you can call collect."

"And did you give him a phone number for the FBI?" >> Yeah. Me and Kevin gave him a phone number to call.

"And did he tell you that he was being threatened in connection with obtaining a statement on the Willingham case?" >> He made a statement to Joe a couple of weeks later that he was hoping to get out -- get time cut or something was supposed to happen with his lawyer in a couple of months; and then he disappeared, because he was working up there on the floor, you know, cleaning. And after May we didn't even see him any more; he didn't even come back up; he wouldn't come in that little cubicle to where, you know, to clean where our three cells were. He just stayed outside, sweeping the floors; and he just disappeared. He never had no more contact with Joe; he -- like he shut off everything at the end of May.

The jury was not allowed to hear from James McNalley.

Interlude

The following quotes are from *The Chicago Tribune*, "Texas Man Executed on Disproved Forensics," by Steve Mills and Maurice Possley, December 9, 2004.

> "He didn't do anything"

> "None of us could see how that would work."

> "They're wanting me to say I can't sleep at night. They want me to say I did wrong. I can't say that."

> "Did anybody know about this prior to his execution? Now I will have to live with this for the rest of my life. Maybe this man was innocent."

> "To me, he was not repentant. He had this attitude and air about him that he was wrongfully charged."

The following quotes are from CNN's AC360°, "A Juror's Doubts," by Randi Kaye, posted October 15, 2009

> "I've got to stand in front of my God one day and explain what I did."

> "I was in the house. I talked to the cops. I talked to the firemen who were there very first on the scene. I looked at the pictures. When you walk through that house, the children's bedroom was set aflame, obviously, by an accelerant."

The following quotes are from CNN's AC360°, "Willingham Juror Now Longer Sure of his Guilt In Texas Case," by Gabriel Falcon and Randi Kaye, posted October 19, 2009

> "When you're sitting there with all those facts, there was nothing else we could see. Now I don't know. I can't tell you he's innocent, I can't say 100 percent he's guilty."

> "I don't sleep at night because of a lot of this. I have gone back and forth in my mind trying to think of anything that we missed. I don't like the fact that years later someone is saying maybe we made a mistake. That the facts aren't what they could've been."

The following quote is from CNN's AC360°, "Did Texas Execute an Innocent Man," by Randi Kaye, posted October 23, 2009

> "In a small town like Corsicana, lots of people knew Doug Fogg."

The following quotes are from a December 2, 2009 Associated Press article by Jeff Carlton, "Cameron Todd Willingham: Jurors Defend Verdict That Led To Texas Execution."

> "A lot of them wanted to vote right away. Me and two other people wanted to go over the facts of the case. It was unfair to go straight in there and decide. We went through everything we could have. All I can go by is what I had seen then."

> "There was evidence of a fire that was deliberate. Not getting the children out of the house. Getting the car out of the way. It was all there."

> "All you can go on when you are on a jury is what is put before you. I stand by my vote -- guilty."

> "We hired [a defense expert] and he said 'Yep. It's arson.' It was really very, very clear what happened in the house. Everybody who saw it, of course, reached the same conclusion."

> "God forbid that somebody was executed who was innocent. Nobody wants that to happen. But for somebody so obviously guilty like Willingham, it's a travesty to make it seem like it was something other than what it was."

> "I never think about [Willingham], but I do think about those year-old babies crawling around in an inferno with their flesh melting off their bodies. I think that he was guilty, that he deserved death and that he got death."

The following quote is from the Dallas Morning News, "Willingham's Innocence in Fire Unclear," by Steve McGonigle, Brooks Egerton, and Gary Jacobson, October 25, 2009.

> "He was a straight shooter, and an honest guy."

For the appellate court decision containing the case summary, see Willingham v. State, 897 S.W.2d 351 (1995)

Lime Street

For a thorough accounting of the Lime Street fire experiment, see "Nightmare on Lime Street: How a Ghastly Jacksonville Fire Forever Changed Arson Science in America" by the online news magazine *Folio Weekly*. Find online using search phrase: Nightmare on Lime Street Jacksonville.

See also *The Devil and Sherlock Holmes: Tales of Murder, Madness, and Obsession*, by David Grann, available from Amazon and other bookstores.

See also "The Lime Street Fire: Another Perspective" by John Lentini. Find online using search phrase: "Lime Street Fire Another" "Video Tape". Include the quotation marks.

Public Defender Pat McGinnis seems to be a spectacular public defender. He is also noteworthy for his work in freeing Brenton Butler. See the documentary *Murder on a Sunday Morning*.

Oakland

For an accounting of the Oakland fires, see "Unconventional Wisdom: The Lessons of Oakland" by John Lentini, David Smith, and Richard Henderson. The article was published in *The Fire and Arson Investigator*, Volume 43, Number 4, in June 1993.

Hurst

For a detailed accounting of Gerald Hurst's role in the case of Sonia Cacy, see the August 28, 1998 *Texas Observer* article "Forensic Fraud: No Motive, Not Witness, and 99 Years in Jail: The Curious Conviction of Sonia Cacy," by Michael Draecher. That article is available from the *Truth In Justice* web site at http://truthinjustice.org/sonia4.htm

For Gerald Hurst's report regarding the Willingham case, see http://www.innocenceproject.org/docs/Willingham_foia.pdf

For discussion of a variety of cases on which Gerald Hurst has helped, see the November 15, 2009 *American-Statesman* article "Arson Scientist Attacks Arson Convictions," by Chuck Lindell. That article is available online from the statesman.com web site. Search using key phrase: "Austin scientist attacks arson convictions" "American Statesman Staff". Include the quotation marks.

For my favorite interview with Gerald Hurst, see the December 2, 2009 *The Observer* article "Fire and Innocence" by Dave Mann. It includes a photo of Gerald Hurst courtesy of Gerald Hurst. I'll dare to include that photo here without specific permission.

Photo courtesy Gerald Hurst

Perry

For the clemency request letter prepared by Walter Reaves, see http://www.innocenceproject.org/docs/Willingham_foia.pdf

For the dates and timing of events in the days and minutes before the Willingham execution, see http://www.innocenceproject.org/docs/Willingham_foia.pdf

The last statements of most of those executed by Texas can be found on the Texas Department Criminal Justice web site. http://www.tdcj.state.tx.us/stat/executedoffenders.htm

The press summaries for many of those executed by Texas and elsewhere can be found on the web site of the Office of the Clark Country Prosecuting Attorney, but not easily. Search using the name of the person executed and append the search phrase: clark county.

My accounting of the people executed under Rick Perry's watch who proclaimed their innocence follows. I include that portion of their final statement in which they proclaim their innocence.

#250 Mark Oran Hill: " I am innocent."

#256 Vincent Edward Cooks: "You people over there. You know what these people are doing. By them executing me ain't doing nothing right. I don't weigh 180 pounds and 5'7"."

#259 Windell Broussard: "I just want to let everyone know that this here is a tragedy. What happened to Diana, Corey, and what is happening to me, it is a tragedy.

#262 Gerald Wayne Tigner, Jr.: "I was wrongfully convicted of this crime ..."

#269 Johnny Joe Martinez: "I know that I am fixing to die - but not for my mistakes. My trial lawyers - they are the ones that are killing me."

#273: Robert Otis Coulson: "I'm innocent. I had nothing to do with my family's murders."

#275: Richard William Kutzner: "I didn't kill your mother. The two guys that worked for me killed your mother and they are still out there."

#279: Toronto Markkey Patterson: "I do not think I should die for a crime I did not commit."

#287: William Wesley Chappell: "My request is that you get yourselves in church and pray for forgiveness because you are murdering me. I did not kill anyone in my life."

#299: Bobby Glen Cook: "It was self defense and I was never able to get up on the stand to tell them. I know this is wrong."

#312: Richard Charles Duncan: "I am innocent."

#320: Cameron Todd Willingham: "The only statement I want to make is that I am an innocent man convicted of a crime I did not commit."

#322: Kelsey Patterson: "I am not guilty of the charge of capital murder."

#336: Anthony Guy Fuentes: "The truth will be known. It didn't come out in time to save my life. ... It is wrong for the prosecutors to lie and make witnesses say what they need them to say. The truth has always been there."

#351 Luis Ramirez: "I did not kill your loved one, but I hope that one day you find out who did."

#363 Jackie Barron Wilson: "Thank you for being there for me and all these people here will find the one who did this damn crime."

#367 Lamont Reese: "And I want everyone to know I did not walk to this because this is straight up murder. I just want everybody to know I didn't walk to this. The reason is because it's murder. I am not going to play a part in my own murder. No one should have to do that."

#372: William E. Wyatt, Jr.: "I would like to say to Damien's family I did not murder your son. I did not do it. I just want you to know that -- I did not murder Damien."

#375: Derrick Wayne Frazier: "I am innocent. I am being punished for a crime I did not commit. I have professed my innocence for nine years, and I continue to say I am innocent."

#379: Willie Marcel Shannon: "I took a father, it wasn't my fault, it was an accident ... I told the Judge the truth it was an accident."

#388: Charles Anthony Nealy: "Kim Schaeffer, you are a evil woman. You broke the law. The judges and courts helped you and you didn't have all the facts. When you look at the video, you know you can't see anyone. You overplayed your hand looking for something against me and to cover it up the State is killing me."

#390 Roy Lee Pippin: "Yes sir, I charge the people of the jury. Trial Judge, the Prosecutor that cheated to get this conviction. I charge each and every one of you with the murder of an innocent man."

#419: Gregory Edward Wright: "I have done everything to prove my innocence. Before you is an innocent man."

#420: Elkie Lee Taylor: "It's bad to see a man get murdered for something he didn't do, but I am taking it like a man, like a warrior."

#426: Reginald Perkins: "I already gave my statement." Prior statement included: "I did not kill my stepmom. I loved her. Texas is going to kill an innocent man."

#427: Virgil Martinez: "I know what you've been told and that's all a lie. John Gomez killed your kids and sister."

#442: Reginald Blanton: "I didn't murder him. ... They want to kill me for this; I am not the man that did this."

#449 Gary: Johnson: "Dell you tell the rest of them what they did was wrong for letting me fall for what they did. I never done anything in my life to anybody."

I do not believe that everyone who proclaimed their innocence was in fact innocent. Nor do I believe that all those who failed to proclaim their innocence were guilty. I do believe it is merely a coincidence that exoneration statistics suggest that 28 people have been executed in Texas under Rick Perry's watch and that 28 of the people executed proclaimed their innocence.

<<>>

I initially calculated the number of innocent people who might have been executed by Texas to be 54. That number has since grown to 55 due to the continuing executions in the state, and the dearth of exonerations.

On my Skeptical Juror blog, www.skepticaljuror.com, I vowed to review all the executions in Texas and identify those individuals most likely to have wrongfully executed. I report occasionally on my progress, assigning a probability of innocence to each person I investigate in detail. It is naturally a slow process, and I am far from finished. Nonetheless, I have so far have the following people to have a greater than 50% chance of actual innocence.

#44:   Johnny Frank Garrett: 91%

#111: David Wayne Spence: 90%

#79:   Robert Nelson Drew: 84%

#33:   Carlos DeLuna: 83%

#229: Richard Wayne Jones: 77%

#127: Davis Losada: 75%

#129: David Wayne Stoker: 73%

#209: Odell Barnes: 69%

#222: Shaka Sankofa, aka Gary Graham: 58%

#367: Lamont Reese: 53%

#239: Claude Jones: 52%

I have not yet scored Cameron Todd Willingham.

Postlude

I obtained the hourly temperature and cloud cover data from the numerically based search engine Wolfram Alpha. Enter search phrase: Dallas, Texas, December 23, 1991.

I used Dallas rather than Corsicana simply because the search engine did not return temperature data for Corsicana. I presumed Dallas was an acceptable analog for Corsicana since the two cities share the same geography and are separated by less than 60 miles.

I obtained Stacy's quotes from David Grann's *New Yorker* article "Trial By Fire." That article, published in September of 2009 substantially heightened public interest in Willingham's case.

"Trial by Fire" is available online. Search using keywords: Trial by Fire Grann.

Dedication

From David Mann's article "Fire and Innocence:"

> Hurst's research leads him to contend that at least one-third, and perhaps even half, of all arson convictions have been based on junk science. In Texas, that would mean between 250 and 400 likely innocent people are sitting in prison at this very moment.

The number of people wrongfully convicted of arson nationwide might be better measured in thousands rather than hundreds.

A Note on Twelve Angry Men

With respect to the case that transformed me into The Skeptical Juror, I did indeed fail to convince two of my fellow jurors to vote Not Guilty. I did indeed realize that the defendant would be re-tried and almost certainly convicted.

I offered my assistance to the defense team, and they accepted. We worked countless hours to prepare for the second trial, and we uncovered the truth behind a crime that never occurred. Together we watched our client walk free, but broken, from the courthouse.

www.ingramcontent.com/pod-product-compliance
Lightning Source LLC
LaVergne TN
LVHW011225080426
835509LV00005B/316